ORDER
AND
CHANGE

ORDER
AND
CHANGE

Essays in Comparative Sociology

Wilbert E. Moore

RUSSELL SAGE FOUNDATION

John Wiley & Sons, Inc.   *New York   London   Sydney*

Library of Congress Catalog Card Number: 67-19449
Printed in the United States of America

PREFACE

It is always a bit pretentious for an author to initiate the publication of a book of his own essays, although those essays have passed various gatekeepers for publication elsewhere. Actually, most of the chapters were initiated by those gatekeepers, and that is part of the rationale for this volume. I have found, for at least the last decade or so, that I have been responding to cues—assenting, perhaps too frequently, to invitations to participate in a lecture series or a joint publication venture. The invitations are always at least faintly flattering, for they imply a judgment of competence and the probability of delivery on schedule— and occasionally they offer other rewards.

Yet it has occurred to me that I was beginning to lose the initiative in my scientific career, and that if anyone—there must be someone, besides eager doctoral candidates under my supervision—wanted to track down my recent publications of less than book length, that earnest soul would have a difficult time indeed.

Thus I have made a somewhat discriminating selection of recent essays, largely from symposia edited by others but with a small sprinkling of journal articles, around some themes that seem to be most lively in the field of sociology.

The contents of this book neither represent my "collected works"—that would be tedious indeed—nor even what might be called selected samples, in a qualitative sense. The principles I have used in choosing essays for inclusion have included (1) coherence, (2) recency, (3) work not superseded by scholarly books, including my own. Thus I have included virtually nothing on demography, because I have done nothing useful in that field lately, and earlier work has been long since incorporated into the standard sources. I have also included virtually nothing from the area of conventional industrial sociology, for I am no longer sure what that specialty comprises, and what I have to contribute to the subject as I understand it is amply represented by several other books of mine. Indeed, the general criterion of selection (not followed with total consistency) has been to choose items that open fresh areas, at least with regard to my own publications, and not to reproduce nice little pieces long since superseded.

I am grateful to the original instigators of symposia and lecture series and to their constituted publishers for permission to assemble the several chapters. In the process of putting this book together, I was faintly dismayed by the redundancy which had infiltrated the seemingly independent sociological endeavors. The original excuse of divergent audiences was probably valid, but putting these pieces together revealed that some basic orientations were reiterated beyond any suitable tolerance in a single volume. I have therefore made drastic deletions from original texts. It was only suitable, since a book ought to be held together by something additional to the glue on the back binding.

The attentive reader will detect that some of the chapters here presented are scholarly in the dual sense of paying grave attention to massive bibliographical sources and of being written for readers somewhat knowledgeable in sociological discourse. Other chapters were originally prepared for oral presentation to "mixed audiences," and that circumstance inevitably affects expositional style. At the risk of being charged, correctly, with unevenness of exposition, I have decided not to edit out those differences. Even the advanced sociological reader may welcome being addressed, intermittently, in the vernacular.

This book evolved while I was unusually busy in other professional concerns, especially those involving the American Sociological Association. The occasion of its completion provides another opportunity to thank my colleagues and the Trustees of the Russell Sage Foundation for the opportunity of doing what it occurs to a sociologist to do. And more than incidentally, it occurs to this sociologist to express warm appreciation to Miss Madeline Dalton for converting a rather disorderly array of manuscript into legible order. She cannot be held truly accountable for content or style. That is my responsibility. But in some sense she did indeed produce the manuscript, and I am indeed grateful.

Wilbert E. Moore

New York and Princeton

February, 1967

CONTENTS

PART **IV**

FORECASTING THE FUTURE

TABLES

ORDER
AND
CHANGE

PART I

GENERAL STRUCTURAL CHANGE

1
SOCIAL CHANGE

Social change is such a prevalent and often disturbing feature of contemporary life that both the specialist and the layman may be tempted to suppose that it is peculiarly modern. Certainly the extensity and rate of change in the modern world are greater than in most past periods, but the static qualities of primitive cultures or archaic civilizations are easily and commonly overstated. Change, at some level and degree, is as characteristic of man's life in organized systems as is orderly persistence.

Indeed, small-scale changes may be an essential component of persistence on a larger scale. For example, given man's biological life cycle, enduring systems like kinship organization or government depend upon orderly patterns of age-specific role performances and the succession of individuals moving through established positions. Likewise, changing patterns on a daily, weekly, monthly, or annual cycle provide a basic and predictable continuity to the patterns of social existence.

Paradoxically, as change has accelerated in the real world of experience the scientific disciplines dealing with man's actions and products have tended to emphasize orderly interdependence and static continuity. Although other reasons for this strange state of affairs will be explored subsequently, the genuine difficulties of dealing with social dynamics cannot be denied. The relationship between small-scale and large-scale change, or between the short term and the long exemplifies analytical and factual complexity. That complexity is necessarily reflected in the formal definition presented here.

Social change is the significant alteration of social structures (that is, of patterns of social action and interaction), including consequences and manifestations of such structures embodied in norms (rules of conduct), values, and cultural products and symbols.

SOURCE. A different version of this Chapter will appear in the *International Encyclopedia of the Social Sciences*.

Preliminary Conceptual Clarification

This definition will encompass the gradual development of a leadership role in a small, task-oriented group, cyclical succession of centralization and decentralization in administrative organizations, or the revolutionary overthrow of a government and the establishment of a new institutional basis for the allocation of power. It will encompass short-term changes in employment rates and long-term changes in occupational structure; growth or decline in membership size of social units; continuous processes such as specialization and bureaucratization or discontinuous processes such as particular technical or social inventions.

The broad definition also comprises both what is commonly identified as *social* change, with a primarily behavioral focus, and *cultural* change, with a primarily symbolic or meaningful focus. The emphasis in the present discussion will be placed on the interplay among patterned behavior, the institutions or normative complexes that guide behavior and relate it to other elements in social systems, and the values that provide the meaning and rationale for activity and restraint. This emphasis cuts across conventional distinctions between the social and the cultural, as they are both intrinsic to the conception of social systems. Though the distinction between social and cultural is useful for some purposes, cultural change requires social actors as agents, and social change is likely to have cultural counterparts.

Yet it is true that changes in certain cultural subsystems—for example, language, the arts, and perhaps theological or philosophical systems—may be viewed in virtual abstraction from human action. This type of abstraction is exemplified in the first three volumes of Sorokin's *Social and Cultural Dynamics*.[1] Similarly, cycles or other fluctuations in the fashions of dress may be viewed "autonomously," though it is also proper to consider such fashions as patterns of appropriate conduct in one aspect of social behavior.

It is often true that modes of abstraction are mere matters of convenience. For example, the steady specialization of vocabularies in language systems may be treated either as a principle of autonomous evolution or related to the expansion of knowledge and to role differentiation in complex social systems. However, there is an underlying problem that should be made explicit. The degree to which cultural subsystems such as language may be traced to structural sources in social systems is a factual question of considerable theoretical importance. Similarly important is the degree to which such subsystems may

be translated into guides for social behavior. If the extent of autonomous variability among coexistent features of a society is substantial,
then a master key to the understanding of order and change will not
work. That appears to be precisely the situation in human societies,
and accounts for the multiplicity of principles relating to structural
regularities and to significant alterations.

It follows from the possibility of autonomous variability and from
the initial discussion of order-producing small-scale changes that a first
requisite for any formalization of dynamic principles is the stipulation
of the structure or component under analysis. Until units or systems
are identified in their principal dimensions one does not know what
is changing. Until temporal and other dimensional specifications are
made, one cannot distinguish significant from insignificant changes.

The Rejection of Singular Simplicity

A further consequence of the possibility of autonomous variability,
again abetted by complexities of scale and time, is that there is no
singular, sovereign cause for changing systems or components. The
quest for simplification, which is an appropriate feature of the scientific enterprise, has led to the identification of some important variables, such as technological innovation or demographic determinants,
but the net result has been the development of "special theories of
change" for specific classes of structures, determinants, and conditions,
and not a master theory that achieves independence from these restrictive variables.

For small-scale structures in general, such as groups or formal organizations, one can only be supremely confident of "fluctuations" in such
components as normative requirements or role performances. If such
structures endure, however, there is a high probability of "evasive
innovation," that is, of modes of action not comprehended by the
established rules of conduct, and consequently the probability of
normative accumulation, the accretion of regulations.[2]

For large-scale systems such as whole societies, one can be confident
that demographic behavior and the vicissitudes of incorporationg infants into the system through socialization will at the very least introduce flexibilities and adjustments if not major structural changes in a
clear direction. However, directionality of change may be inferred from
the universal lack of correspondence between the "ideal" and the
"actual" in social values and normative compliance, and thus the
probability of both technical and social innovation. In summary form,
these innovations are likely to be directed toward "adaptation" to the

nonhuman environment, to which adjustment is never perfect, and toward "social control."

The notion of social evolution is the most general theory applicable to social phenomena. In its simplest form, the theory posits variability of structural forms or components and selective adaptation. Variability in social phenomena may be linked in turn to innovation as well as to fluctuations and unreliabilities in reproduction and socialization. Yet such a general theory will not account for many changes that are otherwise interesting and significant. Social evolution appears to fit the general fate of mankind better than it applies to the transformation of particular societies or cultures.[3]

Changing Theoretical Interests

The predecessors and early exponents of the scientific study of social phenomena were far from impervious to social dynamics. Although people like Frédéric Le Play[4] attempted to establish canons for systematic, contemporary description of social types, a far more prevalent concern in the Nineteenth Century was the attempt to trace the historic paths to the present as then observed. Thus, one form or another of "philosophy of history" was common. Often the history attended to was not universal, but rather the fairly clear antecedents of European civilization. The attempt, generally, was to find order in the succession of civilizations, and occasionally, to account for accumulation. Auguste Comte, who gave sociology its name, was more ambitious both in scope and in content; his "law of the three stages"—the theological, metaphysical and positivist—claimed universality and cumulative directionality in historical change.

The directionality of change, and, in particular, increasing complexity and structural differentiation, came to be a major tenet of evolutionary theories. Following the important intellectual impact of Charles Darwin's works on biological evolution, Herbert Spencer, Lewis Henry Morgan, and others of somewhat lesser stature caught up such notions as selective adaptation to account for both the cross-sectional diversity of societies and cultures and the supposedly sequential stages of social organization. Evolution, in fact, by the end of the Nineteenth Century was a dominant factor in social thought. It appears in the work of William Graham Sumner,[5] despite his predominant relativism: "The mores can make anything right." And it appears in the work of Emile Durkheim,[6] despite his major intellectual influence on functionalism, the explanation of social phenomena in terms of the balance of an interdependent system.

Even Marxism was a variant of evolutionism, particularly in the notion of sequential stages of social organization. But Marxism attempted to supply the mechanism of change by emphasis on technology and its interaction with social organization. In its crudest form, Marxist thought shared with most evolutionary theory a kind of mechanical and, especially, a mindless inevitability in the explanation of the succession of social changes.

Yet some Marxian analysis was by no means as mechanical and mindless as it has been depicted at times, for Marx took fairly full account of the purposive character of social action—and not solely in his theory of revolutionary change. The Marxist position, though correctly criticized for derogating the independent variability and causal efficacy of ideas and ideals, did emphasize interplay of systemic elements and the dynamic consequences. Marx's intellectual heirs were never quite caught up in the extremes of static "functionalism" that came to represent a dominant theme in anthropological and sociological theory.

Functionalism, in the sense of explaining social phenomena by other, contemporary or quasi-simultaneous, social phenomena, entailed the rejection of the "quest for origins." Its proponents (e.g., Durkheim, A. R. Radcliffe-Brown, and Bronislaw Malinowski) in eschewing explanation in genetic terms also tended to suppress all dynamic queries, such as the sources and probable directions of systemic changes. Rather, the demonstration of interdependence came to mean the search for self-equilibrating mechanisms.

Recent revival of interest in dynamics owes something to all of these precedents, including functionalism, from which contemporary theory derives notions of systemic linkages which *may* be sequential, but also some notions of tension and incipient change through the concept of "disfunctions." However, resurgent concern for analysis of change probably owes more to the crude facts of the contemporary world and particularly to the social scientists' involvement in studies of modernization. Although functional-systems models have served rather well as predictors of "eventual" expected changes in elements of social structure "related" to economic development, a kind of sociological determinism may have been pushed beyond probable empirical confirmation in predicting structural similarities in all fully modernized societies. In any event, the mode of analysis has been a kind of comparative statics, offering a before-and-after view curiously discordant with older evolutionary theories: for, the standard treatment of modernization dwells on preexisting heterogeneity that becomes in due course a future homogeneity. Apart from this intellectual anachronism, studies of modernization have led to a recognition of a particular theoretical (and highly practical) weakness in the analytical models employed. A before-and-after comparison diverts attention from mechanisms of change, and entirely suppresses inquiries about sequences and time-tables.

Alternative Models of Societies

Viewing society as a "functional equilibrium system" has advantages in providing agenda for formulating connections and correlations. Whether specifically identified by the scholar or not, this model informs most of the solidly-based principles of social action and structure that comprise contemporary sociology and other social sciences. In the hands of expert theorists, the "functional approach" does not preclude attention to deviance, and does not prejudge either stability or continuity. Indeed, the specification of functional requisites of any society, if not merely definitional of society or simply an heuristic device for aiding comparability amidst conspicuous diversity of social forms, is implicitly an evolutionary theory. Not only do the functional requisites serve as high-level generalizations concerning the common features of all societies, but the survival test implies that past societies have failed to persist for want of one or several operating characteristics.

Viewing society as a "tension-management system" makes order itself problematic and invites agenda for identifying flexibilities, uncertainties, conflicts, and disparities between the ideal and the actual. (The "conflict model" of society[7] on the other hand does not appear to be a comprehensive construction, but only an appropriate emphasis on discordant elements and interests as a counterpoise to various "social integration" models.) The tension-management model identifies structural tension points as probable sites of change. The chief disadvantage of this conceptual scheme is that various commonalities and sheer persistence may be neglected, as attention is directed to intrinsic sources of social change.

Problems of Detection and Measurement

Change takes place in *time*, and observational time is scarce. For the single investigator, time is woefully finite. The "panel study" attempts, over relatively brief periods, to observe alterations in attitude and action while they are in process. For longer periods, historical evidence is required. Here the social scientist commonly turns to the professional historian, and, not uncommonly, in vain. Whether the historians' selective criteria for reporting the past coincide with sociological questions is highly problematic. Historians, for example, have not been very quantitative, and the sociologist interested in rates of change may have to do his own history. Much of the past is of course irretrievably lost. The assembling of social quantities is very recent in man's history, and even yet very incompletely practiced both in terms of areas of cultures of the world and in terms of types of information recorded.

It was earlier noted that the question, "What is changing?" is primary. Determining that question is a theoretical matter. Identifying elements of constructs for observation and analysis stems from intellectual frames of reference. Although opinions may properly differ as to what is significant, there is no general scientific basis for denying, say, legitimate interests in tiny alterations as they occur in small groups, or day-to-day developments in a political campaign. But it remains true that questions of magnitude arise in any case. How much of a change is to be taken as significant, and by what criteria of significance? Were the system-constructs explicitly employed by some social theorists to be taken seriously, this problem would be simpler of solution. Changes could be strictly dichotomized as trivial or tragic[8]: as constituting only variations on a theme within tolerable limits of persistent order, or as so altering an essential social component as to have serious repercussions throughout the system. The empirically verified looseness of social systems and the probability that some changes alter the system by cumulative degrees combine to make the question of magnitude a critical one. How much change, in what, has what predictable consequences for a specifiable class of social phenomena?

Some examples from demographic behavior may clarify the issues relating to significance. Let us suppose that mortality rates are relatively low and temporally stable, and relatively uniform by the standard social categories of residence, ethnicity, occupation, income, and so on. Let us also suppose that birth rates are also relatively low, the modal number of children per family again relatively uniform across social categories. Now let us suppose a fairly rapid rise in birth rates, which in familial terms means a modal number of children of three rather than two. Now such a change will have only minor consequences for the structure of the family, consequences limited to the nuances of generational and sibling relations. But the aggregative effect of the change on the economy, on the density of population, on the demand for schools and teachers, and so on, will be major. (Although some of the assumptions have been artificial, this has been, in effect, the significance of the "baby boom" following World War II.) Now let us alter the assumption of the independence of family size with respect to various social categories. Let us suppose, rather, that over the course

of a few decades the average size of family changes from a distribution
inversely correlated with measures of socioeconomic status to a strongly
positive correlation. Children then become another symbol of affluence.
Here the implications are more complex. In terms of mobility opportunities, it would appear that the relatively small families of the poor
would favor a more favorable distribution of meager resources for
current support and continuing education. Yet the advantages accruing
to the children brought up in well-to-do families are likely to persist,
and to the degree that any inheritance of status operates, the saturation
of the upper ranks would preclude substantial upward mobility on the
part of children of humble origin. Actually, if the fertility differentials
were sharp, only a changed status distribution resembling an inverted
pyramid could avoid substantial downward mobility among the well-
born.

The partially hypothetical illustrations of fertility trends underscore
the importance of looking for both direct and indirect consequences
and for both small-scale and large-scale ones.

The identification and observation of change are methodologically
easiest in proportion to at least four attributes or variables of the
dynamic patterns: scale, brevity, repetition, and mensuration.

"Scale" is a somewhat ambiguous term, possibly referring to the size
of comprehensiveness of the system affected—say the political structure
of a whole society as compared with a local custom relating to court-
ship—or to the degree of alteration. As magnitude in the latter sense
implies at least crude measurement the "scale" variable is most appropriately reserved to the comprehensiveness of the system involved.
(The two senses of scale are of course likely to be positively correlated;
but one can think of small changes in inclusive systems and large
changes in subsystems.)

Changes completed in a relatively short time are likely to come more
readily to the attention of the participant or the observer than those
over the longer term, even if the latter are eventually substantial in
magnitude. Thus there may be very long-term cycles which might be
detected retrospectively if on a sufficient scale—for example, organic
analogies relating to the life cycle of civilizations—but go quite un-
detected if on a small scale and of small magnitude of variation.

Relatively brief changes, even if of small magnitude, have a greater
chance of being observed if they are frequently repeated, perhaps in a
cyclical pattern. Repetition in fact greatly facilitates explanation and
prediction, as chance antecedents may be more readily distinguished
from common and efficacious ones. The repetition need not be confined
to a single social unit, so long as there is some basis of similarity among

units for comparison. Thus some of the social changes related to industrialization are likely to be unique and discontinuous with respect to past trends in areas undergoing modernization, but sufficiently repetitive from one society to another (time for these purposes being only an incidental variable) to permit formalization as general principles.

For large-scale and radical transformations in social systems, as exemplified by political revolutions or rapid industrialization, the quest for quantities may seem an act of supererogation. Yet even here numerical indicators are likely to be useful for comparing cases, and particularly necessary if one is going to speak at all precisely about rates of change. As one moves to less dramatic social transformations, the perception of change may not be uniform, and reliable measurement may be the only way of settling the issue as well as finding at least partial explanation for changes clearly demonstrated. For example, is mental illness increasing in the United States and other modernized societies? By what standardized criteria of identification and diagnosis? If a genuine increase is demonstrable, how can cross-sectional differences in rates—for example by age or income—be hypothetically converted into temporal trends in these same indicators? Failure to exercise both quantitative ingenuity and great methodological caution is likely to produce such unfortunately frequent academic exercises as the spurious explanation for a fictitious trend.

The methodological problems of identification and measurement of change are further complicated by the rarity of the classically neat demonstration of a singular cause producing a singular effect under finitely specifiable and repeatable conditions. Only part of the problem, although an important part, derives from the difficulty or impossibility of fully controlled social experimentation. One must also deal with the further circumstance that at least with present and foreseeable conceptual and observational tools, one is dealing with statistical probability distributions and attempting to explain various "dependent variables" so characterized in terms of various "independent variables" having the same uncertainties. Statistical techniques have been developed for dealing with these crudities, and others are likely to be invented. Most of these techniques are designed for testing relationships among variables in cross-sectional analysis. The problems are further aggravated for sequential analysis, for one must take into account not only the degree to which the outcome is determined by one or another measurable antecedent, but also the important question of the temporal order of critical variables. Smelser has referred to this, by analogy with economic production, as the "value-added process."[9] This methodological principle offers some prospect of moving from necessary to sufficient conditions for change, under favorable circumstances of observation and measurement. The idea resembles various "stage" theories of change, though stages often represent arbitrarily imposed discontinuities in cumulative trends and understate the interaction of variables in the process of transformation. Feldman and Moore[10] have identified one form of the more complex transformation as "cumulative, retroactive evolution" to identify the way later "stages" have a continuing or delayed effect on seemingly earlier ones. The mathematical conception of "stochastic processes" is a more accurate designation for the analytical designation than the reliance on stages, which, however, are useful modes of characterizing sequences that exhibit fairly clear breaks in rates of change, of "emergences" that fundamentally alter the properties of social systems.

The Directions of Change

The principal cause for discrediting the evolutionary theorists of the latter half of the Nineteenth Century was overgeneralization and undue simplification. A rectilinear theory of human evolution took too little account of diversity, or explained it improperly. Although Spencer's distinction of the "super-organic" offered promise of recognition that societies might show some portion of the diversity of plant and animal species, he was too bound by the biological unity of mankind to exploit his fundamental idea. That idea was subsequently exploited to a fault: by de-biologizing the human species and by emphasis on sheer unexplained diversity in complete relativism. This view was no more acceptable than the idea of lining up all of the world's cultures in rank order, the presumably, and often falsely, simpler social organization representing a kind of unexplained primitive survival.

The counterpart in social dynamics of simple, cross-sectional diversity taken as a datum has been the identification of "fluctuations": variability through time with no clearly repetitive or cumulative pattern. Fluctuations do indeed occur: for example chance variability in reproduction and the uncertainties of the intersection of nature and nurture in personality formation. In fact, the vicissitudes of matching recruits with the normative requirements of enduring positions insure some fluctuations in the exact behavioral counterparts of established structures. Sorokin[11] identifies many examples of fluctuations among structural types, though Moore[12] suggests that some of these are more properly viewed as competing principles in a dialectic opposition that leads to quasi-cyclical oscillation.

Cycles introduce a more determinate directionality into social change. A simple pendulum swing between extremes (prosperity and depression, liberalism and conservatism, innovation and accommodation) represents the simplest cyclical pattern. Multistage cycles are likely to rest either on tenuous analogies (the life cycles of civilizations for example), or to share with other stage theories somewhat arbitrary breaks in some variables that on inspection show rather orderly trends. The notion of self-equilibrating mechanisms in functional systems is more readily apprehended in terms of trendless cycles than it is in terms of static continuity, only occasionally disrupted by external disturbances. For example, the tendency in administrative organizations for "indulgent" departures from strict compliance with the rules to grow more extreme until reversed by a renewed insistence on approximate compliance might be characterized as the "cycle of sin and penance." Yet the notion of "self-equilibration" often implies that trends are reversed because of side-effects of actions of the participants. The mechanistic assumption is not always warranted, however. The question as to whether the direction of change is deliberate is always a proper one, and may often be answered in the affirmative.

A further point about cyclical change may be derived from the example of a small-scale repetitive pattern just used. Cycles may be superimposed on an underlying cumulative trend. Thus the "return to the rules" in an administrative organization is unlikely to be complete, and through successive repetitions of the sequence there is likely to be evident a longer-term modification of the norms themselves. On a larger scale, the alternation of relatively high and relatively depressed economic indicators in complex economies may be essentially short-term variations consistent with long-term growth of income per capita or similar measures of economic development.

Cumulation was in fact what misled the evolutionary theorists of an earlier era, who comfortably equated change with "progress." And the cumulation was real, if exaggerated and naive: a point missed by all their relativistic detractors. For various sectors of any social system or for entire systems over considerable periods of time there is evidence of steady or even accelerating growth. The growth in number of rules in continuing organizations is certainly not at a steady rate if very frequent temporal comparisons are made, and probably very steady over somewhat longer intervals. The growth in total human population has been variable over considerably longer temporal periods, and yet cumulative over the span of man's earthly tenure. Rates of technical innovation are variable in time and place (though commonly on a cumulative base). If the invention rate is the unit of observation its trends may appear nearly cyclical over extensive periods of human history. If the sum total of utilitarian knowledge is taken as the basis of observation, the short-term variations in the rate of addition to stock are likely to appear as very minor fluctuations in the long-term accumulation of reliable knowledge at an exponential rate: the more there is, the faster it will increase.

Another methodological aside is here appropriate, already hinted at in the preceding paragraph. Both the rate and the direction of social change are much affected by the time-intervals of observation, including initial and terminal observations. Constant surveillance of ongoing processes is rare outside the laboratory, and nearly impossible for changes over a very long term. Frequent recording of observations tends to pick up cyclical patterns and essentially meaningless fluctuations. Infrequent recording loses such information and points instead to more enduring trends. This is not to argue for less information, as the infrequent observations are subject to grave risks of sampling error in the peculiarities of the situation when observations are recorded. Skilled analysis can sort out mere fluctuations, short-term trends, and long-term trends from a "continuous" series. The fact is, however, that for retrospective views of long-term changes, the opportunity is not commonly offered the analyst. He must take what he can find, and that is more likely to yield "fundamental" trends than the finer processes of transformation that eventually yielded spuriously regular trends.

A further example of great substantive importance may serve to underscore the problems of sorting out the short-term and the long. Contemporary evidence and all reasonable inferences from such historical materials as are available indicate fairly wide short-term fluctuations in death rates and birth rates, but with two clear longer-term patterns. Over the very long term, total human population has grown, and it appears that the growth follows the cumulative, accelerating (exponential) pattern. Examined in somewhat more detail, the shorter-term patterns exhibit greater variability in mortality than in fertility in nonmodern societies and greater variability in fertility in modern societies.

This example may also be pushed somewhat further. The steady decline of mortality followed after an interval by a steady decline of fertility are trends uniformly accompanying economic development. The trends represent a dynamic pattern that is repetitive in space through time, though the pattern seems to operate only once in each economy taken as a unit.

And this example can be pushed still further with respect to the direction of change. The variation in mortality in premodern societies appears to be rather irregular: determined by such "chance" factors as climates and harvests, political vicissitudes, and infectious diseases. Fertility in the contemporary, modernized world on the other hand appears to follow a more nearly cyclical pattern. Among predominantly contracepting populations birth rates are likely to be correlated with *current* economic indicators. But there is more than a slight suggestion that fertility does not function solely as a dependent variable. Prosperous conditions, it may be argued, result in exceptionally high fertility. As these birth cohorts reach maturity they tend to oversupply the then prevailing labor demand, and that serves to increase unemployment and other unfavorable economic indicators. Those economic conditions in turn result in small birth cohorts. Note that if this reasoning has further empirical validation—it fits rather well the fertility behavior of "Western" countries for several decades following the 1930's—we have an example of a self-disequilibrating system. The cycles remain off-phase because of the intrinsic lag entailed in bringing infants to the age of labor-force participation.

The ways in which cumulative trends display themselves are numerous. To the simple, additive (rectilinear) change and the accelerating (exponential) growth should be added one form or another of "logistic" trend. A slow increase accelerates because of an increasing base for combinations to take place, but then "dampens off" as severely limiting conditions are encountered. The size of organizations and even entire populations often display this pattern, though it must be remembered that the parameters or restrictive boundaries are themselves subject to change—for example, by technological or organizational innovation. The limits, moreover, may be lower as well as upper. The decline of mortality is commonly described as a "reverse J-curve," as early and easy improvements in health conditions are followed by more and more difficult lifesaving measures until the limits of biological survival are approached.

The directionality of change can be represented in ways additional to measures of size, incidence, or occurrence. Certain *processes* of change may also be found to have a reliable and enduring direction. Most notable of these in the theoretical literature is the presumable universal tendency toward specialization or structural differentiation. Why this tendency prevails in social systems is commonly left unexplained, the process being taken as a datum. Durkheim[13] and others sought a demographic explanation: growing numbers lead to more complex social arrangements, including positional and role differentiation. Extensive evidence does point to a high, but by no means perfect, correlation between size and specialization, and the mechanism of the relation, the reason for the association, is largely left unexplained.

In Darwinian evolutionary theory, structural differentiation derived from selective adaptation of organisms to their environment. Since environments differ both cross sectionally and temporally, differentiation represents past processes of selection to account for the observed diversity and a way of accounting for continuing change when it occurs. It is surprising that so little use has been made of this conceptual scheme in the theory of social systems, where it appears equally applicable. Population or membership size would then serve as a basis for increased potential variability, and differentiation internal to the system one mode of adaptation of the entire system to its environmental setting. Criteria of efficiency in optimizing goal achievement, criteria which may be made overt and purposive in complex social systems, would then be particular forms of adaptation.

Specialization is not of course an absolutely sovereign and irreversible dynamic process, as its dangers to systemic cohesion may occasionally lead to renewed emphasis on unity and commonality of participating units. Yet the probability of continuing specialization in enduring social systems is high. The cumulative growth of reliable knowledge and technique abets the requirement of differentiated competence.

Structural differentiation does imperil systemic cohesion, as just indicated. Mere interdependence, as Durkheim demonstrated,[14] does not insure "solidarity." Solidarity or systemic cohesion also requires an effective system of norms, which in turn will be justified or rationalized by common values. The *mechanisms* of effecting coordination are chiefly two: exchange, whether through relatively impersonal monetary markets or other forms of complementary reciprocities; and administrative authority, a mode of allocating duties and insuring compliance by the exercise of institutionalized power. The mechanisms are not of course mutually exclusive, as subordination to authority, for example, may be contractual. Now these relationships are essentially structural, but their present relevance is that exchange and "bureaucratization" may be expected to expand *pari passu* with the process of specialization.

Consistently with the position that only "special" theories of social change are appropriate to the diversity of social phenomena, each of the varieties of directionality in change has been illustrated empirically. Although many of these have been offered in the past as master principles of social dynamics, the eclectic view here espoused has clear advantages in factual confirmation, although it thereby suffers loss of simplicity and level of generalization.

A supplementary note on directionality is appropriate. Any of the forms of change we have identified may be associated with ideas of "progress." Progress, which is simply change in an evaluatively approved direction, is of course not itself a scientific principle, but only a possibly relevant social datum as an item of belief. Progress may be viewed by social participants as the continuation of cumulative growth, as the damping of cyclical oscillations and return to a steady state, or even as recapturing an evaluatively superior past state (the concept of "primitivism"). But since social action is partly purposive—a point that will be subsequently explored—the direction of change may well reflect the *desired* direction of change. Thus ideas of progress may be important explanatory elements in accounting for observed dynamics.

The Problem of Discontinuities

Change is most readily perceived as "orderly" where measured trends display a uniform direction or rate, or cycles are repeated often enough to confirm their character. Even "lawful acceleration"* such as the exponential curve, which makes the rate of growth proportional to the extent of the relevant universe at any time, displays an underlying order. From a theoretical point of view such orderly change clearly requires persistence or repetition in the ambient conditions that foster continuity of trends. From a practical or procedural point of view, orderly change provides sufficient time for the identification of causes and the refinement of observation and measurement.

Analytical difficulties multiply when change is in a significant sense and degree "discontinuous." For example, extremely rapid change, even though its antecedents are clear, may have further consequences for altering the fundamental structure of the underlying change-producing conditions. The successor system is then, as it is sometimes expressed, "qualitatively" different. This should not be taken to mean that measurement is no longer possible or appropriate, but only that new variables and parameters must be taken into account. Two illustrations from the contemporary world are in point. Nuclear fission and fusion may be retrospectively viewed as a further step in the multiplying power utilization in man's social evolution.[15] But the implications of that power for international politics, space travel, and economic production introduce new dimensions into the potentialities for further change. At the more strictly social level, the extremely rapid spread of the doctrine of economic development has substantially reduced the cultural insularity of tribal societies and archaic agrarian civilizations,

* See Chapter 14.

and has thus increased the scholarly and practical utility of viewing the entire world as a single system for many purposes.

Closely related to the phenomenon of "emergence" which we have just discussed and which in the past also has been caused by both technical and social innovations—fire, writing, organized technology, and bureaucratic authority, for example—is that of the "threshold." The cumulative and interactive effect of changes that are analytically separable may result in unprecedented transformation. Thus, although there is no precedent for a *rapid* decline of birth rates in the course of economic modernization, several antecedent conditions for a sharp break with the past may be noted: the potentiality and actuality of mortality reductions at a much more rapid rate than in the oldest industrial countries; a nearly universal political adherence to rapid economic development, coupled with growing recognition that economic programs are imperilled by extremely fast population growth; and a steadily changing "technology of contraception" that may greatly increase its economic and esthetic (and perhaps even religious) acceptability.

The concept of the threshold emphasizes sequential rather than factorial analysis of causation. It is equivalent to Smelser's use of the "value added" concept mentioned earlier.[16] It represents an attempt to move from necessary to sufficient conditions in the prediction of change, including those that represent sufficient alterations in direction, rate, or subsequent characteristics of the social system to merit the designation "discontinuous."

Trends may reverse as well as cumulate to new levels. The upswing in birth rates among advanced industrial countries following World War II illustrates completion of a process of change, after which the criterion variables—birth rates or children per family—were determined by previously unimportant factors. The historic decline in fertility rates owed something to marriage rates and age, but chiefly reflected an extending pattern of contraception. As indicated by the then-standard inverse relationship between fertility and socioeconomic status, the leading practitioners of contraception were those families who, on objective grounds, could best afford children. But in the course of time the attitudes and techniques favorable to family limitation became less and less exclusive possessions of upper and middle segments of the status distribution. If, as now appears to be the case, it was chiefly education among the various criteria of status that had the greatest influence on family limitation, it is also noteworthy that it is education that has exhibited the greatest equality of distribution. Once a third or fourth child was no longer putative evidence of ignorance and error, but rather might be interpreted as choice of family size, birth rates began to take on the characteristic trends and distributions of the markets for "consumer durables."

Similarly, although economic modernization is never "complete," its initial, discontinuous impact on traditionally organized societies may be later followed by partial restoration of structures and forms never completely destroyed. For example the nucleation of family units through geographic and social mobility may be followed by partially restored, though discretionary, communication and reciprocities among kinsmen. Likewise, stable exchange or employment relations are likely to lose some of their nominal austerity and impersonality. Note that this is not to say that the *status quo ante* is fully restored, that nothing significant has changed, but only that the conception of an unusually disruptive "transitional period" has some merit.

Fundamental social revolutions represent an extreme form of discontinuous change. Though social scientists have been at some pains to emphasize partial restorations even after major revolutions, it is plainly improper to conclude thereby that revolutions are inconsequential. For revolution in the restricted sense of fundamental change in institutional structure and distribution of social power, a prior indicator is of course *polarization*. Polarization, however, requires explanation in turn. Under the conditions of political centralization, substantial urban agglomeration, and fairly effective communication, polarization is likely to occur when there is an absolute or relative decline in economic well-being or political rights among those already largely excluded from positions of affluence and power. The decline of course must be fairly severe, sharply differential in its impact, and numerically extensive. Although implicitly quantifiable, very little quantitative analysis of revolutionary antecedents has been attempted. Polarization, for example, is typical in the modernized sector in early stages of industrialization. Yet in the majority of historical cases that sector has been too small to provide a clear revolutionary potential, and as it has expanded it has also reduced its polarities. How extensive and rapid must "early" modernization be for one to be able to forecast probable social revolution? The apparently faster change in aspirations than in the means for their fulfillment in contemporary developing areas invites the speculation that the incidence of revolutions may increase in the future. Refining that speculation into a responsible probability distribution awaits comparative data, cross sectional and temporal, not now at hand.

References

1. Pitirim A. Sorokin, *Social and Cultural Dynamics* (New York: American Book Co., 1937–40), 4 volumes. (One-volume abridgement: Boston: Porter Sargent, 1957.)

2. See Wilbert E. Moore, *Social Change* (Englewood Cliffs, New Jersey: Prentice-Hall, 1963), p. 50.

3. See Leslie White, *The Science of Culture* (New York: Grave Press, 1949).

4. (Pierre Guillaume) Frédéric LePlay, *Les Ouvriers Européens* (Paris: Imprimerie Impériale, 1855).

5. William Graham Sumner, *Folkways* (Boston: Ginn and Co., 1907).

6. Emile Durkheim, *De la Division du Travail Social*, 2nd ed. (Paris: Alcan, 1902); English-language edition: Glencoe, Illinois: Free Press, 1960; also, *The Elementary Forms of the Religious Life* (Glencoe, Illinois: Free Press, 1954).

7. See Ralf Dahrendorf, *Class and Class Conflict in Industrial Society* (Stanford, California: Stanford University Press, 1959).

8. See Wilbert E. Moore, *op.cit.*, p. 20.

9. Neil J. Smelser, *Theory of Collective Behavior* (London: Routledge & Kegan Paul, 1962).

10. Arnold S. Feldman and Wilbert E. Moore, "Moot Points in the Theory," *in* Moore and Feldman, eds., *Labor Commitment and Social Change in Developing Areas* (New York: Social Science Research Council, 1960), pp. 360–368.

11. Pitirim A. Sorokin, *op.cit.*, Vol. 4.

12. Wilbert E. Moore, *op.cit.*, pp. 66–68.

13. Emile Durkheim, *De la Division du Travail Social*, previously cited.

14. *Ibid.*

15. See Leslie White, *op.cit.*

16. Neil J. Smelser, *op.cit.*

2
SOCIAL CHANGE AND
COMPARATIVE STUDIES

It is both true and false that we have no general theory of social change. It is true that no singular first cause or monistic determinism has proved valid, and no single formula will encompass small-scale and large-scale changes, the short-run and the long, the persistent trend and the chance fluctuation. Yet the negative position surely has been overstated. Comparative studies of modernization yield a set of related generalizations concerning transformation of societies as they join the contemporary world system; and even notions of long-term social evolution turn out to have merit if made less comprehensive and pretentious than earlier evolutionists were wont to imagine them.

General Comments

The magnitude of contemporary social change, particularly in the structure of societies and their major institutions, and the involvement of virtually the entire world in rapid change that reverberates from one part to another—these set the contemporary era apart from previous periods.[1] Though change is a universal characteristic of human societies, the modern world provides differences in magnitude and rate, as just indicated, and in another respect as well: the high proportion of changes that are either deliberate—a product of purposive intervention

SOURCE. Adapted from "Introduction: Social Change and Comparative Studies," *International Social Science Journal*, 15: 519–527, No. 4, 1963; by permission of the *Journal*, which is published by UNESCO.
In its original form this Chapter introduced a series of papers prepared for the second Inter-American Sociology Seminar, which met at Princeton University in September 1962. I have not removed the references to Latin America, for they serve to provide a context in an area that is newly developing in terms of modernization and also in sociological work.

in the modes of action and organization—or the secondary and tertiary consequences of such deliberate change.

It is not primarily for the analysis of these sweeping social transformations that sociology and its closely related fields have been accorded a measure of scientific respectability in Europe and the United States. That hardly won and barely recognized respectability rests primarily on refinements in theory and measurement used in the study of cross-sectional relations. Just at the time when scholars in Latin America and other developing areas of the world are attempting to push forward in scientific studies of the social order, the order itself is threatening not to hold still enough to be studied. Though the inference that all is in flux is clearly an exaggeration, there is enough truth in it to add a temporal query to the usual spatial one: how applicable are 'established principles' in different settings?

The attempt to push forward a "sociology of development" applicable to Latin America provides an excellent example of several interrelated problems. We may start from the particular and proceed to the general.

The need for more systematic and extensive data-gathering in Latin America is clear, with particular emphasis upon improving and using census materials. At the same time, there is available much material that remains unexploited owing to a shortage of sophisticated sociologists. But what would be the reasonable and proper aim of such intensified effort? If there is indeed a general pattern that encompasses modernization everywhere, would filling in local details be of great significance? Put the other way around, how could the theory of modernization possibly apply to the substantially different economic and political régimes and cultural conditions that characterize so diverse a region as Latin America?

Partially satisfactory answers to these questions can be derived from comments on "levels of generalization." If phenomena generalized about are highly diverse in other, neglected particulars, the generalization may be valid, but lacking in the required specificity for predicting outcomes in rich detail. Taking account of other variables may force reduction of the level of generalization, for example, by constructing typologies. Application of generalizations to cases not previously included may in fact force modification of the principles, as neglected variables turn out to be crucial conditions.

These methodological considerations form part of the rationale for comparative studies. They are quite within the province of "pure science," and have only a partial coincidence with problems of applying general principles to particular policies and strategies of action, for such application always implies taking the particularities of situations into account.

It may indeed turn out that not one but several special "Latin American sociologies" will be needed for predicting the consequences of modernization in a region with great heterogeneity despite some common cultural traditions.[2] Yet modernization has its common features too, in more than a definitional sense,[3] but the exact lines and ratios among the general, the typological, and the particular remain to be clarified by comparative studies.

There is another use for comparative studies that make repeated observations through time as well as under differing conditions from one social setting to another. Our knowledge of the "social consequences of industrialization" rests on a rather extensive use of comparative empirical materials representing the common structural features of highly industrialized societies and the emerging characteristics of newly developing areas. The principles, moreover, have been enriched by theoretical inferences, using "social systems" models, of the structural changes that "must" ensue from major alterations in the structure of production and distribution. Yet the temporal dimensions of change, and particularly the rates and the sequences, the probable leads and lags, remain largely unknown.

The great challenge, therefore, of comparative temporal studies in Latin America is not simply the application and amendment of general theory. In effect, such general theory does not exist. At least it does not exist with adequate empirical grounding. In this respect the 'underdeveloped' state of Latin American social science is shared by North America and Europe as well. The challenge consists of starting with certain developments in theoretical orientations, which lead to the asking of significant questions in a prospectively fruitful way, and thus developing a "sociology of development" that would contribute to social sciences everywhere.

The Uses and Abuses of Dichotomies

The 'classical' tradition in sociological theory does in fact provide the basis for comparative studies. The major theoretical works are replete with the exposition of a fundamental dualism in social organization, which in the currently acceptable mode of discourse may be called the contrast between the "traditional" and the "modern." The criteria or indexes for classification have varied from one author to another, and these variations have some significance. Yet, from a slightly more generalized view, they appear to be variations on a common theme: virtually all attribute to what we now call the "traditional" type of social organization a prominent emphasis on affectivity, consensus, and informal controls and attribute to "modern" forms impersonality, interdependent specialization, and formal controls. The actual dichotomies, of course, differ—for example, community and society (Toennies), or community and association (MacIver), or folk and urban communities (Redfield); status and contract (Maine); mechanical and organic solidarity (Durkheim); sacred and secular societies (Becker). Dichotomies have also figured in more specialized or analytical contexts: for example, the contrast between formal and informal organization that is standard in industrial sociology, or alternative normative principles such as Parsons' "pattern variables."[4] These latter uses, however, figure only indirectly in the analysis of large-scale social change: either in terms of relative incidence of one or another form in traditional or modern societies, taken as given, or as omnipresent dialectical alternatives that constitute points of tension and thus probable sites of change.[5]

Virtually every theorist who has used a dichotomous classification of whole societies or cultures has also made more or less explicit use of the comparative analysis for discussion of the direction of social change. Whether the direction has been viewed with pleasure, dismay, or neutrality, the modern complex social order is seen as contrasting with, but emerging from, more traditional forms of social organization.

Although the safest assumption is that dichotomy is an extremely primitive form of classification, that is, that all dichotomies are in some measure false, the use of such constructed types may still be defensible. In the hands of Germani[6] the global types, traditional and industrial, are dissected into numerous sectors and elements, with the result that a fairly comprehensive check-list for comparative description emerges.

There is a major hazard in this form of comparative analysis, and a major shortcoming in its application to social change. The hazard is that the similarity of concrete societies at both ends of the scale may be exaggerated. (Germani distinguishes, here and there, subtypes of traditional society, and uniformly distinguishes industrial societies following the "liberal" model—approximately that of Western Europe and the United States in the nineteenth century—and "recent transformations."[7]) As a corollary, even if the diversity of premodern societies, richly documented by historians and ethnographers, is given due recognition, the forces of modernization may be depicted as leading to a uniform destination: the creation of a common culture.[8] Now although this hazard may simply illustrate once more the level-of-generalization problem, the ways in which industrial societies differ and are likely to continue doing so are partly at a very general level. Specifically, such societies differ in characteristic modes of tension-management and especially in the political, as distinct from administrative, structure of the state.

The principal shortcoming of the dichotomous classification in the analysis of social change is that it relies primarily on "comparative statics" rather than on processes and procedures, rates and sequences. This is not to say that before-and-after comparisons have no place in dynamic analysis, for at the very least they provide a kind of generalized predictive model for major structural changes that accompany modernization. Such comparisons do not provide either intermediate or terminal time-tables of transformation. And the "final" terminus is arbitrary in a special sense and degree, for once a society moves far enough along the scale to be classed as modern or industrial it will almost certainly, along with others of the class, experience continuing rapid change.

The Models for Change

The challenge to sociological theory which efforts to modernize traditional societies represent has been partially concealed by the development of before-and-after models and by an important additional circumstance: the primary source of change could be viewed as external to the traditional structure. Modernization then becomes a datum, and comparative analysis is used to elucidate systematically the social consequences of this given change.

This procedure has required the suppression of certain otherwise relevant knowledge, or the treatment of certain questions essentially in terms of historical accident rather than in terms of general principles. Thus, little note is taken of the intrinsic sources of change in all societies, or of the circumstance that social change is actively promoted by elements internal to many of the underdeveloped countries. The sources of the original industrial revolutions have been subject to sociological interpretation, but with little applicability to the contemporary world except in the form of special attitudes (for example, towards achievement) and special aptitudes (for example, towards entrepreneurship).[9]

If, however, the destination of modernization is neither uniform nor stable and if the trajectory of transformation differs in space and time, taking account of these variables requires a fairly serious examination of conventional theoretical models.

Conceptions of Social Systems

The model of society that is in most general use by those social scientists interested in comparative social structure may be characterized as the "functional equilibrium system." Representing a departure from global, simplifying theories of social evolution, and, in certain forms, a departure also from a simple relativism that emphasized diversity, the functional equilibrium model has been the main source of propositions concerning relationships and interdependencies. This model thus is the actual mainstay for the impressive body of generalizations concerning the consequences of modernization.

In its relatively pure form the functional equilibrium conception of society results in certain distortions and certain important omissions when applied to modernization. The distortions and omissions are related, for both stem from the circumstance that the model does not attend to intrinsic sources of change, does not predict changes that have persistent directionality (but only those that restore balance if that is disturbed), and thus does not readily handle past changes that clearly affect the current state of the system.

On this point, the distortion may take the extreme form of the "sociologistic fallacy," the view that societies now undertaking rapid modernization were until "yesterday" both intrinsically static and lacking in any prior contact with European civilization.

The conception of society as a functional equilibrium never reigned unchallenged, particularly by some variants of the Marxist tradition. Recently the questioning seems to have become more widespread, with some theorists emphasizing conflict models of the social order,[10] and others the view of society as a tension-management system.[11] The tension-management conception emphasizes intrinsic sources of change, and views change as possibly tension-producing—for example, the lack of synchronization in development measures—as well as possibly tension-reducing.

It would be improper, however, to view the tension-management conception of society as frontally opposed to the functional-equilibrium conception, or as virtuous as opposed to evil. Rather it appears proper to view the notion of tension-management as an amendment to the commonest form of functional analysis. If users of functional analysis tend to neglect conflict and change, users of tension analysis may tend to neglect consensus and continuity.

The tension-management approach does not abandon the important conception of social action in systems, but it makes the order of those systems problematical rather than definitional. Though by no means rejecting the clear evidence of major structural features that modern societies have in common, it also permits recognition of the fact that the characteristic tensions arising in relations between structures (for example, the economy and the polity) are likely to differ, and it invites attention to the continuing dynamics of industrial societies.

A conception of society that makes change normal and posits no steady state for its cessation does not as such tell us anything about the course of modernization. It simply permits thinking in terms of a course rather than a transitory interlude.

Stages: a Partial Solution

Attempts to improve on a simple before-and-after analysis of modernizations may take several forms, including both cross-sectional and temporal typologies. For example, a cross-sectional typology might take into account differences in the relations between populations and resources in preindustrial societies, or differences in the complexity of social organization. A temporal typology might compare and contrast historically "early" and "late" modernization or use a more elaborately graded scale of historical sequences. Thus it has been suggested that the speed of social transformation is correlated with historical time, that is, approximately with position in the ordinal sequence of the start of industrialization,[12] and further that the relative role of the State as an agency of change shows a similar correlation, late arrivals being more political than their predecessors.[13]

Other attempts to enrich the understanding and prediction of modernization involve the notion of "stages" of development. Perhaps the simplest form is the distinction among conditions, concomitants, and consequences of industrialization.[14] Moore has also suggested a sequence in the rates of most rapid growth by different sectors of the economy,[15] and Germani has suggested a six-stage sequence of political participation in the course of modernization.[16]

Since lack of synchronization is the normal state in industrializing and industrial societies,[17] and since some changes may be continuous rather than discontinuous or singular, approximately valid stages may be difficult to detect. Several alternatives are possible: limitation to a single major structure or functional area of society, the use of statistical distributions and rates rather than attributes present or absent, or the use of highly generalized stages with consequent loss of information.

No one of these alternatives is categorically superior to the others. The choice can only be exercised in terms of the scientific purpose at hand.

Sequential Patterns: the Challenge

Although it may appear to the harried official of an underdeveloped country that he must seek to change everything at once, this was certainly not the historic pattern and will certainly not occur even under revolutionary régimes in the contemporary world. Whether for practical policy or for scientific generalization and prediction, the temporal rate and sequence of events need closer identification, along with a distinction among the necessary, the probable, and the unnecessary or irrelevant structural changes. Comparative statics, the careful completion of the cross-sectional analysis of consequences of modernization, may yield a probability table of changes appropriate to various types of societies. Actual examination of the historical course of change and comparison with trends beginning to emerge in the developing areas will be necessary before genuinely dynamic models can be realistically constructed.

It is evident that not all historic rates of change or even sequences must be recapitulated, partly because the products of the past become the ever-richer inventory for the present, an inventory permitting some choice of items and combinations. Those products are social as well as economic, ideas as well as goods. Yet functional connections and limits of resources certainly impose some restraints on choice and temporal priorities.

Some economists have begun to approach development models in terms of "linear programming" and have applied such models not only to elements like power production but also to the supply of teachers for the training of workers in skills needed in the future. Some of the main features of such models have wider utility in depicting sequential connections. When used for planning purposes, however, they are likely to share a fundamental defect of before-and-after comparisons: the assumption of a finite terminal point when change stops.

The sociology of development, it was noted earlier, is still to be built in terms of sequential models. The comparative studies needed for that task will require historical depth and attention to quantities in addition to suitable rubrics for recording evidence across national and cultural boundaries. We are now beginning to ask the right questions, which is no mean achievement.

References

1. See Wilbert E. Moore, *Social Change* (Englewood Cliffs, New Jersey: Prentice-Hall, 1963), especially Chapter 1. The same points have been made independently by Gino Germani. See his *Política y Sociedad en una Epoca de Transición* (Buenos Aires: Editorial Paidos, 1963).

2. See, for example, Roger Vekemans and J. L. Segundo, "Essay of a Socio-Economic Typology of the Latin American Countries," *in* Egbert de Vries and José Medina Echavarría, eds., *Social Aspects of Economic Development in Latin America* (Paris: UNESCO, 1963), Vol. I, Chap. III.

3. See Wilbert E. Moore, *The Impact of Industry* (Englewood Cliffs, New Jersey: Prentice-Hall, 1965).

4. See Talcott Parsons, *The Social System* (Glencoe, Illinois: Free Press, 1951), especially pp. 188ff.; see also Parsons, "Pattern Variables Revisited: A Response to Robert Dubin," *American Sociological Review*, 25: 467–483, August 1960.

5. This is the approach of Moore in *Social Change*, previously cited.

6. Gino Germani, *op.cit.*, pp. 117–126.

7. *Ibid.*

8. See Wilbert E. Moore, "The Creation of a Common Culture," *Confluence*, No. 4, pp. 229–238, July 1955. For a later statement critical of this position, see Arnold S. Feldman and Wilbert E. Moore, "Industrialization and Industrialism: Convergence and Differentiation," *Transactions of the Fifth World Congress of Sociology*, 1962, Volume II, pp. 151–169.

9. See, for example, Everett E. Hagen, *On the Theory of Social Change: How Economic Growth Begins* (Homewood, Illinois: Dorsey, 1962).

10. See, for example, Lewis A. Coser, *The Functions of Conflict* (Glencoe, Illinois: Free Press, 1956); Ralf Dahrendorf, *Class and Class Conflict in Industrial Society* (Stanford, California: Stanford University Press, 1959).

11. See Wilbert E. Moore, *Social Change*, especially pp. 10–11, 70–84.

12. See Gino Germani, *op.cit.*, p. 69.

13. See Wilbert E. Moore, *The Impact of Industry*.

14. *Ibid.*

15. See Wilbert E. Moore, *Economy and Society* (New York: Random House, 1955), pp. 40–41.

16. Gino Germani, *op. cit.*, Chapter 5, "De la Sociedad Tradicional a la Partici-pacion Total en América Latina."

17. *Ibid.*, pp. 98–109.

PART II

THE TRANSFORMATION OF ECONOMIC STRUCTURES

3
SOCIAL ASPECTS OF
INDUSTRIALIZATION

Industrialization has been a major source of both the quickening rate and the geographical spread of rapid social change in the contemporary world. Particularly following World War II economic growth became a matter of political policy in countries already highly industrialized, and particularly in areas previously left behind by the economic transformation of Western Europe and the United States and the later development of Germany, Japan, and the Soviet Union. The breakup of the colonial system and the consequent multiplication of national states hastened the process of making economic development a prime matter of political concern, particularly in areas where prior growth had been small. Economic and technical assistance became a matter of national concern to the advanced countries also, and a major mission of the United Nations and its specialized agencies. England and France particularly took an interest in former colonies. The foreign economic expenditures of the United States and the Soviet Union were strongly influenced by ideological and strategic considerations of the "cold war." Meanwhile, in discussions about the nonindustrial world, the areas that had benefited very little from earlier economic change were first known as "backward," then "underdeveloped," and finally as "newly developing." Though partly a mere semantic evolution in response to supposed political sensitivities in the areas concerned, actual developments in the course of two decades or less gave some color of substance to the more dynamic (and forward-looking) designation.

Industrialization in the strict sense entails the extensive use of inanimate sources of power in the production of economic goods and

SOURCE. A different version of this chapter appears in the *International Encyclopedia of the Social Sciences*.

services. Even so restrictive a definition does not limit the concept solely to manufacturing, as agriculture is also subject to mechanization (as well as other modes of technical rationalization), and so are services such as transportation and communication. It is true, of course, that manufacturing is an essential ingredient, as the machines and instruments used in the production of raw materials or services are likely to be factory produced.

The use of an initially technological criterion of industrialization does not imply a kind of technological determinism. There are clearly institutional and organizational preconditions and counterparts of the scale and efficiency of power utilization. For example, extensive industrialization in the strict sense is quite unlikely in the absence of a highly specialized and coordinated labor force, monetary exchange and rationalized accounting systems, the technology of precise measurement and production control, and so on. These "implications" of industrialization form part of the substantive summary that will be presented in subsequent sections. But technology itself is improperly viewed as a kind of inanimate force. It rather consists of a body of practical knowledge and skills, a social product having social consequences only as utilized through the organized direction of human ingenuity.

Industrialization is often used in a broader sense as equivalent to any form of economic modernization. For this looser usage there is some justification, for there is no example of sustained economic growth (measured, say, by real income per head) without the extensive practice of manufacturing or use of its products. Making industrialization equivalent to economic development runs some risks, however, particularly for somewhat fine-grained analysis of the components of economic growth. Even if the structural integration of economic systems were greater than can be empirically confirmed, the order and rate of change of one or another component in a wide range of "economic factors" would still have significant consequences. The risk is minimized by its recognition, however, and industrialization will be used here in its broader sense except where finer distinctions are necessary and appropriate.

Intellectual Backgrounds

The "classic" writers in economics, who were in the main contemporaries of the early stages of industrialization in England and Western Europe, tended to view the changing technical and organizational characteristics of economic production simply as responses to rational economic interests in an impersonal, competitive market with freedom of contract. About the legal or institutional framework within which an economy would flourish they had remarkably little to say, except negatively in the doctrine of *laissez-faire*. About the kind of property institutions necessary to insure transferability and diversion to alternate uses they were silent, and about the negative implications of the power of property for equality of contractual position they were remarkably obtuse. In fact, the classical model of a competitive economy had a much closer fit, at least theoretically, to an economy comprised of independent primary producers and artisans than to an industrialized system in the strict sense.

Marx's attempted revision of economic theory[1] was much more attentive to the factory as a social system. Although Marx's analysis was, by repeated assertion, "materialistic," it was in effect far more sociological than that of his predecessors. Technology had, it is true, a primary place in the Marxian bundle comprising the "economic factor," but technology interacted with rather than exactly determining the "relationships of production"—relationships, note, primarily governed by property institutions and not by "materialist" considerations in any meaningful sense.

Weber, in turn, attempted a revision of Marxian analysis. He not only analyzed the forms of economic organization in far more comparative detail than Marx had attempted,[2] but also in his famous thesis on the crucial role of Protestantism in the development of capitalism[3] he attempted to assert the importance of values and ideas in economic affairs, elements dismissed as "superstructure" in extreme Marxist formulations.

Marxian and Weberian interpretations remain significant and controversial, but chiefly for the analysis of industrial capitalism in the Nineteenth Century. No one would now seriously maintain that the "Protestant ethic" as such is a precondition of contemporary industrialization, for such a view has been amply falsified by history. The espousal of Marxism by the Soviet Union and other communist states gives a kind of spurious currency to Marxian views of capitalism, for it is primarily the political theory of Leninism that now guides the policies of countries adopting the communist model of economic development, not the kind of historical evolutionism by invariant stages that underlay Marx's view of social change. In many ways Weber and Marx now seem as old-fashioned as the classical economists, for the relative historical success of industrialization alters the relevant environment for latecomers, which, in any event, exhibit a very wide variety of pre-industrial social structures. The preconditions for the original devel-

opment of industrial capitalism are now conditions that already exist—
for example, the essential technology and attitudes favorable to change
—or can be identified and deliberately created, for example, forms of
financial organization and the necessary administrative structure of
the state.

Although scholars with a Marxist intellectual background never
quite lost interest in the relations between industry and society, the
use of historical materials went out of fashion for most other sociologists and scholars in closely related fields, and empirical research,
particularly in the United States, tended to be parochial in its localism.
A resurgent emphasis on comparative analysis, partly growing out of
intellectual contacts between anthropologists and sociologists, may have
antedated a little, but not by much, a much stronger influence on
intellectual concerns. That influence was the actual course of historic
events, including the rapid sweep of the doctrine of economic development through archaic and exotic cultures that until then exemplified
the diversity of the human experience.

As if the crude course of events were not enough to shake the scholars
from their stodgy concerns, another challenge was added on. The quest
for rapid growth, for programmed development, led to a demand for
recipes and time-tables. Although lack of capital was clearly one major
problem in newly developing areas, it was evident in advance to some
political leaders and economic administrators and soon became evident
to some others that money or machines alone would not transform an
economy along modern lines. Technical assistance, beginning with
technology in the narrow sense and with economic and fiscal organization, rather rapidly got extended to civil administration and the broad
range of attitudes, organizations, and institutions that constitute the
web of social systems. Social scientists were asked to give practical
advice, many of them for the first time. But the advice sought was often
at such a level of practicality and detail that the established principles
of the discipline provided little or no help.

Our main and proper concern here of course is to generalize about
the changes in social structure associated with industrialization. Perhaps, however, it is not culpably parochial to note the impact of the
changed nature of the environment on the scholarly world. The dual
challenge provided by rapid change and the attempt to control and
direct it rationally has been a major source for a renewed social scientific interest in social change in all its forms. That interest in turn has
led to a rethinking of equilibrium and social-cohesion models of
societies and lesser systems. The resistances to change that such models
implied turn out to have been fairly uniformly overstated, and the
relativistic view of cultures and their unique value configurations turn

out to be similarly exaggerated at least with respect to the values attached to health, longevity, and material well-being. The "otherwordly" values of the Buddhist or Hindu Far East or of Catholic Latin America have undoubtedly impeded autonomous economic development in the past, and could not be dismissed as irrelevant to the contemporary and future situation, but their strength as factors of resistance can now be called into question with the expectation of answers that force modification of theoretical doctrines of cultural integrity.

Necessary and Probable Relations

The intellectual backgrounds just discussed bring us to the foreground of present theoretical and methodological issues in the analysis of industrialization. The conceptual models of complex social systems, including societies, used by most social scientists involve assumptions about structural determinateness and congruity that need careful scrutiny. In extreme form, such models assume such a close interdependence of elements in social systems that a substantial autonomous (or, more likely, exogenous) change in one component would lead to definite and congruent changes in others. This would be particularly true of such a crucial aspect of social organization as the system of economic production. If this degree of integration could be used with predictive reliability, the "system requirements" of industrialism could be worked out theoretically, and checked against a single established case for empirical confirmation. The actual situation is more complex, however, as the variety in extant industrial societies makes evident.

The rejection of a model involving such complete integration and congruity does not require abandonment of all structural determination and order. Rather, a theoretical approach involving a "system" concept is empirically warranted, but with attention to the *degree* of determination of the structural correlates and consequences of economic transformation and continuing change.

The appropriate cautions in interpretation may be made explicit. First, structural congruities may apply between classes and ranges of structural forms rather than in exact specifications. For example, a strictly hereditary mode of occupational placement is clearly inconsistent with the recruitment of an industrial labor force in the broad sense, if for no other reason than the changing proportions of occupational categories and the appearance and disappearance of occupations from the "market mix." Second, incongruities are probable. Persistent ones—for example, as between labor mobility and employer identification—may be kept within tolerable limits by various tension-management devices, but perfect solutions are unlikely and may be impossible. The low probability of absolutely synchronic change implies incongruities arising from leads and lags. Third, even empirical uniformity is not conclusive proof of theoretical necessity. Structural alternatives simply may not have been tried. The bureaucratic form of authoritative coordination of specialized workers in large productive units seems almost if not completely universal as the standard form of industrial organization. From direct and indirect evidence at hand it cannot be determined whether this is a structural necessity, and if so within what limits of variation, and if not, what are the equally or more viable alternatives. The replication of a standard form of organization may derive from mere imitation, abetted by an untested theory of functional necessity, rather than from successive independent developments based upon experimentation with alternatives.

These cautions do not imply chaos or random variability of social and economic structures. They do, to repeat, bespeak a stance of skeptical inquiry with respect to the theory and evidence available for use.

Correlational and Sequential Analysis

Our theoretical and methodological tribulations are nearing but not at an end. In addition to doubts about the determinateness of functional or structural necessities, an important problem of time presents itself. When are these structural changes associated with industrialization to appear? Immediately or in the "long run"? Can anything be said about the order of their appearance? These are questions that the integration models of society, just discussed, are plainly unsuited to answer. To a remarkable, and indeed dismaying, extent, the "change model" used in the analysis of the social aspects of industrialization has been implicit and clearly unacceptable when made explicit. Characterized and criticized by Feldman and Moore [4] as a three-stage model, only the middle, transitional stage has been seriously studied, the preindustrial and postindustrial stages being implicitly static and "integrated." Although change in preindustrial societies may be relatively slow or infrequent, the assumption of stasis runs counter to evidence that all societies are subject to change from intrinsic sources and to the clear historic fact that most of the "newly developing" areas have had political, economic, and often religious contact with the Western world for periods ranging from decades to centuries. The assumptions of postindustrial stability could only be an implication of scholarly neglect, for it is absurd when made explicit.

The extensive, empirically-based generalizations about social aspects of industrialization are, paradoxically, mainly consistent with this contrary-to-fact change model and with an exaggerated equilibrium or integration model as applied to the stages not directly examined. The fact is that, within limits, common origins and common destinations can be assumed. The errors of the theoretical structure appear when more detail is sought concerning routes and trajectories of change and the varieties of (temporary) destinations, or when attention is turned to the continuing dynamics of industrial societies.

Before-and-after comparisons abound in the descriptive and analytical literature, and gain their validity from the reality of structural constraints on social organization imposed by any of the variant forms of an industrial economy. What is clearly missing in the current state of knowledge, however, is any precision in the temporal order of events, the sequence and timing of structural changes. And since these are no more likely to be invariant than the antecedent conditions or the character of industrial societies, a change-model typology is also missing. The notion that each case is unique, though obviously true in some details, would defeat both generalization and prediction and it is a prematurely pessimistic position. Generalization is indeed possible, as will be indicated in subsequent paragraphs. But the day of "easy" generalizations—easier in retrospect than when the hard-won observations were made, and theoretically easier than was the empirical confirmation—is past.

There is of course still need for cross-sectional data, for establishing the range of conditions and correlates associated with various forms and degrees of industrialization. There is an even more critical need for repeated observations through time, including quantitative trends. As social statistics become more widely available, at least through decennial censuses, the recent course of change in newly developing areas may be compared with the old historic record, which also awaits systematic quantitative analysis. It may be confidently expected that since trends in one or another measurable aspect of economic and social structure are not truly autonomous, somewhat complex "stochastic" models will be needed for analysis of temporal patterns.

Conditions for Industrialization

A review of the circumstances under which industrialization and broader economic development can take place may appropriately start with those most clearly economic in character. It should be noted at once, however, that the distinction between the economic and noneconomic components of social systems is not as sharp as is often assumed for analytic convenience. Industrialization involves, for example, extensive remobilization of the "factors of production," including new supplies of capital, new power sources, "embodied technology" in capital goods and equipment, and new types of labor comprising workers with skills different from those required in the preindustrial economy. But lying just behind these economic inputs or comprising the same requirements in different semantic guise are the organization of capital markets or the investment decisions of the state, a network of relationships between suppliers and manufacturers, an external or internal training system for workers, and so on.

Just how much formal education is a requisite "capital investment" for economic growth is a matter of some conjecture and scholarly dispute. And, given limited investment resources and urgently competing demands on them, there is also uncertainty as between an "elitist" policy of concentrating attention on training professional, technical, and managerial personnel, or a kind of "populist" policy of emphasizing the economic as well as social values of widespread education as a mechanism of attitudinal development along with cognitive learning. The historic record in the now industrialized countries is poorly known and barely analyzed, and in any event might or might not yield precise and applicable answers for countries with largely illiterate populations and extremely short historic backgrounds in the cultivation of the professions and other intellectual occupations.

It is a truism that underdeveloped areas suffer from a shortage of capital and, generally, a surplus of labor. Domestic capital resources may exist to some degree, however, and the problem becomes one of tapping unproductive savings, providing means and motives for diversion of capital from traditional to novel investments, or perhaps a system of "forced saving" through the taxation system and fiscal policies of the state. Labor supplies are likely to represent underemployment in agriculture, but their actual diversion to industrial employment is likely to require a reorganization of agriculture. Improved efficiency of labor in agriculture and some actual increase in farm output are needed to supply the needs for food and fiber of those who will not be engaged in primary production. The supplies of agricultural workers for industry, though numerically ample, are quite unlikely to have the necessary skills—to say nothing of attitudes and habits—for industrial work.[5] Thus some investment in training will be a requisite for new productive systems.

The historic cases of successful industrialization have involved countries rich in territory and resources or else with extensive international trade in capital, raw materials, and products. Many of the new nations are both poor and small, and are not likely to be economically viable without the formation of international trading organizations or actual economic unification across political boundaries.

As to the requisite organizational and institutional structure, we may note some further seemingly economic but more properly normative conditions for industrialization. Property rights must be transferable if land, raw materials, and other material factors of production are to be converted to new uses and passed, say, from supplier to manufacturer to consumer. Nominal ownership by the state changes this condition only in detail, as transfers of power and responsibility over the materials of production are still necessary. Labor, too, must be transferable, as previously noted. Short of reliance on the police power of a totalitarian state, this normally means the establishment of a "labor market" and a system of financial and other rewards to induce workers to move from one economic sector to another, and so on. At the very least, fixed hereditary assignment of economic roles must somehow be broken down. Eventually, a whole new structure of social placement and relative status must be established, but this may be viewed as more a consequence than a condition of economic modernization.

Even exchange relationships, though nominally contractual and perhaps predicated on individual self-interest, are necessarily based on norms of propriety and fair dealing, compliance with promises for future performance, and restraints on competitive strategies that would destroy the system. The classic formulation by Durkheim [6] of the "non-contractual elements in contracts" is a case in point here. The actual organization of monetary exchange relationships must be established where it does not exist. Industry, in particular, commonly involves assembling the factors of production over considerable distances (often crossing political boundaries) and over considerable periods of time. Systems of credit, stabilization of currency and its rates of exchange, and state fiscal policies of some reliability are thus necessary.

Since rules are not always self-enforcing, nor organizational arrangements self-policing even where the appropriate ones exist, a modicum of stable political power is essential. The noninterference of the state in the development of "laissez-faire capitalism" was systematically and hypocritically exaggerated by ideologists for private businesses that generally benefited from direct and indirect governmental assistance. In the contemporary world of the newly developing areas the state is likely to play a prominent, overt, and often dominant part in developmental policies and their concrete implementation. This comes about in part because only the state can muster the necessary capital from domestic and foreign sources and make the other necessary changes in social organization and the legal embodiment of normative codes.

It is also true that industrialization and other measures of economic development have become instruments of national policy in virtually the entire world. And this brings us to the questions of motives and values. The older economic analysis operated with a very simple set of motivational assumptions that individuals would act rationally in ways designed to maximize their own material self-interests. Just what those interests were, beyond health, food, clothing, and shelter, was left vague or the question was simply neglected. Yet, within early limits as this neglect implies, these motivational assumptions appear sounder than the rather exaggerated "value relativism" advanced by anthropological and sociological critics of economic theory. Once some knowledge of the possibility of economic betterment became fairly widespread, discontent with poverty also became widespread. At this level, the motivational requisites appear to be satisfied. But, as usual, the problem is somewhat more complex. The superiority of new employments and styles of life over the old is rarely unmixed, and in some cases evidently not so. A simple quest for improvement does not automatically yield the means for its achievement.

To bring about the capital investment and extensive organizational and technological innovations necessary to transform an economic system, economists have long identified the requisite functions of "entrepreneurship." Their faith was often a little magical, and a little restricted to a free-market economy. Hagen [7] has restated and broadened the case for the importance of creative or innovative personality types. Yet in any case leadership is not independent of the motives of those led. To balance the exclusive emphasis on the innovators or managers, other scholars have argued for the importance of labor commitment—not only performance but also acceptance of the relevant norms—and for the importance of some participation in decisions and actions for the appearance of commitment.[8]

The motives of the ordinary individual participant in economic activities are not necessarily the same as the values espoused by, say, national planners and their spokesmen. Short of terroristic totalitarianism the two presumably have some congruence, but it need not be perfect. Note that industrialization and other developmental measures are always instrumental goals. But for which more ultimate values are they instrumental? Mere improvement of present economic welfare, widely distributed, would presumably best satisfy the aspirations of most participants. But maximizing present returns is likely to be at the cost of sustained future growth, which requires substantial savings and capital accumulation. The long-term view is likely to have little appeal to those who are faring least well in their present situations. The older solution to this problem in terms of profits available for reinvestment rested on the institutionalization of a particular property system, and, like all forms of socially legitimized power, the fundaments of that power were values and nonrational. In societies now just beginning to foster rapid economic development, the proprietary solution has been generally mixed with or superseded by an appeal to national interest and power. Those values, too, are nonrational, but they provide an ideological rationale for present sacrifice or forbearance and an appeal to collective rather than purely selfish interests.

It is perhaps premature to list "nationalism" as a precondition for industrialization, but for reasons just given it would have a high priority among the values precedent to major economic change. Nationalism serves another, correlative function, in providing a sense of identity and meaning for populations physically and socially uprooted. For the economic rewards, even if paid, have social costs, and those too merit attention.

Concomitants and Consequences

The array of necessary and probable effects of economic modernization is so extensive that considerable selectivity must be exercised in brief discussion. Again, it seems appropriate to start with the structural features of society that are primarily economic in form or function, then proceed to the demographic and ecological characteristics of populations rearranged by economic development, and finally to attend to certain outstanding features of social organization.

A monetary basis of exchange is essentially a prior condition for any substantial industrialization, and even remote, small, and isolated manufacturing establishments must either pay their workers wages or set up a commissary. The extension of "custodial" arrangements such as self-sufficient company towns has early limits, including some way of getting external sources of supply.

As economic modernization continues, the "economic calculus" tends to grow in importance. The variety of producers' and consumers' goods makes money the necessary medium for their acquisition and transfer. Perhaps more significantly for the transformation of traditional social forms, both new and old services and reciprocities move through the market. Familial and neighborhood mutual aid either gives way to more specialized, hired services, or if it persists tends to be given a market evaluation. The ubiquity of financial transactions and market evaluation becomes almost total: it affects clubs and religious orders, families and welfare associations, as well as governments, banks, and retail shops.

One of the more ridiculous conventions of traditional economic analysis was to treat labor as an aggregate of interchangeable units, its availability being governed over the short run by a market price translated into a wage rate. Even in the earliest stages of industrialization a quotient of more skilled manpower is necessary, and this demand for differentiated services increases with time. The continuing processes of change in occupational structures that can be traced to industrialization are discussed in Chapter 7.

By very indirect and largely unintentional means industrialization in the broad sense tends to create part of its own labor supply. This comes about by mortality reduction deriving from the whole range of public health, medical, and food-producing technologies. Birth rates, however, are not so immediately affected; they may in fact increase slightly owing to better health and nutrition. The historic record indicates that, after a variable period of rapid transitional growth, fertility also gradually comes under a measure of rational control. The interpretations of declining fertility vary and remain in dispute. That lower birth rates result from deliberate family limitation can scarcely be doubted, but the explanation of the attitudinal and behavioral change is by no means settled. In any event, the immediate effect of rapid population growth may be dampening to rates of economic growth, though not in any simple-minded way, since rapid growth also produces an expanding labor force and, given other favorable conditions, expanded consumer demand. It seems highly probable that fertility declines will eventually happen in newly developing areas, and the combination of official concern and new contraceptive techniques may speed the process as compared with past experience, just as death rates can now be reduced more rapidly than was historically true.

To population growth as a consequence of industrialization must be added a major spatial redistribution. The historic association between industrialization and urbanization was close but not perfect. Large commercial and political centers antedated the industrial era, and, here and there, manufacturing establishments can be operated without large urban agglomerations. Even now, the rate of urbanization in newly developing areas commonly exceeds the rate of industrialization as measured by employment in manufacturing. The urbanization rate displays attitudinal dissatisfaction with present conditions in conspicuous and troublesome ways; the "flight from the land" is an unmistakable "vote with the feet" for better opportunities. And the cities of the world, even if not important manufacturing centers, are not independent of industrialization. The metropolitan complex vends the products of manufacturing, local or otherwise, and depends upon industrial products for communication, transportation, water, sewage, public health measures, and public and private construction. The rate of urbanization is probably increasing everywhere, and it is likely to continue wherever there remain substantial residues of marginal agricultural producers.

As we turn to the historic homeland of sociological and anthropological concern, the principal features of "social structures," the consequences of industrialization are equally evident. Most conspicuous and far-reaching, perhaps, is the impact of industry on kinship and the family, for in many nonindustrial societies the constellation of kinsmen comprises the major source of social position and personal identification. Clearly the required geographical and social mobility of an industrialized economy weakens or breaks the multigenerational and laterally extended "corporate" kin group. The destruction is unlikely to be total, however, contrary to certain interpretations which saw the functional utility of the "nuclear" family in an industrial society, but did not see that such a system was inconsistent with the close bonds between generations and among siblings even in the small-family system. The intergenerational tensions are in fact likely to be sharpest at very early stages of industrialization, as youths are the likeliest recruits to new occupations and styles of life. After a few generations, equality of life chances can by no means be expected, but the disparities are within the "modernized" social systems, not between radically different systems.

At the very time that traditional kinship ties are weakened or broken, the network of other essentially informal relationships is also likely to disappear for the urban industrial recruit. Village or tribal identities may be transferred to the cities temporarily, but rarely survive in important measure among the urban-born succeeding generation. For many of those displaced, there is little social framework between the immediate family and the (possibly remote) state. If either of these links to society fails, and especially if both do, apathy, alienation, and amoral or criminal conduct are likely to ensue. This is a persistent problem of industrial societies, despite the gradual growth or deliberate creation of new formal associations and forms of political participation.

The institutionalization of rationality, an emphasis on problem-solving and impersonal relationships characteristic of industrialized societies, often leads to a kind of "instrumentalism" and lack of fundamental value orientations. The family retains its importance in these circumstances as an affectional and personal set of relationships, permitting legitimate individuality and emotionality. On the larger scale, nationalism and religion compete, uneasily, for nonrational adherence. Both are threatened by secularization, by skeptical questioning of received doctrine, and each attempts to provide answers to the intrinsic doubts and uncertainties of human existence. Nationalism rarely offers a sufficiently personal meaning to death and misfortune to supersede entirely the richer theology of traditional religions.

Social structure is sometimes used in sociological discourse to refer specifically to social differentiation and stratification. For this range of phenomena the consequences of industrialization are, to say the least, complex. The invariant and probably inevitable initial effect of industrialization is a polarization of social status, *within the modernized sector*. The managers and the managed, the innovators and the reluctant followers are likely to represent radical differences in education, income, and clearly, power. This polarization may lead to apathy and discontent on the part of the lower orders, but only rarely to revolutionary disturbances. By the time the modernized sector incorporates a substantial portion of the population its status system has become far more complex. Multiple status graduations, including a disproportionate expansion of "middle positions" are further complicated by multiple criteria of differential valuation and relative position —a "lateral" extension of differentiation. Marx correctly observed the polarities in early industrialization and almost correctly predicted, with some exaggeration, the disappearance of preindustrial strata. Where he was wrong, categorically, was in his expectation of increasing polarization. Yet Max had a certain validity in predicting the characteristics of early industrialization as successive areas enter upon the process of economic modernization. Greater speed of "ideological" incorporation of impoverished populations into the common aspirations of the modern world while actual structural transformations proceed somewhat slowly may well increase the revolutionary potential in newly developing areas.

The political structure of the national state exemplifies and underscores the partial areas of latitude in social systems. It is quite clear by now that rapid industrialization is consistent with a rather wide range of political regimes, though not with all. Political centralization and substantial stability are clearly requisite for continuing growth, but democracy is not. In fact, in the contemporary world the state more nearly shapes the industrial structure than conversely, and the alternative forms of the state may be constructed about as eclectically from a world pool of precedents as technology and economic strategies can be combined in unprecedented ways. Any modern state is likely to hit upon forms of popular political participation as a mode of tension-management under conditions of strain and rapid change. But the manipulative and essentially totalitarian management of such participations appears to be a viable alternative to genuine democracy. Though the ministries of political administration are likely to look pretty much alike in one capital or another, their ultimate accountabilities are likely to differ widely.

Continuities

The theoretically awkward variability of political structures associated with industrialization highlights a weakness in the assumption that industrialization leads to a common social destination. The structural congruities that have made possible the preceding abbreviated summary are real enough. They fall short of a structural determinism. Some persistent differences will be matters of "detail" and not very consequential at a generalized level of analysis. Others cannot be dismissed so lightly; they bear witness to a measure of systemic "openness."

Industrial societies of course have no stable, final destination, and this is part of the problem in predicting the exact consequences of industrialization in areas now beginning the process. Some underlying processes, such as continuous specialization and functional differentia- · tion, are likely to provide sounder bases of generalization than the finer features of social structure at any particular time. Similarly, the substitution of machines for man is likely to be ubiquitous and continuous, with correlative "positive" consequences for occupational upgrading, ambiguous implications for the use of leisure, and "negative" consequences for those displaced or for those unable to fit such standardized selective mechanisms as the school.

Predicting the future of industrial societies has excited remarkably little scholarly, as opposed to literary, attention. That enterprise cannot seriously engage us here, except for one additional point. Paradoxically, and despite political diversity and exceptionally dangerous international tensions, there is a lesson of theoretical importance in worldwide industrialization. The contemporary form of industrialization is not autonomous and "autarchic," country by country, and indeed it never was. But now the new arrivals benefit from accumulated experience, both technological and organizational. The resulting "eclecticism" previously noted has at least two theoretical implications. (1) Novel combinations of structural elements may be expected, some of them viable, and (2) for many purposes the society (approximately equated with the national state) is no longer the most useful comprehensive system for analytic purposes. Even more disordered than the complex modern "society," the world yet must be viewed as a single system if we seek keys to present and future large-scale dynamic processes.

References

1. Karl Marx, *Capital: A Critique of Political Economy* (New York: Modern Library, 1936).

2. Max Weber, *The Theory of Social and Economic Organization* (New York: Oxford University Press, 1947).

3. Max Weber, *The Protestant Ethic and the Spirit of Capitalism* (New York: Scribners, 1930).

4. Arnold S. Feldman and Wilbert E. Moore, "Industrialization and Industrialism: Convergence and Differentiation," *Transactions of the Fifth World Congress of Sociology*, Vol. II, pp. 151–169.

5. See Wilbert E. Moore, *Industrialization and Labor* (Ithaca, New York: Cornell University Press, 1951).

6. Emile Durkheim, *De la Division du Travail Social,* 2nd ed. (Paris: Alcan, 1902) (English translation: Glencoe, Illinois: Free Press, 1960).

7. Everett E. Hagen, *On the Theory of Social Change: How Economic Growth Begins* (Homewood, Illinois: Dorsey, 1962).

8. See Wilbert E. Moore and Arnold S. Feldman, eds., *Labor Commitment and Social Change in Developing Areas* (New York: Social Research Council, 1960).

4

MEASUREMENT OF ORGANIZATIONAL AND INSTITUTIONAL IMPLICATIONS OF CHANGES IN PRODUCTIVE TECHNOLOGY

The problem of interplay is basic to the theoretical interpretation and the empirical measurement of the implications of technological change. Like the division of a functional system into categories or aspects, the selection of a starting point is somewhat arbitrary. If changes in productive technology have social consequences, they also have social sources. Technological determinism, including the famous conception of "culture lag," may be dismissed simply and categorically as having neither empirical nor theoretical support worth any small fraction of the attention it has been accorded. The methodological excuse for taking technological innovation as a starting point is the greater possibility of identifying and measuring first-order (economic) consequences and thence proceeding by direct and indirect routes to trace out paths through the web of social behavior. The practical or pragmatic excuse is the recognition that changes in productive technology are requisite to programs of economic "development," mixed with some concern for predicting, measuring, and possibly controlling various indirect consequences. In the modern world most changes in productive technology are deliberate, the product of purposive and evaluative human conduct, and are fostered, guided, or limited by anticipations of indirect, noneconomic implications.

SOURCE. Adapted from "Measurement of Organizational and Institutional Implications of Changes in Productive Technology," *in* International Social Science Council, *Social, Economic, and Technological Change: A Theoretical Approach* (Paris: 1958), pp. 229–259. By permission of UNESCO, copyright owners.

Since a "complete" description of the social implications of technical change is a scientific impossibility, and any attempted approximation would prove extremely uninteresting for any purpose, some selective criteria are needed. The obvious ones are *importance* for some theoretical or practical purpose, the existence of some hypothetical bases for alleging that *linkages* exist, and finally, the possibility, real or hypothetical, of *measurement*, both as a means for establishing the dimensions of change and as a partial test of the theoretical connections.

The problem of assessment of organizational and institutional "implications" suffers to a high degree from measurement difficulties. For the most part the measures suggested are possible *indexes* of the hypothetical connections, leaving open the possibility that the index runs in the expected direction for the "wrong" reasons, or, in other words, that alternative theories would encompass the same observations but also offer proof of the mechanism of relationship. For example, it is suggested that the growth of membership in "management associations" would constitute an index of the development of "organizational technology," which is derived, step by step, from the idea of "instrumentalism" in social affairs, a subcategory of a more general extension of the idea of natural control to social control, providing a final "cultural" link to changes in productive technology. Now this inferential chain would not be *proved* by the particular index, and alternative explanations of "management associations" might have greater theoretical and empirical rigor. Obviously the shorter the inferential chain and the more open to inspection its links, the easier is the demonstration of the connection between its ends. Yet the attempt to operate in partial obscurity seems required if we are to move toward a greater understanding of social systems and toward prediction of patterns of change.

There is one seeming alternative to measurement by index, and that is measurement by enumeration. Several lists have been compiled indicating the "social effects" of particular inventions. However, without rigid and essentially arbitrary ways of assuring the homogeneity of the items, and of limiting the pursuit of indirect effects, the task is endless, and useless for any purpose except to emphasize that technological innovation may have many effects.

We are thus forced to adopt a posture of bravery before largely unknown dangers and to reject safety to no purpose.

A Note on Organization of the Discussion

Tracing the organizational or institutional implications of changes in productive technology involves at least two ranges of variation:

(1) the directness or indirectness of the links, and (2) the type of social unit to which the effect or "implication" is attributed. Thus changes in physical goods, which may have many consequences for patterns of social behavior, are more clearly linked to productive technology than are changes in attitudes toward social relations, which may have even more important consequences for patterns of social behavior. Either the closely or tenuously linked consequence of technical change may have implications for individual personality, family life, community organization, the shifting bases of social stratification, or the size and nature of the state and society.

If we are to proceed with the discussion of measurement of relations in some orderly fashion, some clarity on the directness of the alleged connections and on the social unit of observation is mandatory. The procedure adopted here is to make the "unit of observation" the prime variable, cross-classified by the degree of linkage with technical change. The following chart (Table 4.1) illustrates the organization and the range of hypothetical implications that may be subject to measurement.

For example, changes in productive technology in the United States have made possible the production of many household appliances, some of which are "labor-saving" for the housewife. Given a level of income adequate to purchase these appliances (an income level at least partially conditioned by the physical efficiency of production), the time budget of the housewife is affected, and her social roles inside and outside the family probably altered in measurable ways. This constitutes accordingly a fairly direct connection between productive technology and one or more social subsystems.

A much more tenuous hypothetical relationship pertains between the implications of changing technology and habits of social thought (the "rational spirit"), on the one hand, and the development of deliberate social manipulation and innovation by the agencies of the state, on the other. Yet it is precisely some of these more indirect relations that challenge our theoretical and technical equipment for analysis.

It will be apparent that the difficulties of demonstration and proof increase as one moves from top to bottom on the chart, and likewise as one moves from left to right. Analysis would be even more complicated and hazardous if an attempt were made to establish diagonal links, which, however, certainly exist. For example, the widespread distribution of comic books and radio and television programs for children affects not only the structure of the family, but, possibly, later attitudes toward national policy and organization.

In the following discussion various kinds of "measures" will be suggested. Some of these are easily made "operational," given either official

TABLE 4.1 Illustrative Chart of Hypothetical Implications of Changes in Productive Technology for Social Organization and Institutions

Level of Linkage with Technical Change	Unit of Observation		
	Subsystem	Social Structure and Stratification	Nation or Society
Physical Products	Household appliances and the role of housewives; Transportation and suburbanization; Communication techniques and formal organizations	Mass communication and development of common standards; Consumption goods as status symbols and their degradation	Communication, transportation, and the size of centralized political units; Tools of political power
Work Roles	Specialization, role conflict, and the fractionated individual; Leisure: the individual, the family, and voluntary associations	Competing bases of leadership between old and new skills; Specialization and the "blurring" of class lines; Leisure and its use as a symbol of status	Group specialization and the fractionated society: interdependence vs. integration; Leisure and political participation
"Rational Spirit"	Organization technology; "Rational" mate selection, marital adjustment; The "techniques" of individual adjustment	Educational trends and status distributions; The new elite: thinkers, manipulators, coordinators	Social instrumentalities of social power: propaganda, thought control; Rationalization of administration and bases of authority; Deliberate social innovation

data or, in many instances, the opportunity to carry out field surveys. Others, such as various complex indexes, would require considerable ingenuity to translate into operational components and their inter-relation. Thus an index of "national power" or "weapon potential" has certainly been attempted in scholarly and official circles, probably with small reliability. Some of these more complex measures are never-theless suggested as possible end-products of simpler and more direct, if partial, procedures. In order to avoid lengthy and necessarily dis-cursive discussion of each of the many measures suggested, their ap-proximate applicability is graded "A," "B," or "C" by the following code:

A—measures applicable where official or similar statistical data exist;

B—measures applicable through field surveys;

C—measures requiring indirect observation and inferential analysis.

The organization adopted here does not readily permit a further distinction that has considerable practical importance, namely, the "stage" of technological development being considered. In the con-temporary underdeveloped areas modern technology is being intro-duced "from outside" with far-reaching and partially unknown consequences. Since recapitulation of past developments in the indus-trialized West is not to be expected, and since the affected societies differ in many respects, genuinely common functional or sequential relations must be rather highly generalized. The bias in the ensuing discussion is toward the measurement of relations in highly industrial-ized societies. The justifications are two: a longer record and a some-what more complete availability of quantitative data. Some of the measurements suggested, however, are at least in principle applicable to less developed areas. Indeed, some of the theoretical and methodo-logical problems are partially simplified in such areas, precisely because the productive change is in some sense "intrusive," and its implications may be readily and unambiguously traced without as much interde-pendence and circularity of influences as pertains in societies long committed to technological change.

Implications for Social Subsystems

Changes in productive technology may have various effects on the structure and operation of groups, communities, formal organizations, and so on. The awkward expression "subsystem" is used as no other

single term such as "group" will encompass the range from the socialized individual (the personality as a system) to such entities as communities. The unit of observation referred to by the term is, however,
in every case a *concrete* system, not an *analytical* system such as "power
structure," which is an aspect of all social systems.

Changes in Physical Products

Among the most obvious and pervasive consequences of technological change are the changes in the variety and quality of physical
goods available to consumers. Availability is of course partly a question
of effective demand and therefore of price or the distributive system,
and thus indirectly a function of productive efficiency. Given the circumstances that some changes in productive technology are likely to
result in more goods, of more kinds, of variable qualities, and at prices
that have a downward tendency, what can we say of the implications
for various social subsystems?

Since the family or household is generally the consuming unit, its
organization and activity is a good place to look for implications. At
early stages of industrialization household activity is likely to be
radically altered by the decline or disappearance of handicraft production, and an alteration of roles and relationships within the family.
The immediate consequence may be a greater subordination of the
position of women through partial loss of economic function.

Measures: Time budgets of behavior and their trends
         (B).

         Indexes of "relative power" within the family
         (C).

In highly industrialized economies, and particularly in the United
States, mass production of household appliances has presumably helped
to alter the position of the housewife, especially by giving her more
leisure for "self-cultivation," passive participation in the mass culture,
or active participation in various kinds of activities outside the home.

Measures: Time budgets of behavior (B).

         Participation in voluntary associations (B).

Of course many other goods enter the household unit, some of which
like canned, frozen, and other packaged foods may be assumed to have
consequences similar to the use of household appliances. Others, such
as private automobiles, may radically alter the behavior of the family

as a unit, or the distribution of rights and responsibilities within the family.

Measures: Passenger-car statistics, including types of use
and users (A, B).

Still other physical products may alter family activity in ways ranging from the utilitarian (sewing machines and woodworking shops) to the expressive (the former, plus various "nonutilitarian" hobbies such as photography and "craft" work in various materials).

Measures: Sales of workshops and craft hobby supplies
(A).

Time budgets of behavior (B).

"Value added" by household producing-and-
consuming units (B).

The development of new means of communication and transportation also affects the family in complex ways. Thus, urbanization is generally pictured as breaking up the family in terms of common activities, but the radio and especially television may have an opposite effect. Likewise, the development of suburbanization through rapid transportation, which will be discussed below in terms of community structure, may provide the basis for a more "integrated" family structure than exists in central cities.

Measures: Time spent in the household unit or with the
family as a group (B).

A still more indirect effect on family structure, but still partially traceable to ease of transportation, is the relation between geographical mobility and the development of the conjugal family (the effective unit being the married couple and their children, with minimal relations between adult generations and adult siblings). Such a family system tends to develop as a corollary of economic modernization, as it is functionally related to systems of status achievement and occupational mobility. Of course rapid transportation and communication allow the maintenance of contacts among geographically separated kin units, but it is suggested that geographical separation is still of considerable importance in the relative independence of family status within the kinship system. Moreover, even marital selection itself is likely to be less subject to precise considerations of the status of parental families if the young, who comprise the bulk of opportunity-seeking migrants, operate in partial ignorance of or unconcern over such considerations.

Measures: Kinship composition of households, including trends (A).

Indexes of geographical separation of kinsmen, related to intergenerational and differential sibling occupational or status mobility (B).

Indexes of "class heterogramy" related to geographical mobility of marital pair (B).

Frequency of visits related to distance among geographically separated kin units (B).

Changing residence patterns are linked to changes in productive technology both by the requirements of economic organization, and by the facilities of transportation and communication. The implications of urban living are many and widely ramified. The extensive literature on urbanism has exhibited a quite uneven and haphazard use of social measurement. The disorganizing and demoralizing effects of city life have received more attention than have the ranges and types of social contacts made possible and even necessary by congested living.

One principal set of theoretical problems concerning urbanism is that of the relations among size, location of social activity, and function. Thus size is presumably directly related to specialization of social roles and organizations. As cities grow outward through suburbanization and extend their influence to established small communities in their surrounding areas, some functions are likely to be centralized while others have greater immunity to absorption. Urban transportation systems bring together people whose residencies are often widely scattered, and make possible social participation (whether in formal associations or in informal visiting) on occupational and similar bases rather than on a primarily residential basis. Commutation affects not only the life organization of the commuter, his family, and his residential community, but presents central cities with problems of providing services for daytime populations that may be much larger than their residential populations. The tendency for the functioning metropolis to extend beyond its political boundaries is likely to prompt new forms of political organization for the control of problems common to the region.

Measures: Daytime population in ratio to residential population of cities by size (A or B).

Growth of metropolitan "authorities" (B).

Residential versus occupational bases of social activity (formal and informal) (B).

Ecological "gradients" for various urban activities (B).

Indexes of loss of local functions in small communities (consolidations of schools, churches, fraternal organizations) (C).

Ratio of special-interest associations to size of community or city (C).

The development of communication and transportation, which we have used as the primary link between changes in productive technology and the growth of cities, also has clear implications for the internal functioning of urban centers. Urban life both broadens the potential and probable range of social contacts among the inhabitants, and tends to narrow the interdependence and mutual control resting on personal and "primary group" relations. It seems likely that this effect of urbanization has been overstated in the standard literature, but its theoretical and practical importance is such as to suggest the need for further precision in conceptualization and measurement.

Measures: Ratios of law enforcement agents to number of inhabitants by size of community (A).

Average and differential ratios of "primary" to "secondary" social contacts by size of community (B).

Limited, largely specific and impersonal contacts and the presumed diminution of "primary" controls in the city have led social scientists and laymen alike to view city life as "disorganizing," or at least to put in doubt the "integration" of cities. And clearly this range of social problems underlies the somewhat naive hopes that currently underdeveloped areas may have economic development without urbanization. The combination of congestion with the loss of traditional bases of integration and control may of course facilitate crowd and mob behavior, although the substantial record of rural and small-town mobs indicates again that some of the theory may be more persuasive than true.

Measures: Differential "integration" of areas within the city, as measured by indexes of social and personal "disorganization" (crime, delinquency, marital desertion, suicide, mental disorders) (A).

Indexes of community knowledge and participation (B).

Incidence of mob action by size and type of community (B).

General indexes of urban integration (C).

The growth and structure of the modern city in industrialized countries is substantially different from other urban agglomerations, and can be linked back to changes in productive technology. Once again, however, the direction of influence is not unilateral. Urban traffic congestion constitutes a pressing challenge to invent new modes of moving people and goods. Population concentration and its effect on land values constitute challenges to innovations in building materials, and in architectural techniques. Urban zoning, planning, and slum-clearance projects may be viewed as indirect consequences of past technological developments, and an attempt to control or undo those consequences.

The "social subsystems" discussed so far have been primarily the family and kinship organizations, and the "locality group" or community. Changes in physical products, but especially in communication and transportation facilities, have at least partial effects on at least two other major types of organizations—the formally constituted association and the administrative organization. These effects would appear to be increased potential size, possible geographical dispersion, and a correlative tendency to centralize some of the common interests and functions of local units at "headquarters" level. The internal structure of such organizations is of course also affected by mechanical means of communication, computation, record-keeping and even routine "decision-making."

Measures: Number of "national" associations (A).

Number of membership "groups" without meetings (B).

Expenditures for office and business machines, by organizational size (B).

Indexes of organizational centralization and dispersion (C).

Changes in Work Roles

The effects of changing productive technology on work roles, previously traced in their economic and demographic aspects, also include implications for individual personality, social groups, and organizations. Questions of occupational specialization have been approached chiefly in terms of measures of productive efficiency, although more recently some attention has been given to measures of work satisfactions and morale. Viewed from the standpoint of the personality as a system, the appropriate questions include the effect of role specialization and possible role conflict on personality integration, the relation between work satisfactions and individual need-dispositions, and the implications of uncontrolled and perhaps unpredicted changes in work roles for emotional balance and security. Extreme views hold that many individuals get "fractionated" in modern life, with occupational specialization a major source of this tendency, and exhibit various personality disorders. But occupational specialization covers at least two different processes—the division and dilution of job requirements, and the diversification and addition of requirements. And there is some reason to guess that the strains on various executive and professional roles are as great as, if different from, the routinized but changeful obligations of the semiskilled worker.

Measures: Occupational distribution of positive work satisfactions (B).

Indexes of apathy, alienation, and mental disorder by types of occupation (B).

If jobs become decreasingly interesting with technical innovation, which is by no means proved as a measurable average tendency, it could be argued that increased leisure provides partial compensation. Thus there is some theoretical basis for thinking that gambling behavior may be strongly associated with routinized occupations, and that spectator sports events are chiefly appealing to those that have jobs that provide "perfect" predictability of outcomes. On the other hand, leisure may be viewed less as an escape from routine than as disposable time and energy. Thus participation in voluntary associations, the development of "creative" hobbies, and affective involvement with the family may be considered as made possible by the fact of increased leisure, or as made "necessary" because of the character of work roles.

Measures: Indexes of participation in gambling, passive
               entertainment, voluntary associations, creative
               hobbies, family, as related to types of work
               roles (B).

Turning from the individual to various groups as the focus of
attention, it is clear that many organizations and patterns of activity
depend for their existence or incidence to a considerable measure on
the available leisure of workers and housewives, and possibly for their
support on the routinization of productive assignments. The family
deserves special attention in this connection, however. Usually viewed
as "losing" functions with economic development and its concomitants,
a more theoretically adequate view is that the family is at the same
time loaded with additional burdens of providing affection, primary
controls, and a legitimate display of emotion. The extension of fractional, impersonal relations elsewhere at least heightens this standard
function of the family. At the same time the greater leisure of the
housewife and the breadwinner make possible more choice in family
activities, but does not guarantee harmony or integration of individual
preferences.

Measures: Indexes of affective involvements in the family,
               and of desertion and divorce, as related to
               types of work roles (A and B).

Occupational mobility is functionally related to the reduction of
effective kinship ties beyond the immediate family, as earlier noted in
connection with transportation and geographical mobility. Both the
mobility aspirations of parents during early years of marriage and their
aspirations for educational and similar advantages for their children
tend to primary emphasis on the immediate family and to family limitation. To these influences of changing work roles on the family we
may add another. That is the negative effect of expanding employment
opportunities on the cost and supply of domestic servants, and thus
on the composition of the household units. The sacrifice of domestic
servants for middle-income groups appears to be a universal penalty of
economic modernization.

Measures: Time-trends of proportion of domestic servants
               in labor force, and by income-rank of house-
               hold employers (A).

Work roles, being central to both the activity of the worker and
the income of his family, naturally have an influence on other organizations also. It appears likely that upward income-and-occupational

mobility will be accompanied by residential mobility, at least between residential areas in the same metropolitan district. Some areas may be marked by a sufficiently high turnover of residents to permit us to extend the metaphor of "bedroom suburbs" to the concept of "transient hotel suburbs," with the attendant problems of community identification and participation. Residential location is of course related to family income, but it appears probable that selection and segregation of residential areas extend to other occupational dimensions, including that of high career mobility.

Measures: Residential turnover by types of residential areas (distinguished in part by occupational structure) (A or B).

Finally, various organizations and activities may have different symbolic and prestige values, not directly determined by membership dues or costs of participation. Thus Protestant religious denominations in the United States have differential prestige, at least at the community level, and there is some indication of changes in affiliation with career success.

Measure: Relation between income-and-occupational mobility and changes in number and types of associational memberships (B).

Growth of the "Rational Spirit"

We come now to an order of implication of changes in productive technology that is the least precise and demonstrable, and yet of great potential importance. The theoretical derivation can be stated simply. It can be argued that historically in the West, and in most primitive and agrarian societies, technological change was largely fortuitous and often successfully resisted when introduced from without or accidentally developed from within. Deliberate change, rewarded by income advantages and prestige, is a relatively rare and largely recent phenomenon. Such change, particularly the expanding technology that underlay the Industrial Revolution and was in turn magnified by new productive organization, was initially focused on control of the non-human environment (inanimate sources of power and raw materials and selective breeding and utilization of plants and animals).

Now, the argument proceeds, the development of productive technology entailed not simply an accumulative growth of practical knowledge, for there was also required a "habit of mind." That habit of mind may, with full recognition of the hazards of a sort of cultural

mysticism, be called the "rational spirit." Its hypothetical essentials
are the use of demonstrated fact and logic for the solution of problems, a questioning of traditional solutions or even of traditional
identification of problems, and a deliberate attempt to master "nature"
as well as understand it. Although the roots of this view are very old
in human experience, its *active* and *deliberate* implementation as an
agency of change has certainly got its greatest impetus over the course
of the last few centuries in Western societies.

The final stage in this argument is that over a much shorter length
of time, and with a growing volume of effort and treasure, the "rational" or technological view of nature has been extended to human
motivation, organization, and control.

Although this theoretical statement is foreshortened and in considerable measure speculative, it permits the derivation of a number
of hypotheses concerning the forms and directions of social change.
Until the links in the theoretical derivation are independently established, complete confirmation of the derived hypotheses would not
constitute proof of the theory. But this is by no means a unique
situation, nor one that needs to give us pause for long.

Against this background, what kinds of evidence are there of the
implications of what may be called "calculated control" in various
subsystems? At the personality level, we should expect an emphasis
on the "techniques of adjustment," and on the "rational" solution of
emotional and other personality conflicts. Thus "mental health" is
increasingly viewed as a technological problem, not, for example, as a
religious one.

Measures: Trends in ratios of psychotherapists to popula-
              tion (A).

              Trends in sales of personality self-help
              books (A).

              Trends in incidence of personal counselling by
              secular and religious counselors (B).

Similarly in mate selection, family adjustment, occupational choice,
and "career management" we should expect emphasis on the use of
"rational" techniques, "how to" guides, and reliance on professional
counselors.

Measures: Trends in sales and readership of career self-
              help books (A).

              Trends in use of "marital happiness" tests (B).

Trends in number and incidence of use of marital and career counselors (B).

It is perhaps in the large work organization that "social technology" is most apparent and pervasive. Engineers have increased rapidly, but so have administrative and personnel experts, teachers of "human relations," advisers on effective communications, career planners and executive developers, liaison men and bargainers. All this is a far cry from older and simpler notions of master-servant or contractual relations of employment. Social cooperation has become at least as problematical as mechanical efficiency. It is of course possible that the problems of *securing* cooperation have genuinely increased owing to the spread of the questioning habit of mind throughout the population, and not simply that the recognition of "manipulative" possibilities has been confined to executives, professionals, politicians, and public administrators.

Measures: Trends in occupational structure (A).

Membership in "personnel" and "management" associations (B).

Implications for Social Structure and Stratification

Some aspects of the impact of technological changes are most conveniently viewed with reference to social structure in its distributive sense, including social stratification. This unit or level of observation differs from various subsystems in that it is not necessarily organized around personalities or membership units. It differs from the nation or society by emphasis on distributive and differential characteristics, not on the large collectivity as such.

Changes in Physical Products

Here again we may start with the implications of new physical products for social structure and stratification. The simplest relation is that between income and the number and quality of physical goods that the consumer can and does afford. But there are also interesting complications. In the process of industrialization, the substitution of manufactured for handicraft goods and the addition of new articles of consumption may more nearly mark off the "old" and "new" socio-economic sectors than they differentiate "superior" and "inferior" strata. (The notion of the superiority of hand-made products persists in some degree in all industrial societies, although it is commonly not borne out by utilitarian criteria.)

Measure: Trends in differential distribution of handi-
            craft and manufactured goods (B).

Since consumption goods reflect income in some degree but also take on symbolic value with reference to social status, the effect of productive changes is a complex one. Generally speaking one effect of technological change is to reduce costs of production, bring the product within the reach of more consumers, and thus subject status symbols to rapid degradation. (This is of course a universal law, the principal variable being time.) On the other hand, rapid changes in form and function of consumer goods may differentiate income and status groups in their purchase of latest models and styles. We have thus the somewhat contradictory tendencies of increasing equalization of general standards of physical-goods consumption, and the steady appearance of new status symbols that may or may not be directly income-determined. (They may be primarily a reflection of differential standards of taste and sensitivity to changes in fashion.) The shift from goods to services in higher-income groups may be viewed as an extension of this principle.

Measures: Trends by income or socioeconomic status, in
            the physical-goods composition of family in-
            comes (B).

            Obsolescence rates of consumer durables, by
            socioeconomic status (B).

Changes in transportation, and particularly communication, may have implications somewhat analogous to those just noted. The development of mass-communication media, although initially differentiating those who have access to them and those that do not, appears to have the long-run effect of promoting a "mass culture." This means that many status and regional differentials are subject to pressures for uniformity.

Measures: Audiences of mass media (B).

            Trends in distribution of nationally advertised
            products, and in common sources of news and
            views (B).

With the progress of economic development in all parts of the world, despite differential rate, success, or long-term prognosis, it appears probable that even national differences in standards and types of physical consumption will inevitably narrow. Those who take pride in "cultural" differences dislike and would like to prevent this consequence, but it does not appear likely that they will be heard or can succeed in preserving archaic patterns.

Changes in Work Roles

Just as old and new products may differentiate sectors of a society undergoing modernization, so old and new occupations may cleave the system of social stratification. New occupational roles, related to new modes of productive organization, do not so much provide new positions or new competitors for leadership in an existing system of stratification as they provide a new and competing system—a system that has generally won in the long run.

Measures: Representation of "old" and "new" leadership
in governmental organs (B).

Proportions of population in competing "systems" of differentiation, and rate of change (C).

Within the "modern" sector of the society, and particularly in contemporary underdeveloped areas where industrialism and its technology are "intrusive" rather than "crescive," the early impact of this form of productive organization is to accentuate "class" differences. Workers are, almost inevitably, unskilled. Managers, technicians, and even supervisors are likely to be drawn from sectors of the social structure (or a foreign one) quite different from the places of labor recruitment.

At later periods of industrial development occupational specialization, coupled with intergenerational and career mobility, tend to blur class lines. Income inequalities may well increase in range, but on the basis of a continuum that allows only arbitrary separations. Differences in occupational prestige and other bases of judging social status may vary somewhat independently. Occupational differences, and their changes in direct or indirect response to changing technology and economic structure, do not permit clear identification of what constitutes "capital" or "management" and what "labor."

In other words, the historical and comparative evidence indicates that the Marxian view of increasing polarization of owners and workers is exactly backwards. It may even be speculated that the persistence of the view is partially a by-product of its acceptance by managers rather than by "workers," and of policies that attach primary importance to one among many actual and potential cleavage points in modern societies.

Measure: Indexes of class differences and class cleavages, and their trends, including class-oriented memberships, political affiliations and voting behavior, memberships in occupational associations as compared with "industrial" unions or "management" identifications (C).

An important by-product of specialization is the creation of occupations that are highly technical in their qualifications and duties and in their titles. Specific occupations or their functional importance is thus often not known or understood beyond a very limited circle. In other contexts of community or society more general classificatory categories are used for purposes of judging rank. Even such classifications do not necessarily produce a unitary system of differential valuation, but seem rather to produce a vague and plural system of stratification. In these circumstances social class may be more of a dull analytical tool of the observer than a meaningful part of social structure.

Measure: Tests of knowledge and consistency of prestige-rating of various occupations (B).

The obsolescence or dilution of technical skills clearly affects social status, and the apparent risk of such changes during a career is a possibly important element in the rating of an occupation at any given time. Whether from the individual point of view or that of the society's interest in optimal use of labor resources, the problems of potential obsolescence involve decisions as to the amount of education to be given before entrance into the labor force, and its relative distribution between general and specialized training.

Measures: Trends in general educational levels (A).

Data on occupational demand as related to educational supply (B).

Leisure has long been recognized as a privilege and symbol of superior social position. A "leisure class" is never likely to be very numerous, and must always be distinguished from involuntary unemployment or the urban phenomenon of part-time work by those who "live by their wits." Length of the work week and the enjoyment of holidays and vacations is the more important differentiating variable. However, like other status symbols it is subject to degradation by equalization. And it is by no means true that positions with high income and/or prestige uniformly afford extensive leisure also.

Measure: Normal work periods by occupational dimensions (B).

How leisure is spent, although partially limited by income, is likely to be related to occupational roles and used as a symbol of social status.

Measure: Temporal trends in various leisure-time activities (B).

Growth of the "Rational Spirit"

The theory that a long-term implication of changing productive technology has been an attitude or habit of mind favorable to deliberate social manipulation and control leads to several hypothetical trends in general social structure and patterns of behavior. It should perhaps be stipulated that falsehood, deception, and fraud are not modern inventions, and that differential control of knowledge has always been an element in social power. What is being suggested here is that the widespread and self-conscious use of differential knowledge for power, influence, or social manipulation is especially fostered by an instrumental view of the social universe.

If this argument has at least speculative merit, it should be expected that education would be increasingly secularized, both in sponsorship and in content. The content should increasingly emphasize psychology, group adjustment, and "social studies." Budgets and enrollments in higher education should exhibit trends toward social science, administration, methods of education, and advertising and marketing. The occupational structure should be characterized by increasing proportions of "social technologists" in the broadest sense of the term.

Measures: Public school attendance and budgets (A).

Changes in occupational distributions (A).

Distribution of advanced students by fields of specialization (A).

Changes in standard curricula (B).

Research and "information" budgets by broad
fields of knowledge (B).

In terms of social status and power, the theory being argued here
would lead us to expect, if not a rise of a new elite of "social
manipulators" (advertising experts, managers, propagandists and public relations experts, social workers, "influence" salesmen, bargainers
and arbitrators, and opinion and attitude samplers), at least their more
prominent representation in various elites. Engineers have not necessarily declined in influence, but social technologists seem to have risen,
and traditional forms of leadership and influence have suffered at the
hands of both.

Measure: Trends in social and educational backgrounds
of formally recognized leaders (B).

There is a kind of paradox in the developments suggested here.
On the one hand, the "manipulators" presumably gain a differential
advantage from superior knowledge of psychological and social principles. The advertiser attempts to learn unconscious motivations of
potential customers and make rational use of such knowledge by appealing to the consumer's irrationalities. The manager adopts a
deliberate program of human relations, with all its emphasis on sentiment and informal organization, in order to improve output and
reduce turnover or absenteeism. This leads to a kind of picture of the
philosopher-kings and the prelogical primitives. On the other hand,
the very social system that fosters such views also encourages their
extension and equalization. Discovery of the program and its "informa-
tional" sources either automatically defeats their effect, or gives rise to
countermeasures (so that all sides are represented by their own
"experts").

Measures: Time periods in the use of various "instrumental" techniques, and their sequence (C).

The circulation of manipulative elites and the possible tendencies
to equalization of cynicism do not, of course, provide a very cohesive
social system, or one in which status differentials rest upon commonly
accepted criteria. It is perhaps fears along some of these lines that
plague leaders in underdeveloped areas.

Many of the types of social relationships in a society that is mobile
and undergoing rapid and often deliberate changes are momentary
and fragmentary in their very nature. Despite the emphasis on the
development of a kind of amoral manipulative attitude, industrial

societies have generally developed norms and codes for the guidance of conduct, and rules of honesty and fair play. Some of these norms, summarized as "ethical universalism," apply to strangers as well as friends, competitors as well as cooperators. Such rules are subject to the pressures of the sort previously discussed, but failure to recognize the existence and operation of norms would represent a serious misunderstanding of the nature of society.

Measure: Tests of acceptance and practice of universalistic norms (B).

Implications for the Nation and Society

Some of the most important implications of changes in productive technology relate to the largest standard unit of observation—the society, or its collective political aspect, the nation. The difficulties of measurement are correlatively great. This is true partly because of extended causal links, partly because of the difficulty of keeping the unit of observation clearly in view as a collective entity. Because of the existence of formal agencies of government, the state is an easier unit of observation than the society. Because of the importance of concepts of "culture" and "society" in sociology and social anthropology, and the wide use of the distinction between "industrial" and "nonindustrial" types of social systems, as well as distinctions within these categories, we should make some attempt to deal with the more abstract units also.

Changes in Physical Products

For the character of the state and society, the two most obviously important types of products strongly affected by technological change are communication and transportation and the tools of coercive power.

Communication and transportation have a clear theoretical relevance for the size of political units and the effectiveness of internal control. However, except for the technological basis of colonial empire-building in the past, the size of actual political units appears to have scant if any relation to the technological level of the several economies. That the intensity or effectiveness of internal political control is related to technological development in communication and transportation appears at least sufficiently plausible to warrant investigation.

Developments in the ease and speed of transportation and communication should be expected to increase the influence of the central government as compared with the government of all political subdivisions. By the same token, the effective legal rules and the degree and manner of enforcement should tend to increasing homogeneity throughout the territory of the national state.

Measures: Trends in proportionate budgets and person-
              nel of national and local governing units (A).

              Indexes of differential law enforcement, related
              to distance from capital (C).

The control of "mass" communication media by the government is an important component of maintenance of power in nondemocratic political systems. Secrecy, distortion, and positive and negative propaganda depend not only on the control of communication media, but presumably also on their changing technological efficiency.

Measure: Effectiveness of "propaganda" in competitive
             and monopoly situations (B).

The "tools of power" for the maintenance of order and law enforcement include not only rapid communication and transportation but also the paraphernalia of "scientific" crime detection and the attempted monopoly of increasingly efficient weapons. If this linkage of political power to productive technology were the only one operating, we should expect an increasing efficiency of law enforcement as judged by the size of police forces. Actually of course other influences operate, including the probable increase in crime rates and reliance on formal social sanctions in urban-industrial settings.

Measures: Trends in law enforcement officers per capita
              (A).

              Indexes of "crimes known to police" that are
              solved (A).

The relation of the technology of armament production to national power is theoretically obvious, but difficult to measure in any precise way. If national power could be measured without the test of war, which in any event is fought by coalitions difficult to appraise separately, it might be possible to relate that measurement to armament expenditures or some other index of weapon potential.

Measure: Index of national power related to index of
             weapon potential (C).

If we turn from the nation to the society, it is clear that rapid communication and transportation, and particularly the development of "mass media" provide the basis for increased homogeneity of language and "cultural" standards throughout the society. National marketing of manufactured goods tends in the same direction. This has led some scholars to refer to the development of a "mass society" or a "mass culture." Indeed this trend goes beyond national boundaries, with the products of industrial manufacturing achieving something like worldwide distribution and the consequent increasing standardization of some parts of consumption and social behavior. Although some of this standardization may be relatively superficial, the introduction of cheap manufactured goods may displace local craftsmen, destroy archaic forms of social organization in production and consumption, and contribute to the process of separating economic transactions from other significant social patterns. The spread in availability and use of manufactured contraceptives has far-reaching effects on family organization and demographic trends, the eventual outcome of which may be greater uniformity rather than increased diversity. Despite persistent and pronounced differences in values and ideologies, the long-term trend in the spread of Western forms of economic production will certainly be the reduction of social and cultural differences at the level of daily activity.

Measures: Audiences of mass media (B).

Indexes of "cultural homogeneity" within and between societal units (C).

Changes in Work Roles

Work roles may again be viewed in two ways—the significance of growing specialization, and the significance of increasing leisure.

For the nation, specialization and diversification of economic "interests" are likely to produce a shifting basis for political alignments and pressures. Regional interests may become less divergent, while interests that cut across the boundaries of political subdivisions may seek representation. If formal political representation continues on geographical bases, one should expect a growth of informal representation of occupational and other economic interests.

Measure: Trends in political "lobbying" (C).

The productivity of a highly specialized economy is presumably an advantage for national power, but this may be offset by increased vulnerability, not only to enemy attack but to internal tension, disaffection, and conflict. Ideological appeals to disaffected elements in the occupational structure becomes thus a potential weapon in "psychological warfare." The special significance of specialization is that the "strategic" occupational groups are very numerous, and the critical membership in any one may be rather small.

Measures: Linear programming matrixes, occupations being taken into account (C).

Indexes of national morale and differentials by occupation and interest groups (C).

As long recognized in sociological theory, an interdependent system is not necessarily a "solidary" or "cohesive" one in terms of common beliefs and values or the absence of deviation and tension. A society with high occupational specialization does not necessarily show a persistent "class" cleavage in the traditional sense (and is indeed unlikely to do so), but rather is likely to have fairly extensive internal tensions and deviant patterns. Control and adjustment of these tensions has both political and wider social implications, including tendencies for both deliberate change and somewhat unplanned "drift" in societal structure. Just as the individual may be fractionated by discordant role demands, the society may be fractionated by discordant groups and pressures.

Measure: Various indexes of "social disorganization": crime, divorce, interest-group conflicts (C).

The principal significance of leisure at the national societal level is the potentiality it offers for extending the basis for "social participation," including political participation. This makes possible, but does not guarantee, representative government on the basis of a wider electorate and also a more active popular participation in electoral campaigns and the debate of issues of political and social policy.

Measure: Trends in extension of political suffrage and in indexes of political participation (C).

Growth of the "Rational Spirit"

We have now reached the most attenuated and speculative link of the chain that theoretically leads back to changes in productive technology. If the theory that an attitude favorable to deliberate social control derives in part from extensions in physical technology is at all tenable, then the implications for political organization and practice and for the nature of society are manifold.

In the political sphere, we should expect increasing emphasis on devices for measuring *and influencing* public opinion, including at the extreme, extensive exercise of "thought control." This does not necessarily involve the neglect of emotional or affective aspects of motivation and social relations, but rather the manipulative "rational" use of others' emotions as a means of control. We should also expect the legal system to exhibit an increase in the number and complexity of laws, and a marked shift from a simple criminal code to an elaborate civil and administrative code.

Measures: Proportion of national income spent on civilian administration (A).

Trends in budget and personnel devoted to internal governmental "propaganda" (B).

Trends in surveys of public opinion (B).

Trends in proportion of criminal cases brought under traditional, customary, or common law offenses as compared with those comprising technical and statutory offenses (C).

The so-called social movements directed at protest and reform have a considerable history, but their incidence seems to have at least a crude temporal correlation with the development of deliberate economic innovations. These social movements generally have been interpreted as *reactions to* economic changes. The point of view adopted here is that they may be more significantly viewed as extensions of those changes. Even the development of legislative bodies, which constantly revise and expand formal rules of social conduct, appears to be relatively recent, their predecessors having been more nearly judicial or emergency-solving bodies.

Measures: Trends in proportion of legislative officeholders (A).

Number and membership of protest and reform groups (B).

Here we face once more, and in a crucial way, the thorny problem of the integration of a specialized, interdependent, fractionated, "rationalized," and manipulative social order. That the integration is problematical seems clear from many crude indicators, whatever the source of the difficulties. In the theoretical approach adopted here it is not accidental that modern industrial societies, and even those just starting rapid change, exhibit both an extension of "rationality" and the appearance of new "irrationalities" in the form of virulent nationalism and patriotism, the recrudescence of emotional religious movements, loyalty tests, and appeals to the fundamental and traditional verities. These may be interpreted simply as reactions to the tension and uncertainty produced by rapid social change. But this explanatory principle seems too simple and too sterile. The more elaborate set of functional relations in a dynamic system used in this discussion seems to offer some prospect of both theoretical fruitfulness and partial measurement.

Postscript

Changes in productive technology are both accidental and deliberate. It is a special feature of industrial societies that deliberate change represents so large a segment of the total significant changes in physical technology and in the social order itself. Now this means that change is undertaken with *anticipated* consequences, although there is always a considerable likelihood of secondary and tertiary *unanticipated* consequences. The latter category tends to be unstable, as constant efforts are directed at increasing predictability and control.

Among the social scientists, sociologists and anthropologists appear to have the strongest vested interests in emphasis on the unanticipated results. This emphasis presumably derives from their conceptual and theoretical concern for social systems as complex functional entities. But the existence of unanticipated consequences presumably always constitutes a challenge to the adequacy of theoretical systems. The looseness of all known social systems is such as to give rise to the probability that this challenge will not be completely met, for reasons inherent in the phenomena themselves. (It may be well to remember that astrophysical systems are not perfectly predictable either.)

The use of social science for purposes of prediction and control in practical affairs thus illustrates once more the extension of the idea of purposive intervention in the social order. To the extent that past unanticipated consequences of technical change can now be not only anticipated but directed, modified, or prevented, social science can be, in a limited way, self-defeating, for its use distorts the phenomena to be observed. The fact remains, however, that purposive intervention is also limited in the control of functional relations, and most technical change in underdeveloped areas, for example, will have to be instituted because of or despite the consequences, but not with an avoidance of them.

5

DEVELOPMENTAL CHANGE IN URBAN-INDUSTRIAL SOCIETIES

The most conspicuous common characteristic of advanced industrial societies is their rapid rate of change. Yet the sources and directions of their change remain virtually unexplored by sociologists and other social scientists. This neglect derives in large part from the limitations of standard theoretical usages explored in previous chapters. Even in the extensive studies of modernization, a particular protocol of analysis has inhibited both a quest for universal dynamic principles and, especially, any substantial attention to the great importance of deliberate change.

These two neglected areas are linked in the concept of "developmental change," for universally the gap between the ideal and the actual is likely to lead to acceptance of some innovations, including those that are exogenous or have to be viewed as "accidental." This same gap gives rise to deliberate change, whereby conscious intervention in the natural and social world becomes organized and institutionalized.

Developmental change in economically advanced societies comprises two principal components: the *continuation of orderly trends* that may be properly called "progressive" because they correspond to universal or more specialized values, and *planned change*. The assumptions underlying the expectation that trends will continue should be noted. In one sense trends extrapolated into the future imply some form of autonomous or quasi-autonomous dynamics, segmented into the distinct components of social systems. Thus population growth, urbanization, college enrollments, or family budgetary behavior can be con-

SOURCE. A substantially different version of this Chapter will appear in a symposium on Developmental Change, edited by Arthur Gallagher, Jr., to be published by the University of Kentucky Press.

sidered as separate building blocks of a future social structure. Viewed more sharply, such confident predictions are likely to assume a continuity in fundamental values and a large measure of persistence of institutional arrangements.

Were we also to include newly developing areas in our purview, we should want to add to our kit of prophetic tools the possible *replication of historic sequences,* for some repetition is to be expected despite the social speedup that a common world experience affords. Were we also interested in concrete social forecasting, we should have to include *persistence,* for there are predictable elements of stability, as I suggested with respect to orderly trends. And for realistic forecasts on a global basis we should also want to take into account the potentiality of sharp discontinuities in the rate and direction of change, for this most challenging aspect of social prediction must be assumed to display lawful qualities also (discussed in Chapter 14).

Once we recognize that developmental change *is* an outstanding characteristic of urban-industrial societies, and we have gained a moderately respectable intellectual position for talking about it at all —the attention to "autonomous" trends and deliberate innovation— the ways of segmenting a social system may become rather conventional. The focus here is highly selective, and designed to illustrate the approach rather than provide a tidy summary of all aspects of developmental change. The two topics selected are consumption and education. (Changes in occupational structures also exemplify developmental change, and will be discussed in Chapter 7). Both consumption and education link the economy with other aspects of social organization, and are marked by both autonomous trends and deliberate change.

Consumption

Since growth in real income per capita is commonly used as a definitional measure of economic development, I shall not attempt to document once more that income differs in industrialized and newly developing areas, or that income has shown a long-term increase in industrial societies. Rather I should like to note some trends in income distribution, changes in patterns of consumption, and certain aspects of social welfare in affluent societies.

The Shares of Income

A rising per capita income can give a quite spurious sense of increasing general welfare if in fact the income is highly uneven in its distribution. In some newly developing countries it very nearly appears that the rich get richer and the poor, if anything, get poorer. Whether this augurs well for the longer-term future in such societies depends on whether the wealth of the rich is invested in ways that will eventually yield wider economic benefits.

In his comparative and historical studies, Kuznets has shown that there is in fact greater income inequality in underdeveloped countries than in developed ones.[1] This is despite the fact that income inequality in most countries, developed and underdeveloped, for which data are available shows less inequality in the agricultural sector than in nonagricultural production. Thus, it does indeed appear that the rich get richer precisely in the modernized portions of underdeveloped countries, and that income inequality is likely to be most extreme at the earliest "stages" of the development.

Some historical trends bear out the assumption that economic development is marked by a reduction in income inequality,[2] though the trend toward decreasing the share of the highest groups and increasing the share of the lowest ones is a matter of decades, if not of a century or more. The improvement "from the bottom up" has been less marked than the decline "from the top down."[3] Thus, as we might have inferred from occupational trends, it is especially the large "middle" sector of income earners that has benefited most from developmental change.

There are, of course, some remaining or new pulls toward the minority extremes: for example, the "new millionaires" in oil and executive positions in some large corporations, and the "new proletariat" of migrant farm workers and technologically displaced industrial workers in the United States. Poverty has not been abolished in the wealthiest country in the world,[4] and the rate of technological displacement among lower skill categories in agriculture and manufacturing, and even in such services as finance and distribution, indicates that the problem is not about to disappear. The very fact that this is a minority phenomenon tends to delay public action to retrain and relocate workers.

We may, in fact, be in the midst of an unprecedented polarization: a majority of the population affluent and a minority comprising the "hereditary poor." The problems of poverty have lately come to national attention in the United States, and it may be expected that those left behind in the process of modernization, or discarded after becoming fully incorporated in the industrial labor market, will constitute a problem for *all* advanced economies, including the Soviet Union and its satellites. The communists talk a great game about the utilization of human beings in constructive and liberating ways, but thereby conceal pockets of old poverty and pockets of new poverty.

In general, the few poor among the many rich bother the conscience but not the power of the latter. However, Rex Hopper advances a persuasively disturbing argument that the incipient technological displacement of previously affluent and influential cadres of white-collar personnel may in fact have revolutionary potential. Because of the prospective source of leadership and other peculiarities of the American political situation, Hopper thinks a rightist revolution has a higher probability than thunder on the left.[5]

Meanwhile, upgrading and bureaucratization have surely resulted in a rising proportion of the labor force with relatively *secure incomes,* and for many, *secure mobility,* with rising incomes through a normal career. Thus, if a somewhat reasonable anxiety about the future pervades the entire Western world, the anxiety is based more on international political uncertainties than on the time-honored concerns for mere economic well-being. I do not mean to discount status anxieties in a mobile and competitive labor market, but I am suggesting that the longitudinal view, the hope for the future, tends to offset the relative disappointments of the present for substantial portions of the population.

After Affluence, What?

An increase in financial well-being can be said to lead first to relative satisfaction of life's "necessities," growth in expenditures for "comforts and conveniences," and finally the indulgence of various "luxuries." This seems simple enough until we realize that the definition of standards and categories is social as well as physiological, and thus variable within and between societies and through time. Comforts have a way of becoming necessities, and what may appear to be luxuries, such as the support of rather showy religious and political activities and monuments, may be regarded in particular settings as having priority over all other obligations.

Despite these difficulties, there are some regularities in the association of consumption patterns and developmental change. Kuznets presents data[6] showing that expenditures for food range from 27 per cent of the total consumer outlay in the half-dozen most prosperous countries to nearly 50 per cent in an equal number of poorest countries for which data were available. (Inclusion of beverages and tobacco, as luxury items, narrows the differential slightly, the percentages being 37 and 57, respectively.) Of course, this does not mean that the rich eat less—per capita expenditures for food are nearly five times as high in the wealthy countries as in poor ones[7]—but only that the *proportions* spent for food decline with prosperity.

American data show a decline from 32 per cent of consumption expenditure for food and beverages in 1909 to 27 per cent in 1957.[8] This relative decline took place despite a radical "upgrading" of the quality of food consumption, particularly a marked increase in consumption of meat, the year-round consumption of fresh fruits and vegetables, and a larger proportion of food costs represented by processing, packaging, and distribution.

Engel's law,[9] to the effect that food expenditure proportions are negatively related to income, was formulated on the basis of cross-sectional data. It also operates through time. Of the traditional trilogy of food, clothing, and shelter, the first two conform with the expectation that "necessities" recede in relative importance with greater affluence. However, that part of housing and household operation that constitutes mere shelter cannot be disentangled from comparative statistics. Rich countries spend larger proportions on this mixture of necessities, comforts, and luxuries than do poor countries.[10] In the United States housing and utilities appear to have declined and then risen again in this century, while household equipment and operation show a slow but fairly steady upward course in consumer allocations.[11]

How is growing affluence reflected in consumer behavior besides upgrading their dwelling-places? In the purchase of "things," the automobile stands out clearly among all of the toys and gadgets available for people who do not have "everything." Consumer transportation, including public fares as well as private cars, by the middle 1950's in the United States exceeded clothing and personal care.[12] With increased travel (as well as multiple car-owning), this proportion is likely to go on increasing. Recreation other than travel also combines "goods" and "services," and is certain to increase further. Medical care and insurance is another prominent way that increasingly prosperous American consumers allocate their resources. On the other hand, health services, education, and various welfare expenditures represent prominent areas of governmental action, and I shall return presently to the rising cost (and perhaps benefits) of government in prosperous economies.

In discussing the main outlines of shifting budgetary behavior of consumers, I have not commented on the qualities of life that these imply. The crudities of "consumership," the supposed materialism of Americans and of those who seek to emulate our prosperity, or the alleged deadly standardization fostered by mass consumption in response to the stimuli of mass media—all these social criticisms strike me as highlighting social problems and simultaneously distorting them. As I have written elsewhere, "Money is useful for whatever it will buy, which may be quite non-material and even philanthropic. The world's materialists are perforce the have-nots and not the haves . . . In a prosperous economy . . . money becomes increasingly essential for maintenance of the good life . . . and a decreasingly reliable predictor of exact consumption expenditures. . . ."[13] As to standardization, this seems to me clearly greater in broad terms of reducing regional or ethnic differentials—or rather, incorporating many of them in a growing pool of options—than in the precise preferences exercised by consumers. In the same book from which I just quoted I referred to the possibilities of "mass produced individuality,"[14] noting the possibility that the very wealth of goods available, including components for optional assembly, reduces the likelihood that consumers will in fact all choose the same units or aggregates of goodies.

The Market versus The Fisc

One implication of what we have been observing with regard to changing consumption patterns is that the demand for services is likely to rise more rapidly than the demand for goods. Indeed, it is possible that Engle's Law with respect to food could be extended to all goods, as satiation with mere things is at least imaginable but satiation with services and experiences scarcely so.

The steady movement of services into the market is one of the well-established trends in developmental change. Here, however, we must recognize that there are at least four organizational options: self-help and informal mutual aid, private but organized philanthropy, the impersonal market, and the state through its power of taxation and transfer. I think it is unquestionable that the last two have grown steadily at the expense of the former two, and that the market *versus* the "fisc" is now the chief option available in pluralistic societies.[15] (In fact, it is unlikely that socialist or communist states will entirely abandon market mechanisms for allocating at least some services, such as recreation and travel.)

Although it seems clear that prosperous countries spend more of their national income on social security than do the few very poor countries that provide programs and data, the variation among prosperous countries is rather wide. American social security expenditures amount to around 5–6% of national income, but Italy's is about twice as high, and West Germany's runs around 20%.[16]

All prosperous countries have become "welfare states" in varying forms and degrees, providing both direct construction and services through the power of taxation, on the one hand, and acting as "trustee" for contributory social insurance on the other. Yet the major share of growth in the American governmental budget is of course accounted for by military expenses and international relations. Table 5.1 shows the phenomenal growth in total budget of all American governmental units in this century, and the more than threefold increase in the share allocated to "defense." By comparison, the budget for education, though greatly increased in absolute amount, takes a smaller proportion of the total tax dollar now than at the beginning of the century. It is, perhaps, fairer to appraise education (or other "welfare" expenditures) with respect to nondefense budgets, and on that basis education in 1957 accounted for 19% of expenditures compared with 17% in 1902.[17]

TABLE 5.1 Total, Defense, and Educational Expenditures of all U.S. Governmental Units, 1902–1957

Year	Total (Millions)	Defense (Millions)	Per Cent of Total	Education (Millions)	Per Cent of Total
			Expenditures		
1902	1,660	165	9.9	258	15.5
1957	125,463	45,803	36.5	15,098	13.1

Source: U.S. Bureau of the Census, Historical Statistics of the United States, Colonial Times to 1957 (Washington: 1960), p. 723.

Galbraith[18] seems to think that the fisc is destined to win over the market with respect to most relatively "impoverished" or newly assertive demands: education, health, highways, and perhaps even housing. Certainly any substantial reduction of military spending would produce a clamor for public assistance and adult retraining for displaced persons, and would produce the opportunity for an attack on the poverty that remains amidst general prosperity.

Planned change in consumption has not been eschewed in the capitalist, pluralist democracies, but it has achieved public acceptance as a governmental function only in terms of war and defense and, somewhat reluctantly and intermittently, in terms of aiding those conspicuously disadvantaged. To match the hard core of poverty there is a hard core of political opinion (especially in the United States but also in Western Europe) that represents a kind of crude Social Darwinism: the poor deserve their fate, for they have fallen back in (allegedly fair) competition. They are thought to lack ambition or ability, or both. Perhaps the greatest contemporary policy significance of the social sciences has been the attack on the easy and self-serving assumptions of the fortunate. The implications are unmistakable: deliberate, problem-solving programs aimed at equalizing opportunity.

Education

The relation between education and economic development is so commonly known as to seem to need little documentation. Literacy rates, school attendance rates, or median years of school completed will, in a cross-sectional comparison, rank countries approximately in terms of their national income per capita. There are, however, some anomalies. England achieved economic growth and the world's greatest empire with remarkably little investment in higher education and rather modest enrollments in secondary schools until recent years. Egypt, on the other hand, combines a low general level of literacy and a relatively high proportion of college graduates: educational attainments representing essentially a "shaft" rather than the "pyramid" that would be more symbolically suitable to the Egyptian landscape.[19]

The correlation between education and development also needs examination from the point of view of causation, for the degree to which expanded education has been a causal factor in developmental change is not readily distinguishable from the degree to which education is a valued "consumer service" made possible by economic growth. Economists[20] have begun to view education in terms of personal or public investment, and the conviction that education is a major requisite of growth is certainly widespread in developing areas.

There can be no doubt about the growth of education in the highly developed countries and little doubt about the functions of formal education in allocating labor to more or less skilled and well-paid employment. For the school-age population in the United States, only 47.2% were enrolled in school in 1850,[21] and the commitment to education was certainly greater here than in England or Western Europe. Each subsequent decade in the United States showed a steady increase to 78.7% in 1950 and 87.7% in 1957. Nonwhites showed a more marked increase than the total for white males. Thus, nonwhite females moved from 1.8 to 74.9% over the 1850–1950 century, and nonwhite males from 2.0 to 74.7%. By 1957 the lowest category (nonwhite females, 85%) was very close to the highest category (white males, 90%).[22]

In Britain only 40% of 10-year-olds were receiving full-time education in 1870, but that percentage had moved to 100% by 1902.[23] The percentage of 14-year-olds in school moved from 38 in 1938 to 100 in 1961. Only 2% of the 19-year-olds were in school in 1938, and 7% in 1962.

The British investment in higher education is thus advancing rapidly, but in the 1950's the enrollment in higher educational institutions (151 per 100,000 population) was still lower than that of virtually every country in Europe, excepting only Albania and Malta.[24] For the same period American college enrollment rates (1,816 per 100,000 population) were twelve times as high as the British, and almost three times as high as those of the closest rival, the Soviet Union (613 per 100,000 population).[25]

There is every reason to expect a rising *rate* of college attendance in economically advanced countries as well as in those developing areas where college enrollments have been very small. Postgraduate education is also certain to increase, at least in the advanced countries, as new and old professions go on growing.

A rising average, and perhaps minimum, level of education of the labor force in the course of economic development appears probable in view of trends in education, but precise temporal comparisons for particular occupations or occupational categories are not yet possible. We do know that poor education is probably an important factor in unemployment. For example, in the United States in 1960, the median years of school completed for unemployed males over 25 was more than two years less than that of the male labor force as a whole (8.8 years as compared with 11.1). Though in the total male labor force 44% had 4 years of high school or more education, the proportion with such educational levels among the unemployed was just half as high.[26]

Trends in educational levels may be inferred from differing educational levels by age. American data for 1960 show, for example, that male "operatives" aged 20–24 had a median educational attainment around the 12-year level that would imply completion of secondary school. The medians then decline steadily with each age category to a level of 7.9 years for the oldest group.[27] Virtually every occupational group displays a similar age pattern, with two notable exceptions: Professionals have a median educational attainment over the 16-year (college) level for all mature age groups except those 65 and over, for whom it is only slightly lower, and nonfarm managers and officials have median attainments under the 12-year (secondary) level only for ages 55 and over.[28]

The educational factor in occupational classification is shown in Table 5.2, which confirms the ordinary "prestige" ranking of occupations from professionals down to farm laborers. Of professionals, 34.9% had postcollege education.[29] The "professional" category is of course rather heterogenous. A surprising 2,058 persons (but only 0.1%) had no years of school completed, and 9.2% had less than a high school education. A considerable proportion of these was not in "established" or "learned" professions. Of all "professionals" with less than a high school education, 38.8% were in the "other" category,[30] including such occupations as actors, airplane pilots, artists and art teachers, athletes, dancers and dance teachers, entertainers, funeral directors, and musicians and music teachers. On the other hand, professionals included a major proportion (around three-fourths) of all those with postcollege education.

TABLE 5.2 Occupational Categories by Median Years of School Completed, United States, 1960

Occupational Group	Median Years of School
Professional	16.4
Managers, Proprietors, and Officials	12.5
Sales Workers	12.5
Clerical	12.3
Craftsmen	10.3
Operatives	9.1
Service Workers	9.1
Farmers	8.7
Nonfarm Laborers	8.3
Farm Laborers	6.8

Source: U. S. Bureau of the Census, Population Census, 1960. Subject Reports: Educational Attainment, Final Report PC(2) 5B (Washington: 1963), Table 8.

It is, additionally, worth noting that there is a clear and almost uniform positive correlation between education and income within occupational groups.[31] In other words, even if there are no *formal* educational requirements for entrance into an occupation, the better educated do in fact earn higher incomes.

It is, of course, impossible from these data to distinguish the relative influences of supply and demand. Does the labor market "require" rising educational levels, or merely "benefit" from the education provided for other reasons? The latter possibility cannot be totally rejected, as there is some ground for suspicion that employers may insist on particular educational specifications in recruitment that are not in fact required by the performance specifications of the positions to be filled. Educational levels by age and occupation for other countries and at successive periods would be a desirable check on the virtually unique American data.

The growing emphasis on education as a criterion for employment has some potentially negative by-products that should be noted. Though expanding educational opportunities may lead to some increases in the openness of social structures in terms of intergenerational mobility, it may result in the successive reduction of alternative avenues of social placement. What of the individual who does poorly on standardized ability tests, whose talents are not highly verbal, whose athletic or artistic or mechanical aptitudes are poorly adapted to the academy?[32] Some of the pluralism of pluralistic societies may disappear if the measurement of merit gets too rigidly standardized.

On the other hand, the occupational sorting accomplished by the school may be too precise. Nothing is less practical than a practical education if the result is a trained incapacity for adaptation to change, or continuous learning, and for some degree of creativity. The school will fulfill its function as an agency of developmental change only if it prepares its graduates for a somewhat uncertain world, where no niche is absolutely secure and few niches even hold their shape well.

Education is a major component of planned change in modernizing and advanced economies. Yet remarkably little is known about the school as an agency of change, as an attitude-forming environment as well as an instrumentality of technical training. For the misfits—those not yet incorporated into an industrial way of life or discarded from it—there will be a powerful temptation for educational planners to attempt to equip their unfortunate clients with very narrowly specified skills. There may be no perfect solution to the problem, but at the very least it is appropriate to recognize that being a misfit is likely to be a recurrent rather than a singular situation.

Concluding Comment

It may be objected, with some justice, that by focusing attention on changes in occupational structure, consumption, and education, I have presented an overly optimistic view of the present and future. It is true that I have said nothing of such conspicuous problems as urban congestion, juvenile delinquency, mental health, or divorce, or such subtle problems as that of maintaining privacy in the fact of ecological crowding and electronic invasion of the home and the mind. And I should not want to deny that some of these problems are genuinely greater than in the past as well as more commonly recognized. Much of what we have been calling developmental change is goal-oriented and deliberate, and the one clear moral we may draw from the negative items is that problems multiply along with partial solutions. The tensions of societies change in character or relative urgency as societies evolve, and there is no prospective future time when life will be simpler than the past for the citizen to act upon or for the scholar to think upon.

References

1. Simon Kuznets, "Quantitative Aspects of the Economic Growth of Nations, VIII. Distribution of Income by Size," Supplement to *Economic Development and Cultural Change*, 11, No. 2, January 1963.

2. *Ibid.*

3. *Ibid.*, p. 59.

4. See J. N. Morgan et al., *Income and Welfare in the United States* (New York: McGraw-Hill, 1962).

5. Rex D. Hopper, "Cybernation, Marginality, and Revolution," in Irving Louis Horowitz, ed., *The New Sociology* (New York: Oxford University Press, 1964), pp. 313–330.

6. Simon Kuznets, "Consumption, Industrialization, and Urbanization," in Bert F. Hoselitz and Wilbert E. Moore, eds., *Industrialization and Society* (Paris and The Hague: UNESCO and Mouton, 1963), pp. 99–115.

7. *Ibid.*, p. 108.

8. See *Historical Statistics of the United States, Colonial Times to 1957* (Washington: U.S. Government Printing Office, 1961), pp. 178–179.

9. For reference to the classic work of Ernest Engel, see Carle C. Zimmerman, *Consumption and Standard of Living* (New York: Van Nostrand, 1936), pp. 24–41.

10. See Kuznets, paper cited in Reference 6.

11. See Reference 8, pp. 178–179.

12. *Ibid.*

13. Wilbert E. Moore, *The Conduct of the Corporation* (New York: Random House, 1962), p. 274.

14. *Ibid.*, p. 270.

15. For an analysis of private and public welfare services, see Margaret S. Gordon, *The Economics of Welfare Policies* (New York: Columbia University Press, 1963).

16. *Ibid.*, pp. 15–16.

17. See Reference 8, p. 723.

18. John Kenneth Galbraith, *The Affluent Society* (Boston: Houghton, Mifflin, 1958).

19. For international data on education, see United Nations, *Report on the World Social Situation* (New York: 1957), Chapter V., "Education."

20. See, for example, Theodore W. Schultz, *The Economic Value of Education* (New York: Columbia University Press, 1963).

21. See Reference 8, p. 213.

22. *Ibid.*

23. Robbins Committee Report: Committee Appointed by the Prime Minister under the Chairmanship of Lord Robbins, 1961–1963. Cmd. 2154. (London: HMSO, 1963). All data in this paragraph are from this report.

24. See Reference 19, pp. 84–85.

25. *Ibid.*, pp. 82, 86.

26. U.S. Bureau of the Census, *U.S. Census of Population: 1960 Subject Reports, Educational Attainment,* Final Report, PC (2)—5B (Washington: U.S. Government Printing Office, 1963), Table 4.

27. *Ibid.*, Table 8.

28. *Ibid.*

29. *Ibid.*

30. *Ibid.*

31. *Ibid.*, Table 9.

32. See David A. Goslin, *The Search for Ability* (New York: Russell Sage Foundation, 1963).

6

THE IMPACT OF TECHNOLOGICAL
CHANGE ON INDUSTRIAL
ORGANIZATION

There is a very popular notion abroad in the land that technology is an automatic, autonomous, and indeed sovereign source of social change. This idea is, of course, much admired by technologists, for after all that makes them leaders, but it will not pass muster as a social theory. To a remarkable degree, in the modern world every economy or society gets about the technology that it deserves, or at least what it is able and willing to support. But I have also previously argued [1] that each stage of economic development gets about the kind of organizational theory that it deserves, as sensible administrative policies vary not only with the state of technology but also with the qualities of the inhabitants of administrative organizations.

These *caveats* are relevant to my task here, for although I shall start by considering technology as an independent variable that has important and specifiable consequences for the character of industrial organization, I shall conclude by turning the relationship about, and

SOURCE. Adapted from "The Impact of Technological Change on Industrial Organization," in Wroe Alderson, Vern Terpstra, and Stanley J. Shapiro, eds., *Patents and Progress: The Sources and Impact of Advancing Technology* (Homewood, Illinois: Richard D. Irwin, Inc., 1965), pp. 159–169; by permission of the publisher.

Some years ago I wrote a paper on this subject: "Technological Change and Industrial Organization," in International Social Science Council, *Social Implications of Technological Change.* (Paris: 1962), pp. 199–209. In the present effort I shall be repeating some points expressed there, but here I give greater attention to the interplay between productive technology and administrative technology, and take a closer look at technology as a dependent variable, that is, as useful innovations often created within the industrial organizations themselves.

briefly consider industrial organization as a source of technological change. For the sake of clarity it should be noted that by industrial organization I shall mean the networks of positions and roles, the goals and rules of conduct comprising productive units. The term is thus approximately equivalent to the firm in an enterprise economy, with somewhat more difficult but not impossible identification of comparable units in socialist and communist states. I am not concerned here with the effect of technology on the allocation of other factors of production or on the competitive position of firms, industries, or sectors of the economy. For this range of problems I regard the term "industrial organization" as ambiguous and improper.

Technological Change as an Independent Variable

The most conspicuous consequences of technological change for industrial organizations are to be found in their general "shape," as reflected for example in the numerical distribution of various skills and responsibilities, and in critical dimensions of internal relationships such as the interaction of men and machines and the ways in which expert information flows and authority is exercised.

Changes in Occupational Structure

Successive improvements in man's attempt to adjust to his environment and extend his mastery over it give substance to conceptions of social evolution as comprising *part* of the changeful qualities of social life. In an industrial economy technological change is exceptionally rapid, being both organized and institutionalized, and thus deliberate in high degree. Its impact on the allocation of productive tasks, that is, occupations, is multiple, and from an evaluative point of view, mixed. Negatively, technological change often results in the breaking up of skill combinations, which we may call skill dilution, and outright skill obsolescence. Though the distinction is not always clear in practice, skill dilution is most commonly attributable to changes in productive processes, and skill obsolescence to changes, and especially to substitutions, in industrial products. Less noticed by social critics but of crucial importance in industrial evolution is a third change in occupational demand, which is the need for new skills and new skill combinations, which results generally in occupational upgrading.

Since technology itself is highly diverse, and since the "latest" technology may not be instantaneously and generally adopted, all of these processes may be going on simultaneously. Certainly, the overriding long-term trend has been that of upgrading, with well-known human costs for those left behind in the transformation.* Within industrial organizations this process is reflected in the proportional shifts of production workers from the unskilled to the semiskilled and skilled; shifts from blue-collar to white-collar positions, and from supervisory to technical personnel. The geometric shape of the organizations comes more nearly to represent a diamond sitting on its point than a pyramid sitting on a broad base, and with lateral diversification growing relatively to vertical distinctions of skill and administrative power.

As we all now know, it is not just the men at the machines and benches that are threatened with technological displacement or challenged to acquire needful new skills. Automation and computerization threaten the job security of clerical workers and even junior managers, while demanding new design and maintenance services of a high order of trained competence.

We are, in my opinion, far from the automatic factory for most industrial processes. The machines are not self-designing, self-reproducing, self-installing, or self-maintaining. But as we move somewhat closer to the factory without workers, we should speculate a bit on the possible implications of continuous operation for the possible needs for expansion of technical personnel and possibly even for increase of policy-level executives.

Changes in Man-Machine Relations

Early forms of industrial technology made overt the subservience of the production worker to the machine in terms of both task and temporal rhythm. Subsequent developments in task subdivision and in more sophisticated machines and sequential flows of materials (and therefore sequential dependence of workers on their productive predecessors) heightened the seeming servitude to the machine. Still later changes in productive processes have substituted mechanical for muscular work, and in the course of those changes the remaining workers have been restored to machine mastery. In many industrial situations the worker now manipulates the machine, with an impressive level of what one is tempted to call dexterity, or monitors a control panel with perhaps little manual manipulation but a high requirement of responsibility.

Yet note that this sequence of changing relations of men and machines was not solely a result of changing technology in the narrow

* See Chapter 7.

sense of applications of physical and chemical principles to practical uses. Machine technology and what we may call administrative technology have been interdependent all along. The social technology of wage employment, organizational design, task allocation, temporal coordination, and administrative decision and discipline antedated the technology of machine pacing. Industrial discipline and task specialization have made possible the development of mechanical substitutes for mechanized men. Technologists in the narrow sense have often responded, sometimes tardily, to cues given by organizational planners, aided and abetted by such expert advisers as cost accountants.

Meanwhile, the organization of the work place in a highly mechanized operation bears little resemblance to the factories of our common experience or to the factories comprised of work teams and their informal relations so extensively documented in the literature of industrial sociology. For the remaining workmen, the physical setting of work is often socially sterile. The cost of achieving machine mastery is the loss of human contact, except during rest periods or out of hours. Yet the manipulator of the machine and certainly the maintenance man becomes a problem-solver and not an automaton.

Indeed the problems may become so complex that a new wave of higher-level specialization is likely to set in, with diagnosticians and varieties of therapists necessary to deal with the mechanical ills of the new technology. And note that the men manipulating and monitoring the machine, as well as their supervisors and higher management, may not fully understand the processes involved. They can appraise results but not procedures, for in effect they are dealing with experts at one remove by dealing with the products of the experts' creation.

Changes in the Demand for Experts

This brings us to the growing demand for a battery of experts in the administrative operation of industrial organizations. At a minimum, experts serve as suppliers of current information on technical developments. By one view, even the hardware scientists and technicians in research and development units have chiefly a defensive function, that of alerting policy-forming executives of possibly significant external developments. But as an over-all view this cynical interpretation suffers the same fatal, logical defect as the explanation of social conformity solely in terms of the expectations of others. In the present context, the defensive view would not account for the actual rate of technical innovation. That rate, within any industrial sector, is likely to be approximately proportional to the size of firm. In some fields without a highly developed theoretical system and corresponding scale of technical excellence—chemistry is a good example—the rate of innovation may be closely proportional to the man-hours of research time expended.

In the nature of the case, experts must face "outward" and be in close contact with their own professional peers, and in many cases must also represent various external clienteles within corporate councils. The latter is especially the case of the multiplying "relations specialists," but external relations includes law and marketing, for example, as well as dealing with labor and cultivating a public image. Both the peer identity and the representation of clienteles introduce necessarily diverse and rather commonly discordant notes into the symphony of organizational kinship and loyalty. This probability gives rise to managerial problems that I shall note below.

The increasingly technical character of everything from metallurgy to accounting and investment means a great "technification" of managerial organization taken as a whole, and helps account for the proportional increase of "staff" positions relative to "line" positions. The burden this places on central administration is a further problem to which I now turn.

Changes in Managerial Tasks

Time was when there was a normal presumption that the various levels of management corresponded to degrees of competence on a single scale, the higher-level executive being in their lofty positions as a result of competitive selection and accumulated experience. Though the manager as a generalist is still a widely shared conviction and a goal of selection and various attempts at advanced training both in the corporation and in the academy, it is becoming increasingly difficult to maintain. At the very least, it has to be recognized that the manager is not the fount of wisdom and technical knowledge for his subordinates. Often the reverse is true. The manager becomes the coordinator of experts, each of whom is likely to outrank his superior in specialized knowledge, each in his own field. Such a situation distinctly damages the cherished stereotype of the executive as a leader of men, an innovator, and a kind of exemplar of energetic virtue. Energetic and virtuous the manager or executive may be, and even, within narrow limits, an innovator, but he can scarcely lead in the sense of instruction and example. Whom could he fool?

Note that these developments radically change the managerial role, but they scarcely make it simpler or even degrade it. The manager's tasks now prominently include a cultivated ability to comprehend the information and advice that stem from basic knowledge and procedures that he could not duplicate. And since the experts represent *different* bodies of knowledge and technique, there is no reason to suppose that they will speak with a single voice. They may all try to talk at once, true enough, but that scarcely qualifies for the phrase "in unison." There is indeed a notable tendency for the expert on industrial payrolls not only to welcome the request that he be practical, but to insist on it. The difficulty is that as many solutions to problems will be offered as there are experts consulted. The manager's task in dealing with experts is simply to make simultaneous sense out of discordant and contradictory advice. At the same time, of course, he must attend to all of his other responsibilities and accountabilities as a representative of his superiors, or, if he is high enough in rank, his directors and various clienteles and publics, and to a myriad of organizational controls and pressures.

Although I cannot demonstrate the point conclusively, I think the technical and deliberately changeful environment in which the modern manager operates has as a minimum effect a steady decrease in reliance on experience and precedent for current decision. The injunction to "find the better way" tends to operate more and more pervasively.

In my book *The Conduct of the Corporation*[2] I have written disparagingly of the pretensions to professionalism on the part of business managers: ". . . Until there is established a body of abstract principles capable of application in a wide variety of situations, and until training in these principles readily distinguishes the true professional from the amateur or the man qualified only by a limited range of experience that he cannot generalize, the attempt to 'professionalize' management must be regarded as rather incomplete."[3] I also noted the virtual absence of ". . . a binding code of ethics, protective of both professional standards and of clients, and enforced chiefly by the professional body itself."[4]

In the short time since those views were written there has not been sufficient change in the great world of corporate management to force a radical revision of my views. However, I think careful and weighty attention should be given to such hopeful signs as the questioning or abandonment of the case method of business-school instruction, the increasing frequency of mid-career advanced study, and the development of training in rather elaborate rational-decision models using complex data inputs and analytic schemes for arriving at disciplined judgment. If this sort of thing goes very far, the merely experienced manager may be as technologically unemployable as some of us are beginning to feel in our own scholarly disciplines.

Diversification versus Linear Evolution

The long-term historic trends in technology can be partially cast into an evolutionary model, which allows both diversification through selective adaptation and cumulative or directional change as judged, say, by growing mastery of the environment.

The world technological pool, however, reduces the prospects for replication of historical developments in areas now industrializing. This is a principal justification for the idea of cumulative change. The available technology might be likened to the shelf-stock in a super-market, from which the shopper is free to choose without regard to the sequence in which the goods were acquired and displayed. Thus selectivity, eclectic combinations, and new adaptations are all possible and probable. There are, however, some structural constraints: increased power may break the machine rather than increase its output, mass production is uneconomic without a system for mass distribution, and so on. More interesting are the sequential constraints. In newly developing areas capital is scarce and dear, and labor is cheap though inefficient. The temptation to import the latest laborsaving technology is strong in the nationalistic environment of new nations, but time is still required to upgrade the labor force and develop industrial traditions. Thus though the organizational evolution of modern industry as we know it may be foreshortened by benefit of exceptional effort and learning from past experience, it is not likely to be reversed. With perhaps distressing frequency the factories in developing areas are likely to resemble those in Manchester in the early Nineteenth Century, and with the same radical disparity between the manager and the managed—a disparity that has been reduced and made increasingly ambiguous by the sorts of changes we have been discussing. We are now confronted with the ironic fact that Marx has proved to be radically wrong on the continuing course of industrialized societies, but repeatedly reconfirmed as a correct analyst of the earliest stages of modernization.

The Production of Technology

I now turn to technological change as a dependent variable, as the outcome of deliberate efforts at creative innovation, backed up by deliberate decisions to allocate time, talent, and money to the organized production of new knowledge.

Scientific Management versus The Management of Scientists

"Scientific management," as enunciated in the works of Frederick W. Taylor and his followers, assumed that both technical and decisional skills were exclusively managerial properties. Workers as Taylor observed them were inexperienced and without industrial traditions and often without formal education. In Taylor's view they required close supervision, including instruction and discipline. He also assumed them to be "economic men," and though I have joined, if I did not help lead, a chorus of criticism of Taylor's administrative theories,[5] I now think he was essentially right for the time, technology, and labor force that he experienced. This is an example of the assertion that each stage of industrial development gets about the administrative theory that it deserves.

An upgraded and committed labor force requires more coordination than supervision. Even at the level of first-line supervisors, the foreman may be less technically qualified than his subordinates.

Introducing technically-trained experts, and particularly of organized research, within the industrial organization brings the change in appropriate administrative styles into sharp focus.

The role of professionals in organizations is intrinsically ambiguous, as I have already noted. Relational experts are necessarily "two-faced,"[6] since they cannot represent the company to its clients without representing the clients to the company. And researchers are necessarily peer-oriented as well as somewhat organizationally responsible. This lack of total organizational commitment is a principal, though not the sole, source of line-staff conflict, which is a ubiquitous and intrinsic feature of industrial and indeed of all administrative organizations.

The organization and administration of scientific research has received considerable scholarly attention, most recently and effectively by Kornhauser and Marcson.[7] Two problems are especially worthy of comment: (1) The administrative scientist, such as the director of a research laboratory, commonly has to be a scientist in order to get his position and steadily loses his current claims to scientific authority as he exercises administrative authority. (2) The conditions for creativity are still not firmly known, but two firm findings are that freedom is necessary and that peer orientations must be indulged. I should add a third, less firmly grounded condition, that security of position is more conducive to creativity than is anxiety.

Problems of Communication and Implementation

The effective production of technical innovation encounters at least two pervasive problems of administrative organization, namely communication and managerial or "line" decisions.

Jargon, argots, and patois abound in industrial organizations. Thus there is a very general need for translators and interpreters if coordination is to take place, and particularly if technical innovations are to be appraised at decision-making levels. It is not surprising, therefore, that large industrial research laboratories find it advantageous to have technically-trained "salesmen," whose mission is not to deal with external customers but rather with managers of product divisions and general managers who have to be convinced that there are practical, economically advantageous opportunities in new technical developments.

Like their kind everywhere, these salesmen often do not succeed. Acceptance and implementation of an innovation in either product or process requires positive decision and positive action. The larger the organization, presumably the larger the flow of innovative suggestions from the legitimate trouble-makers, and, I fear, the larger the number of company officers who have and often exercise veto powers. Those line officers above the potential innovator in relative rank are legitimately empowered naysayers, for whatever sensible, nonsensical, or merely neurotic reasons. If the decision is affirmative the innovator's path is still rough. Managers down the line, who have ordinarily not been consulted on implementation, cannot normally exercise official vetos. Their power (though not their authority) is that of sabotage— of conscientious withholding of cooperation—and at that they are often adept.

I cannot prove it, but I firmly believe that actual product innovations, as distinct from changes in process alone, are disproportionately introduced by small and indeed often by new firms. This is their mode of entry into the market. The bureaucratization of research, if it does not destroy creativity, is likely to thwart it at the level of positive action.

Distortions of Defense

Investments of men and money in new technology are now strongly influenced by national support and in the industrial sector especially by defense spending. This means that some technologies are favored while others languish, thus again disproving merely technological primacy in social change.

The support of technology in the name of defense also means that governmental contract negotiation becomes a major managerial activity. Moreover, the government becomes the sole and insistently monopolistic customer for some technology. Changes in technology and choice of producers may be made on political as well as economic and technical grounds.

This is a major part of the contemporary production of technology. The situation affects not only industrial organization, but it also affects the way one must rationally view the relations between government and industry. The old shibboleths about keeping government out of business were tainted, and their contemporary reiteration plainly shocking. The relations between private corporations and agencies of government are multitudinous and run from cooperative interdependence to competitive or combative redefinitions of rights and responsibilities. But the ideologues of business who speak out against big government, and that includes an alarming proportion of otherwise responsible executives along with irresponsible writers of speeches and copy for institutional advertising, must speak with a forked tongue. Indeed, they must either be hypocritical or dangerously naive, knaves or fools. That is not the way the modern technological or political world is organized, or could be, and it is surely high time that a little measure of responsibility on public issues intruded itself into the thinking of the producers of technology who are also, along with the rest of us, its somewhat reluctant beneficiaries.

References

1. Wroe Alderson, Vern Terpstra, and Stanley J. Shapiro, eds., *Patents and Progress: The Sources and Impact of Advancing Technology* (Homewood, Illinois: Richard D. Irwin, Inc., 1965), pp. 207–209.

2. Wilbert E. Moore, *The Conduct of the Corporation* (New York: Random House, 1962).

3. *Ibid.*, p. 12.

4. *Ibid.*

5. Wilbert E. Moore, *Industrial Relations and the Social Order*, revised ed. (New York: Macmillan, 1951), pp. 170–184. The same materials appeared in the first edition in 1946.

6. See Wilbert E. Moore, *The Conduct of the Corporation*, previously cited, Chapter XIII, "Two-Faced Experts."

7. William Kornhauser, *Scientists in Industry: Conflict and Accommodation* (Berkeley and Los Angeles: University of California Press, 1962); Simon Marcson, *The Scientist in American Industry* (New York: Harper, 1960).

7

CHANGES IN OCCUPATIONAL STRUCTURES

One of the most direct links between modes of economic production and social structure is of course to be found in labor-force participation and types of economic activity. As an economy shifts from a highly decentralized "subsistence" production to a highly interdependent production of a wide range of goods and services, the human or social counterpart is a series of shifts in work roles. Here I want to explore various facets of this transformation, identifying several interdependent but analytically distinct "processes" of change. I shall use the concept "occupational structure" in a broad sense to include a number of ways whereby economic performance roles are differentiated and organized.

Since our focus is on structural changes in the course of economic modernization, some introductory comments are in order regarding the view of social change that informs the subsequent discussion.

The degree to which changes in economic structure determine other changes in societies may have been exaggerated by analytical models that attend to interdependencies but not to autonomous variability in subsystems. Thus the attempt to generalize about the social consequences of economic development and the attempt to increase the precision of predictive generalizations, though laudable, may encounter some unbreachable barriers. Differences in preindustrial social patterns

SOURCE. Adapted from "Changes in Occupational Structures," *in* Neil J. Smelser and Seymour Martin Lipset, eds., *Social Structure, Mobility, and Economic Development* (Chicago: Aldine Publishing Co., 1966); by permission of the editors and publisher.

I wish to express my thanks to W. Lee Hanson, whose written discussion of the original draft emphasized the economic bases for changes in labor demand; to Mrs. Karen Many, for helpful editorial suggestions; and to Neil J. Smelser, who pointed out the interdependence of processes of structural change.

do have lasting consequences, and there are options in politicoeconomic regimes. Precise replication of historic changes may not be expected in some aspects of contemporary modernization because the experience of the past may be forthrightly adopted or rejected, with resulting changes in both timing and sequence.

These initial *caveats* are meant to be disarming, but are also less critical with respect to occupational structures than with respect to, say, the forms of the polity.

Specifically, we shall be arguing that several trends in occupational structures are closely associated with economic growth, as measured, say, by rising real income per capita. Thus some international cross-sectional data will be used for want of historic series, and the particular features of occupational structure being examined are inferentially additional indicators of economic development.

A further implication of the use of cross-sectional and temporal data as direct or putative trends merits display. This implication is that economic growth may be properly treated as a continuous (and enduring) kind of transformation. Although some sharp transitions and discontinuities cannot be denied, they are generally exaggerated by "before-and-after" comparisons or by three-stage models that mark off modernization as a dynamic era distinct from preindustrial or post-industrial economies.

Our mission, then, is to examine structural changes in the disposition of human labor as a framework within which social mobility may be examined.

The Mobility Problem

Changes in social location or position are generally identified by the general term mobility. (A semantic case can be made for the use of "mobility" to mean readiness to move, and some other term, say, "movement," to refer to actual changes. This argument is likely to fall on deaf ears, and I shall continue to use the term conventionally and improperly.) Mobility thus comprises changes in location (locus), relative position (status), sector, industry, or "lateral" occupational segment (situs) or in employer (patronus).[1] Distinctions are also drawn for status mobility between intergenerational shifts and changes within a career. For reasons that probably could be traced to the intellectual history of their discipline, sociologists concerned with mobility trends have concentrated primarily on intergenerational movement, and have commonly espoused the view that the only significant question about such movement is the comparative "openness" of systems. Rogoff, for example, made a study of comparative mobility rates a generation apart, and "standardized out" changes in occupational structure—the "demand" side of the equation—by computing expected frequencies.[2] In fairness it must be added that she concluded that she had thereby eliminated the major factor in mobility changes between 1910 and 1940.

Now the analytical separation of mobility accounted for by changes in the distribution of occupations within the socioeconomic structure from that accounted for by changes in the distribution of opportunity or accessibility is a perfectly legitimate procedure. But there is no reason to say that only the second datum is interesting. Marsh, in fact, has suggested that the manifestly greater intergenerational mobility of industrial societies may be entirely explained by changes in occupational structures rather than in terms of values and norms that encourage mobility aspirations and merit recruitment.[3] For example, if a survey of current farmers reveals that virtually all had farmer fathers, it would be quite improper to conclude that there is very little mobility out of agriculture: the proportions of farmers in the total labor force may have declined by half in the course of a generation and a fair proportion of farmers' sons thus be in some other economic sector and occupation.

The present discussion relates to changes in demand for types and grades of economic activity. Hypothetical directions of change will be noted, together with kinds of desirable data. Here and there references to actual quantities will be noted.

Sources and Types of Structural Change

The demand for labor by industry, occupation, location, and employer may be viewed in economic terms as the resultant of two other classes of variables: the demand for goods and services, and the relevant factor proportions of capital, labor, and, especially, the state of the appropriate technology. Even at a given level of "available" technology, capital may within limits be substituted for labor—that is, machines for men. Though the occurrence is rare, the converse substitution of men for machines is of course theoretically possible. The supply and price of labor presumably influence employers' decisions on "factor mixes," including investments in technological change with the immediate or later aim of displacing some proportion of workers or avoiding dependence on certain skilled occupations in short supply.

To these elementary principles of economic interdependence we should add that the supply of labor is affected not only by current demand but also by past demographic behavior of the relevant population, ease or difficulty of migration, by institutional determinants of labor-force participation, and notably by the efficacy whereby the schools and other training agencies produce the requisite manual skills or intellectual accomplishments. Thus the focus here on changing structures, on the "demand" for labor somehow filled by movement of individuals from their social, geographical, or occupational origins, is not intended to make of occupational changes a sovereign determinant. It is only intended to redress the balance of customary discussion, which, we have noted, tends to view mobility solely as a sorting of persons into given positions.

The types of structural change attended to here are: the initial formation of labor market and its expansion at the "expense" of subsistence production or traditional modes of exchange; sectoral relocation, particularly the proportional growth of nonagricultural employments; specialization, the process of subdividing complex skills but also multiplying the kinds and levels of skill needed; upgrading the long-term process of proportional shifts to higher skill categories, possibly accompanied by higher minimum-skill levels; and finally, bureaucratization, the organization of specialized labor into large administrative units that secure "political" (or disciplined) coordination rather than relying solely on the impersonal controls of the market.

Although these processes will be discussed seriatim, they are all structurally related to economic growth and to each other. It is hard to imagine, for example, extensive economic development without a great expansion of non-agricultural production and labor. The variety of goods and services that characterizes the advanced economy bespeaks specialization, but specialization also occurs because of considerations of efficiency and rationalized organization. A rationalized organization, plus the adaptation to change and its deliberate creation, demands increasing managerial, clerical, and technical services, and the coordination of the manifold specialties (most of which do not yield a single product but only a share in a complex productive and administrative process) could scarcely be effected without "political" coordination. But political coordination supplements rather than supersedes the market. The formation of a labor force paid in wages and salaries is the way specialized producers become generalized consumers for themselves and their dependents.

The interdependence of structural changes does not of course assure their perfect synchronization. For example, migrants from "subsistence" agriculture may swell the ranks of the urban unemployed, and the supply of "upgraded" aspirants turned out by the schools may exceed the rate at which the demand for their skills is expanding. Specialization may be carried to extremes that place complex processes in jeopardy from the failure of a single workman, and bureaucratization may add more to the employment opportunities in "administrative" posts for otherwise unemployable scions of an archaic elite than to efficiency in mobilizing human resources for productive tasks.

With respect to the interdependence of structural changes I shall have little more to say, but I shall attempt to note the implications of the several processes for occupational mobility.

Market Participation

The first change in occupational structure associated with modernization is the creation of a labor force in the technical sense. That is, the separation of "work" from other, possibly useful, activities requires the operational definition of financial remuneration,[4] and thus the creation of a labor market and/or its indirect equivalent in a commodity market.

On this point national statistics are extremely unsatisfactory, for the category "agriculture" fails to distinguish between market production and "subsistence agriculture," with products and participants that are scarcely part of the market system. For many areas of Africa and Asia it would be valuable to have temporal trends in the assimilation of subsistence production into the national economy and of producers into the labor force. Some data on Sub-Saharan Africa indicate that less than half of the potential male labor force may be actually involved in the labor market either as workers or commercial producers, though the ratios vary widely from place to place.*

It should be noted, however, that such data as are available (not very recent in most instances) indicate that a minority of African males at the time of a given enumeration or survey are engaged in wage labor, but such data leave out of account both commercial activities and self-employment in services, and give no hint at the extent of commercialization in agriculture.

Trends in labor-for-participation rates by age and sex also warrant examination. It is probable that participation rates under age 18 are negatively correlated—cross-sectionally or temporally—with indicators of economic development. Put another way, the median age of labor-force entry should be positively correlated with economic advancement. Labor-force participation of the aged may also have a (probably

* See Chapter 9.

low) negative correlation with advancement. (Though advanced economies offer a wider variety of employments that are not very physically demanding, they also generally afford institutionalized retirement systems.)

Female labor-force participation is more strongly affected by institutional variation than is male participation, but the problem of cross-sectional or temporal comparison is further complicated by variations in concepts and statistical procedures. In particular, the "unpaid family worker" is an attempt to represent statistically an economic role that the market itself does not record. Obviously such quasi-participants in the labor force are most numerous in economic activities where the family as such retains functions of production other than self-consumed services. This form of linkage between the family and the economy is thus most prominent in agriculture, and secondarily so in various commercial services, though handicraft "putting-out systems" involving multiple participation by family members are not unknown. Unpaid family workers represented 19% of agricultural workers in the United States in 1950, less than 1% (0.008) of nonagricultural workers. By 1962 the proportion had fallen to 16% in agricultural but had risen to slightly over 1% in nonagricultural employment.[5] Although the family inevitably retains many economic functions in an urban-industrial economy, including consumption decisions, major influences on vocational choice and occupational placement of the young, and various services that could be commercially evaluated, unpaid family workers are in a sense anachronistic, for they represent an incomplete development of an individualized labor market.

With respect to direct, compensated female participation in the labor market, it may be hypothesized that rates will increase with economic growth, and that has been the American experience. If we take into account intrafamilial female work and the growth of non-familial production, it is somewhat more accurate to say that the initial impact of commercialization of labor, an impact that endures for considerable periods, is to reduce the economic contributions of women, which are then increased through the rising rates of direct labor-force participation. As far as release of married women from domestic household functions is concerned, it is clear that the major, and perhaps only important, labor-saving device has been the contraceptive, which permits limitation of the number of children and especially of the duration of childbearing. The increasing labor-force-participation rates of American women over the age of 45 are testimony to the combined effectiveness of family limitation and the school as the daytime custodian of children and youths.

TABLE 7.1 Proportions of the Economically Active Population in Agriculture, Various Countries, Around 1950

Country[1]	Date	% in Agriculture
Haiti[2,3]	1950	88
Thailand[2,3]	1947	81
India[2,3]	1951	69
Pakistan[4]	1951	62
Brazil	1950	58
Mexico	1950	58
USSR[5]	1950	56
Costa Rica[4]	1950	55
Ceylon[4]	1946	53
Egypt[4]	1947	51
Hungary	1941	50
Spain	1950	49
Japan	1950	48
Finland	1940	47
Italy	1954	41
France	1950	32
Chile[4]	1952	31
Ireland[4]	1951	31
Norway	1950	29
Argentina[4]	1947	25
Denmark	c. 1950	23
Canada	c. 1950	21
Sweden	1950	20
Switzerland	1941	20
Netherlands	1947	19
New Zealand[4]	1951	18
Australia[4]	1947	15
United States[6]	1950	12
Belgium	1947	11
United Kingdom	1951	5

Source. Unless otherwise indicated, Simon Kuznets, "Quantitative Aspects of the Economic Growth of Nations. II. Industrial Distribution of National Product and Labor Force." Supplement to *Economic Development and Cultural Change,* 5, No. 4, July 1957, Table 4, pp. 82–95.

[1] Arranged in descending order of last column.

[2] Males only.

[3] United Nations. *Statistical Yearbook,* 1955 (New York: 1955). Table 6. Males only.

[4] United Nations, *op. cit.* Both sexes.

Sectoral Relocation

One of the best-established generalizations concerning structural changes related to modernization is the shift from agricultural to non-agricultural activities. Table 7.1 represents the proportions of the economically active populations in agriculture in various countries around 1950 (still the most recent data available for most countries). In order to show the cross-sectional progression from countries which can properly be called economically backward to those that are advanced, I have arranged the countries in descending order of the agricultural labor force. The intermediate position of France, where "peasant" agriculture remains important, perhaps requires less comment than do Chile and Argentina. Though by no means truly "advanced," by many economic and social indicators these South American countries do have highly commercialized farming, involving considerable mechanization, especially in Argentina.

Actual historic trends in the decline of agricultural employment are also interesting. Table 7.2 presents for several countries the long-term changes in agricultural employment, with the final column representing the simple arithmetic mean annual rate of decline implicit in the before-and-after comparisons. This unsophisticated measure reveals some interesting differences between countries. It invites a somewhat speculative generalization to the effect that the later an economy enters on industrialization the more rapid is the shift from agricultural to nonagricultural occupations. The relatively rapid declines in Japan and the Soviet Union at one extreme and the slow declines in France and the United Kingdom at the other lend some credence to the generalization, but more precise formulation of how the "onset" of modernization is to be measured and dated would be needed for effective confirmation or disproof.

Changes in trends through time within countries also hold some interest. An inviting hypothesis would allege a height-slope relationship comparable to the temporal course of mortality rates, whereby high rates decline rapidly and low rates decline slowly, with a resulting reverse J-curve temporal trend. Again the Soviet or Japanese extremes

5 Warren W. Eason, "Labor Force," in Abram Bergson and Simon Kuznets, *Economic Trends in the Soviet Union* (Cambridge: Harvard University Press, 1963), pp. 38–149; data from p. 77.
6 United States Bureau of the Census, *Statistical Abstract of the United States,* 1962 (Washington: 1962), Table 280, p. 215.

106   The Transformation of Economic Structures

TABLE 7.2 Long-Term Rates of Decline in Agricultural Labor Force,
Various Countries, and Periods

Country	Beginning Date	% in Agriculture	Ending Date	% in Agriculture	Mean Annual % Decline
USSR[1]	1925	85.5	1959	48.4	1.09
USA[1]	1820	71.8	1960	7.1	.46
France[2]	1846	57.0	1954	22.5	.32
United Kingdom[3]	1801	35.9	1951	5.0	.21
Denmark	1870	54.0	1940	29.0	.36
Ireland	1841	51.0	1951	31.0	.18
Sweden	1840	71.0	1940	27.0	.44
Japan	1872	85.0	1936	45.0	.63
Brazil	1872	78.0	1950	58.0	.26
Mexico	1900	70.0	1950	58.0	.24
Puerto Rico	1899	63.0	1948	39.0	.49

Source. Unless otherwise indicated, Simon Kuznets, work cited in Table 7.1.
[1] Warren W. Eason, work cited in Table 7.1, footnote 5.
[2] J-C. Toutain, La Population de la France de 1700 à 1959, Cahiers de l'Institut de Science Économique Appliquée, Suppl. No. 133, Paris, Janvier 1963, pp. 54–55.
[3] Phyllis Deane and W. A. Cole, British Economic Growth, 1688–1959, (Cambridge: Cambridge University Press, 1962), p. 142.

as compared with British experience would be consistent with the hypothesis, but the joker is that there is no numerical magic at work here. Real development has to take place to permit the sectoral relocation to occur: Witness the relatively slow decline from initially high levels in Brazil and Mexico.

An examination of somewhat shorter periods for the United Kingdom does indicate some "coasting off" of the rate of decline (from the rather low levels of agricultural participation prior to substantial industrialization). Had we started the comparison with 1851, when the percent in agriculture was down to 21.7, the annual rate of decline over the ensuing century would have been lower (0.17) than over the whole 150 years. The 1901–1951 decline, from a 1901 level of 8.7% in agriculture, was even lower (0.07).[6]

On the other hand, the rate of decline of the agricultural labor force in the United States appears to have accelerated through time. For the Nineteenth Century the average annual rate of decline was 0.43%, for the period 1900–1950 the annual rate was 0.51, and for 1950–1960 the rate was 0.67.[7] Nevertheless, unless we move to the "automatic farm," a slowing rate of movement out of agriculture will eventually come about.

There may be cases in which development, or at least early development, does not reduce the agricultural labor force. If the Indian data cited by Kuznets[8] are believable, there was an increase in the percentage in agriculture from 51 in 1881 to 63 in 1911, with perhaps no reduction thereafter. One possibility which I suggested years ago in another connection is that cheap manufactured goods may displace the handicraft producers more rapidly than they can be absorbed by expanding employment opportunities in manufacturing.[9] Bauer and Yamey note the correlative possibility of rising unemployment rates in the cities.[10]

There are descriptive materials and data relating to urbanization rates that suggest that urban unemployment or entrance into marginal "service" activities are more probable than an increase in agricultural proportions. Thus an alteration of one historic pattern seems to be occurring. The Colin Clark formulation[11] was to the effect that economic growth is accompanied by a large proportional shift into secondary (manufacturing) production, followed by proportional increases in tertiary (service) production. It now appears in many developing countries that urbanization is proceeding at a more rapid pace than the expansion of manufacturing employment, with the result that there is a direct shift out of agriculture into services.*

"Industrial" classifications of the labor force appear to be more extensively available than other structural features of the labor force. The changing proportions engaged, say, in construction and production of capital goods as compared with those engaged in consumer-goods production may or may not show a uniform trend regardless of economic regime or historic era. Uniformity appears unlikely, but cannot be summarily denied, and a reliable and predictive typology is not quite at hand. Kuznets' analysis of international and temporal differences indicates, aside from the shift out of agriculture associated with economic growth, a probable increase in transportation and communication. Services as a whole are not highly unequal, though clearly changing in quality and type within the category.[12]

Though the shift from agricultural to nonagricultural activities may

* Bauer and Yamey, noting similar points, miss completely the invariant association between economic development and transfers out of agriculture. This leads them to the idiotic statement (Reference 10, p. 42), ". . . the thesis connecting changes in occupational distribution and economic progress is not established, and . . . occupational statistics are an infirm foundation for any generalization."

be hard to appraise in terms of status, it is a form of mobility of great significance for social organization and styles of life. It is a prime example of change of situs, missed by exclusive attention to changes of occupational rank. Most rural–urban migrants are youths and young adults. This pattern confirms what would be expected from the demand side: namely, that occupational mobility between sectors favors the young, who can in general more readily acquire the unfamiliar skills. The transitional process will work "smoothly" only if the relocation is proportional to the rate at which the young can be spared from agricultural labor, or seek to leave it in any event. When technological displacement is very rapid, as in the contemporary United States, the young still provide most of the recruits to growing sectors (technical services, for example), but the older worker may lose his place in the labor market altogether.

Specialization

The continuous expansion of the number of occupations is a widely noted dynamic feature of developing and industrial societies,[13] yet remains unmeasured. For measurement one would need serial recording of the gross number of distinct occupations, though rate of change as distinct from total magnitude might be derived from successive sample surveys comparably drawn from the universe of those economically active. Grouping and reclassifying of occupations inevitably appeal to census officials, and defeat calculations of trends. Even if one had, say, successive compilations in various countries such as the *Dictionary of Occupational Titles* prepared by the United States Employment Service, one would still have to be cautious. A recorded increase in occupations might represent a mixture, in unknown proportions, of genuine increase and improved identification—similar to the classic problem of interpreting temporal trends in the incidence of diseases.

The sources of specialization are several: increased size of interdependent economic (and other social) units, making possible the classically recognized efficiencies of division of labor; technological changes, requiring new performance criteria; new products and services. It is useful to distinguish skill dilution—the subdivision of performance roles—and new skill combinations, often associated with the growth of knowledge.

The process of specialization makes *exact* occupational inheritance increasingly unlikely, a circumstance that is concealed by grouping occupations into white-collar and blue-collar,[14] or only slightly more elaborate classifications.[15] Specialization even invades occupations that appear to persist, such as various professions (which thus become in a sense occupational groups).

Assessing the relative importance of the sources of specialization is not likely to be possible from census data, for reasons noted, and even repeated surveys would have to collect data wisely and interpret them cautiously. Yet by taking into account the way various ages may represent changes through time, a single survey might yield substantial additions to knowledge. This would, incidentally, permit testing the hypothesis that there is a correlation between the historic "age" of an occupation and the mean age of its occupants, and conversely that genuinely new occupations tend to be filled by new or recent entrants to the labor force.

Were a moderately satisfactory "index of specialization" to be constructed, it would not only be possible to add some precision to long-term trends, but also would make possible certain other calculations: for example, the influence of labor-force size. And despite the hypothesis concerning the importance of youth in manning new occupations, it should be supposed that a correlation would be found between the index of specialization and within-career occupational mobility when observed in appropriately fine detail. This should be true not only for the "mechanical" reason that the rates of mobility will be strongly associated with the number of categories distinguished, but for the somewhat more interesting reason that a highly specialized labor force presumably increases the chances of a fit between role requirements and individual aptitudes and interests. It may be supposed that mutual selective processes will not be perfect, with resulting further sorting. And it may also be supposed that as individual interests and capabilities change, further occupational mobility may occur.

Such attention to detail can scarcely be dismissed as trivial in the large sweep of socioeconomic changes, since the steady progress of specialization greatly increases the probability that the labor-force participant will have a career marked by one or more changes in occupational role and associated social attributes.

Upgrading

It appears that economic growth is accompanied by a long-term shift from manual to nonmanual occupations in nonagricultural occupations. Data for constructing historic trends, however, are surprisingly scanty even for this dichotomous classification of "skill" categories. Incidentally, the increase in the number of engineers and such occupations as skilled servicemen for complex business machines makes the manual/nonmanual distinction a fuzzy one. I agree with Duncan's[16] comments about the predominantly manual components of some white-collar occupations. Just why a typist is a "head" worker and a linotypist is a "hand" worker is by no means clear. Despite these strictures, it is *generally* true that those occupations commonly classified as non-manual require somewhat higher educational levels and—though with considerable overlapping of the distributions—yield higher incomes.

Table 7.3 presents data for a number of countries representing a considerable range of economic advancement. The countries are arranged in the order of the proportions of white-collar workers in the labor force. Except for the anomalous (and unbelievable) figures for Burma, the order of the countries is not radically different from what one would expect. Varying degrees of census accuracy and varying statistical conventions impair the comparability of the data presented, and no confidence could be placed in the exact rank order.

The proportion of "professionals" in the labor force is probably subject to fewer errors and differences of definition. The range presented in the last column of Table 7.3 perhaps results in a somewhat more accurate ordering of the countries involved. (The alleged "over-supply" of professionals in some developing areas is, I should think, unlikely to be true of the category as a whole, but of particular occupations such as lawyers.)

Even the "professional" category is remarkably heterogeneous in exact occupational composition. In American census practice, for example, not only are various "technicians" included, but also entertainers and other occupations that may have no formal educational requirements. The median number of years of school completed for all American male "professionals" 25 years of age and over in 1960 was 16.4, just beyond the college level.[17] About one-fourth (24.5%) of the group had less than a college education.[18]

Some examples of historic trends in "upgrading" occupational distributions are in order. White-collar workers represented 28% of all non-agricultural occupations in the United States in 1900, 42% in 1950.[19] By 1960 the percentage had almost reached 50, and for the white labor force had slightly exceeded that proportion.[20]

The rate of professionalization in the United States has been even more rapid. Professional and kindred workers represented by 4.2% of the total labor force in 1900, 8.6% in 1950, and 11.2% in 1960.[21] Though American nonwhites had much lower representation in professional categories, the percentage increased from 3 in 1950 to 4.7 in 1960.[22]

In France, the "liberal professions" changed from 9.4% of all services

TABLE 7.3 White-Collar and Professional Workers as Proportions of Economically Active Populations, Selected Countries, Around 1950

		(In Thousands)			Percent	
Country[1]	Date	Econ. Active (1)	White-Collar (2)	Profes-sional (3)	White-Collar (4)	Profes-sional (5)
Burma	1953	1,075	420	39	39	4
South Africa[3]	1946	889	321	—	36	—
Israel[4]	1958	319	111	37	35	12
U.S.A.	1950	60,037	21,213	4,736	35	8
Canada	1951	5,300	1,761	376	33	7
New Zealand	1951	740	235	53	32	7
United Kingdom	1951	22,578	6,447	1,387	29	6
Sweden	1950	3,120	843	219	27	7
Japan	1950	35,574	8,362	1,634	23	5
Chile	1952	2,188	445	92	20	4
Austria	1951	3,361	652	181	19	5
Denmark	1950	2,063	325	121	16	6
Mexico	1950	8,345	1,304	207	16	2
Costa Rica	1950	272	40	9	15	3
Paraguay	1950	437	55	13	13	3
Brazil	1950	17,117	2,107	286	12	2
Yugoslavia	1953	7,838	683	225	9	3
Pakistan	1951	22,393	1,765	224	8	1
India	1951	101,725	7,487	1,586	7	2

Source. United Nations, Demographic Yearbook, 1956 (New York: 1956), Table 13, pp. 338–418.
Percentages were computed prior to rounding population figures to thousands.
1 Arranged in order of magnitude of column 4.
2 Excludes unpaid family workers.
3 European population.
4 Jewish population.

in 1856 to 11.9% in 1936.[23] Though no later data are presented because of discontinuities in definitions, Toutain comments on the rapid growth of the professions after World War II.[24]

Eason presents data[25] showing an approximate doubling of the Soviet "intelligentsia" with a higher education as between 1926 (8.6%) and 1956 (17.0%) and more than doubling of the proportions with a technical secondary education (10.6 and 32.4%, respectively). However,

Eason also presents data[26] for workers in industry which show virtually
no decline between 1928 and 1959 in the proportions of "wage earners" (around 85%), though a slight increase in engineering, technical,
managerial, and salaried personnel (from 9 to 13%); declines were
registered in the initially small proportions of apprentices and service
personnel. Administrative personnel in industry showed an actual
decline, 1954 to 1959, from 14 to 10%, but Eason thinks this primarily
represents some reduction in the governmental superstructure, and that
the relatively low proportions of administrators as compared with
American experience represents a genuine difference in the degree of
"advancement" in the respective industrial structures.[27]

A rising average, and perhaps minimum, level of education of the
labor force in the course of economic development appears probable
in view of trends in education, but precise temporal comparisons for
particular occupations or occupational categories are not yet possible.
Differing educational levels by age provide a reasonable basis of inference, however. In 1960 in the United States, for example, male "operatives" aged 20–24 had a median educational level around the 12-year
level that would imply completion of secondary school. The medians
then decline steadily with age categories to 7.9 years for the oldest
group.[28] Virtually every occupational group displays a similar age
pattern, with two notable exceptions: professionals have a median
educational level at or just over the 16-year (college) level at all mature
ages, and nonfarm managers and officials have median levels under the
12-year (secondary) level only for ages 55 and over.[29]

If primary attention is paid to the formal schooling of the young as
the method of meeting the rising skill demand of the labor market, the
schools are clearly the principal agency of social mobility. The coordination of the curricula of the schools with *current* demand is quite
unlikely to be perfect, since school curricula and counselors tend to get
the vocational word tardily. As for prospective demand, a few years or
a few decades after the completion of formal schooling, exact mobility
preparation would be both unlikely and incorrect for the interim. The
continuous capacity for learning, which is probably highly correlated
with sheer level of education, is a prime requisite for multiple movements. The shortages of particular skills, which are an endemic feature
of modernizing and advanced economies, are likely to lead to pressures
on the regular schools to solve the mobility problem. Accumulated
adaptive experience, and formalized adult retraining are likely to be
necessary if rapidly changing occupational demands are to be met
without a built-in generational lag.

Bureaucratization

Bureaucratization is a process of structural change in the labor force that may, over time, reduce certain kinds of mobility (for example, from manual to nonmanual occupation via an independent business, or movement between employers) and increase others (such as promotion to higher levels of skill or responsibility and essentially "lateral" transfers within a "family" of related occupations). The simplest measure of bureaucratization is the proportion of wage and salary earners in the labor force. This proportion appears to show a long-term and relatively steady increase in "capitalist" countries,[30] but of course it is nominally complete in Soviet-type economies. Independent workers in nonagricultural occupations in the Soviet Union decreased from 28.3% in 1928 to a mere 3.1% in 1959.[31]

Table 7.4 presents for a number of countries the proportions of wage and salary earners among economically active males, the countries being ordered once more in terms of the magnitude of the percentages.[32] The proportions reflect in some degree the varying importance of "peasant" agriculture, and it might have been preferable, where possible, to confine the comparisons to nonagricultural participants in the labor force. This would of course have reduced the range of variation, but not by any means radically changed the order. In this connection, the radical decline in United States agricultural employment, 1950 to 1960, from 7,507,000 to 5,723,000 was accompanied by an absolute *increase* (from 1,733,000 to 1,806,000) in wage and salary earners and a decline in the self-employed from 4,346,000 to 2,802,000.[33]

For France, Toutain,[34] presents the following proportional distributions by "employment categories."

Category	Percent	
	1906	1936
Employers	30.3	29.2
Salaried	11.8	15.6
Workers	33.7	34.6
Self-Employed	20.1	13.7

In French manufacturing[35] the proportion of workers (ouvriers) appears to have risen from 56.0% in 1906 to 66.8% in 1931, then to have fallen to 60.0% in 1936; however, the rate of unemployment had

TABLE 7.4 Wage and Salary Earners as Proportions of Economically Active Males, Various Countries, Around 1950

		(In Thousands)		
Country[1]	Date	Males Econ. Active[2]	Wage and Salary Earners	% Wage and Salary Earners
United Kingdom	1951	15,647.3	14,028.0	90
U.S.A.	1950	42,906.0	34,265.0	80
W. Germany	1950	13,483.0	10,831.0	80
Sweden	1950	2,188.0	1,673.0	76
Belgium	1947	2,525.8	1,903.0	75
Canada	1951	3,994.8	3,011.0	75
New Zealand	1951	567.0	423.2	75
Switzerland	1950	1,417.3	1,069.9	75
Australia	1947	2,454.8	1,827.0	74
Austria	1951	1,882.4	1,371.0	73
Netherlands	1947	2,757.0	2,025.0	73
Spain	1950	8,087.0	5,885.0	73
Czechoslovakia	1947	3,528.0	2,551.0	72
Argentina	1947	5,022.0	3,564.0	71
Denmark	1950	1,369.0	975.0	71
Portugal	1950	2,382.0	1,699.0	71
Costa Rica	1950	205.5	144.7	70
Norway	1950	1,010.0	708.0	70
France	1946	12,668.0	8,538.0	67
Bolivia	1950	360.6	234.0	65
Italy	1954	12,879.0	8,113.0	63
Ceylon	1946	2,042.0	1,206.0	59
Brazil	1950	12,209.0	7,064.0	58
Japan	1950	18,510.0	10,360.0	56
Venezuela	1950	1,273.9	696.0	55
Mexico[3]	1950	7,372.0	3,831.0	52
Philippines	1948	4,443.0	2,197.0	49
Yugoslavia	1953	3,940.0	1,914.0	49
Egypt	1947	5,957.0	2,626.8	44
Paraguay[3]	1950	364.3	144.4	40
Haiti	1950	635.1	129.9	36
Pakistan	1951	21,026.0	3,375.0	16

Source. United Nations, *Statistical Yearbook, 1955* (New York: 1955), Table 6, pp. 56–61.

[1] Arranged in order of magnitude of last column.
[2] Excludes unpaid family workers.
[3] Both sexes.

markedly increased in 1936, and could be expected to bear most heavily on this group. Salaried workers (employés) over the 1906–1936 period more than doubled in proportions (3.6 to 7.7%) and the self-employed have been reduced by about half (25.3 to 13.9%). On the other hand, the proportions of self-employed in services remained about constant at around 15–16%.[36]

In the United States the proportion of self-employed workers outside agriculture was as low as 11.6% in 1950, and fell to 10.4% in 1955, but held virtually constant in 1960 and 1962.[37]

Shifts in type of self-employment should also prove instructive. In nonagricultural activities I have the impression in the United States that self-employment is decreasingly common in construction and manufacturing, in financial operations and distribution, and even in the "liberal" professions, but perhaps increasing in repair and advisory services.

Whether in newly developing areas an acceleration principle in bureaucratization may be expected to operate is perhaps too hazardous a speculation. Yet the strong degree of governmental decision-making for the economy would lead to the expectation of a fairly rapid extension of government services and perhaps a rapid reduction of self-employment, at least outside of agriculture.

A Retrospective Comment

The processes of structural change in economic activity that we have discussed represent the "demand side" of various forms of occupational mobility. Though much ingenuity has been spent on detecting trends in the "supply" side, particularly the degree of openness of systems despite differences in social background, the studied neglect of structural changes is no longer tolerable. Surely no one would pretend that equal opportunity prevails in any advanced industrial economy, whatever the political regime. Yet, to assert that mobility rates over the last half-century or so have changed very little, as some researchers have done, or even that the American social structure has become more "rigid" since the turn of the century or after the First World War, as is frequently asserted in sociology and social history texts, is in total disregard of the structural changes noted here, and particularly the process of upgrading. Whether this process can go on indefinitely, and at what cost for those left behind in the process, are theoretically interesting and practically significant questions. The lack of synchronization that is observable in areas newly emerging from relatively slow-moving structural changes has no prominent, tidy resolution in the course of continuing economic development. The stable future is surely as mythical as the stationary past.

References

1. See Arnold S. Feldman and Wilbert E. Moore, "The Work Place," in Moore and Feldman, eds., *Labor Commitment and Social Change in Developing Areas* (New York: Social Science Research Council, 1960). Chapter II.

2. Natalie Rogoff, *Recent Trends in Occupational Mobility* (Glencoe, Illinois: Free Press, 1953).

3. Robert M. Marsh, "Values, Demand and Social Mobility," *American Sociological Review*, 28: 565–575, August, 1963.

4. Wilbert E. Moore, "The Exportability of the Labor Force Concept," *American Sociological Review*, 18: 68–72, February 1953.

5. United States Bureau of the Census, *Statistical Abstract of the United States, 1962* (Washington: 1962), Table 297, p. 226.

6. See Source cited in Table 7.2, footnote 3.

7. See Source cited in Table 7.1, footnote 5.

8. Kuznets, work cited as source in Table 7.1.

9. Wilbert E. Moore, *Industrialization and Labor* (Ithaca, New York: Cornell University Press, 1951), p. 305.

10. See P. T. Bauer and B. S. Yamey, *The Economics of Under-Developed Countries* (London: James Nisbet & Co., 1957), Chapter VI.

11. Colin Clark, *The Conditions of Economic Progress*, 2nd ed. (London: Macmillan, 1951), pp. 395–439.

12. Kuznets, work cited in Table 7.1.

13. See, for example, Neil J. Smelser, "Mechanisms of Change and Adjustment to Change," in Bert F. Hoselitz and Wilbert E. Moore, eds., *Industrialization and Society* (Paris and The Hague: UNESCO and Mouton, 1963), Chap. 2.

14. See, for example, Seymour Martin Lipset and Reinhard Bendix, *Social Mobility in Industrial Society* (Berkeley and Los Angeles: University of California Press, 1960).

15. See S. M. Miller, "Comparative Social Mobility," *Current Sociology*, Vol. IX, No. I, 1960.

16. Otis Dudley Duncan, "Mehtodological Issues in the Analysis of Social Mobility," in Neil J. Smelser and Seymour Martin Lipset, eds., *Social Structure, Mobility, and Economic Development* (Chicago: Aldine Publishing Co., 1966).

17. U. S. Bureau of the Census, *U. S. Census of Population: 1960, Subject Reports, Educational Attainment*, Final Report PC(2)-5B (Washington: 1963), Table 8, p. 136.

18. *Ibid.*

19. U. S. Bureau of the Census, *Historical Statistics of the United States, Colonial Times to 1957* (Washington: 1960), p. 74.

20. *Statistical Abstract of the United States*, 1962, Tables 297 and 299, pp. 226, 227.

21. 1910 and 1950 figures from Reference 19, p. 74; 1960 figure from *Statistical Abstract*, Table 297, p. 226.

22. *Statistical Abstract*, Table 229, p. 227.

23. Toutain, work cited in Table 7.2, footnote 2, at p. 147.

24. *Ibid.*, p. 148.

25. Eason, work cited in Table 7.1, footnote 5, at p. 64.

26. *Ibid.*, p. 89.

27. *Ibid.*, p. 90.
28. U. S. Census report cited in Reference 16, at pp. 136–137.
29. *Ibid.*
30. Hoselitz presents some data on this and on the increasing importance of large productive units. See Bert F. Hoselitz, "Some Problems in the Quantitative Study of Industrialization," Essays in Quantitative Study of Economic Growth, *Economic Development and Cultural Change*, 9 (3): 357–549, April 1961.
31. Eason, work cited in Table 7.1, footnote 5, at p. 82.
32. A somewhat comparable compilation for an earlier period, taking wage and salary earners as a proportion of males 15–64, is presented by Moore, article cited in Reference 4.
33. *U.S. Statistical Abstract*, 1962. Table 297, p. 226.
34. Toutain, work cited in Table 3, Reference 2. Table 66 (p. 166, not numbered).
35. *Ibid.*, Table 80 (p. 176, not numbered).
36. *Ibid.*, Table 90 (p. 184, not numbered).
37. *U. S. Statistical Abstract*, 1962, Table 297, p. 226.

8

NOTES FOR A GENERAL THEORY
OF LABOR ORGANIZATION

The actual diversity of labor organizations and forms of "industrial relations" is matched or exceeded by the diversity of descriptive studies, empirical generalizations, and theoretical interpretations. This rich variety in the real world and in the scholarly world may imply that any discussion of general theory is pretentious. Yet it does appear worth while to state some simple aims for general theory, and to record some notes on the kinds of variables that appear essential for making sense out of experience.*

The Quest for a General Theory

A general theory of labor organization should be derived from characteristic forms of cohesion and division among the gainfully occupied in a "modern economy."† To attempt to account for the unique or

SOURCE. Adapted from "Notes for a General Theory of Labor Organization," *Industrial and Labor Relations Review*, 13: 387–397, April 1960; by permission of the New York State School of Labor and Industrial Relations, Cornell University.

* In addition to references noted throughout this article, this discussion draws on some previous papers published over the last few years: Wilbert E. Moore, "Occupational Structure and Industrial Conflict," in Arthur Kornhauser, Robert Dubin, and Arthur M. Ross, eds., *Industrial Conflict* (New York: McGraw-Hill Book Co., 1954), Chapter 16; Moore, "The Nature of Industrial Conflict," in H. D. Woods, ed., *Industrial Conflict and Dispute Settlement* (Montreal: McGill University Industrial Relations Centre, 1955), pp. 1–31; Moore, "Management and Union Organizations: An Analytical Comparison," in Conrad M. Arensberg and others, eds., *Research in Industrial Human Relations* (New York: Harper, 1957), Chapter 8. The attempt to view labor organization in broad comparative and dynamic perspective derives mainly from joint work with Arnold S. Feldman in *Labor Commitment and Social Change in Developing Areas* (New York: Social Science Research Council, 1960).

† Schneider gives as his opinion that the existing theories and the empirical phenomena "are too complex to be placed under the rubric of one theory. . . ." Eugene V. Schneider, *Industrial Sociology* (New York: McGraw-Hill Book Co., 1957), p. 331. See Chapter 14 on "Theories of the Labor Movement" for a useful and concise summary.

even the rare event is to set an impossibly high standard for theory. To attempt to generalize for all productive systems, including those of exotic tribes, is to exaggerate an already formidable task. It does appear appropriate, however, to require that a "general" theory should be applicable to various "stages" in the process of economic transformation, historical and contemporary, and valid across national boundaries. Thus the theory should aim for more than a persuasive interpretation of American labor organization and its history.

The aim, stated in minimal and thus possibly realizable form, is to use a limited conceptual apparatus for propositions of some generality and some interdependence. These propositions should be limited by peculiarities of time and place only where essential. At the same time, such propositions should not achieve generality at too great a cost in substance; such propositions risk being true but trivial. For example, we do not gain a grasp of great leverage on an unattractive array of phenomena if we conclude that some form(s) of labor organization will be found among some sector(s) of the gainfully occupied in any industrial society.

There is a crude and a subtle sense in which most of the scholarly literature on labor organization is too empirical. In the crude sense, the multitude of "case studies" and other descriptions of particular structures, relationships, and events have not used either concepts or procedures permitting replication, comparative analysis, or substantive additions to theory. In the subtle sense, even broader historical and comparative interpretations have been too much preoccupied with labor unions or the "labor movement,"* with occasional side glances at *part* of the "unorganized" workers but not at others, including those who may be highly organized but in different associations with different names.

The essential character of the preceding complaint is that the studies and interpretations, despite their rich store of information and hypotheses, have exhibited a too ready acceptance of conventional divisions between "management" and "labor," without adequate critical examination of such a division and without much attention to persons thus excluded entirely. It is rather remarkable that "management" has now generally superseded "capital" as confronting labor in the language of polite scholarly discourse, but only as a linguistic transformation and without raising substantive questions concerning the actual transformation in the organization and conduct of enterprises. The

---

* This criticism applies to Perlman's classic treatise as well as others. See Selig Perlman, *A Theory of the Labor Movement* (New York: Macmillan, 1928; reissued by Augustus M. Kelley in 1949).

corporate revolution is at last having some small effect on the economic theory of the firm, but virtually none on the economic or sociological theory of labor. The implicit theory underlying most of the "labor movement" literature is vulgarly Marxist, whatever its superficial orientations.

The "notes" appended to this introductory broadside are intended to provide some substantiation of grievances, but also some redress.

A General View of Sources of Cohesion and Division

Two kinds of competing loyalties or bases of allegiance are generally recognized in discussions of industrial relations. The one is between employers and unions, the other between occupation (craft) and general status (the industrial union or labor party). However, the crossing currents that emerge in groups and collective relations can be better understood by identifying four bases of loyalty and identification: the productive organization, the industry, the occupation, and general status. Now the fundamental point about these is that they are not mutually exclusive. On the contrary, all or nearly all are simultaneously present and operative—operative to produce tensions of both individual and collective character. Even where two principles, or their exponents, are in overt conflict (thus *organizationally* requiring preclusive identification) there is likely to be a covert conflict of loyalties.

The Productive Organization

The business firm, or its approximate equivalent in socialist forms of organization, provides a perfectly normal focus of worker loyalty. (In large enterprises, the identification may be with divisions or other units, and there are interesting interplays between "local" and general allegiances.) The productive organization is the source of the worker's livelihood, the place where he spends his working hours, and in many cases, the source and locus of expected future upward mobility. The loyalty may extend to the organization as against competitors or various sources of "outside interference."

There is reason to suppose that loyalty to the productive organization may be both collective and distributive. The loyalty to the organized unit and its various symbols may be supplemented by identification with other members—"laterally" and "vertically," that is, with and without considerations of rank and authority.

The reality of some commitment to the firm permits us to relate various bits of empirical experience. The most obvious of these bits is the characterization of the labor union (and by sensible extension not usually made, the professional association) as competitive with the employer for the loyalty of the worker. This competition shows up in another guise within the multiemployer union, where there are recurrent tendencies to conflict among "locals."

The competition between some form of occupational identification and organizational loyalty does not coincide with the conventional division between "management" and "labor." It is a pervasive source of tension between "line" officers (coordinators) and "staff" officers (information suppliers). The latter, unless gradually socialized through long tenure, tend to be minimally identified with the current employing organization.

It was hinted a few lines back that one element in loyalty to the productive organization may be acceptance of the system of authority. The legitimacy of power is carefully, if not always completely successfully, cultivated in all stable organizations. To put the case extremely, the administrative costs of terror are probably greater than the costs of indoctrination and concessions to various motivational interests, such as the desire for some self-determination. The central point here is that some acceptance of authority is normal. The fact that legitimate power is limited and circumstantial binds executives, too, and encourages their "downward" organizational responsibility, often performed patronizingly. This attitude of *noblesse oblige* stems from a somewhat irrational or neurotic identification by the executive with the firm as such, as coincident with the life-space of the principal official.

The Industry

An entire industry or "economic sector" may be relatively weak or amorphous as a source of cohesion. This is true for several rather disparate reasons. First, under private or state monopoly conditions, the industry is simply coextensive with the firm or its equivalent, and thus loses independent variability as a focus of allegiance. Second, under other circumstances, the industry may not be "organized" as an entity comprising all interests, and thus may lack precise boundaries and visible symbols. Third, and correlatively to the lack of comprehensive organization, industrial identification tends to rest only upon the recognition and calculation of economic interests.

Industrial allegiance is likely to be weakest among production workers, strongest among market-oriented managers who form trade associations and employer associations because of common interests in commodity and labor markets. Industrial unions also, in a sense, have a common labor-market orientation. Although the basis of union organization and jurisdiction is primarily derivative from considerations of collective bargaining, the industrial union may still develop an identification with the market interests common to the industry. This potentiality is most likely to be realized where there are clear interindustry shifts in factor allocation and thus in economic opportunity. Competing fuels, such as coal and oil, and competing means of transportation, such as trucking and railroads, come to mind as illustrations.

Where an industrial union bargains with employers on an industry-wide basis, something like an organization for the industry is established, and some form and degree of cooperation are likely to emerge and persist despite recurrent contract negotiations.

It should also be noted that various skills and many quasi-professional and staff positions tend to be industry-specific rather than employer-specific, so that occupational and industrial identification may coincide.

Although industry in an enterprise economy is more extensive than the firm, in another sense it may also be smaller. Put more exactly, the matching of firms and industries is difficult for large multiproduct firms. It follows that, in these situations, identification with industrial interests is not simply an enlarged version of loyalty to the employer; rather, the possible collision of interests within the firm is greatly enhanced.

Occupation

The sources of occupational identification are many. Those who share specific occupations are likely to have a nearly common education and training, common working standards, relatively narrow income ranges, a common interest in maintaining (at least) income differentials, and possibly common career patterns.* The occupational peer group is also frequently the source of tolerable judgments of competence and performance.

It follows that the strength of occupational cohesion is likely to vary directly with skill levels (measured in training time) and thus with relatively narrow ranges of horizontal transferability without loss of status. Thus occupational identification is not likely to be highly salient among unskilled and semiskilled workers. It is also questionable among managers (that is, coordinators) to the extent that their skills are in some sense more general and widely transferable than are those of

---

* Perlman, *ibid.*, being primarily concerned with an interpretation of unionism, saw the central strength of occupational identification as consisting in the control of occupational opportunity. The present interpretation is closer to that of Frank Tannenbaum in *A Philosophy of Labor* (New York: Alfred A. Knopf, 1951).

other workers of equivalent rank and income levels. The attempt to achieve professional status and identification for business managers may be regarded as a search for occupational identity.

Status

Given any structure of authority, there is a potential and probable coalescence of interests by rank. This does not mean necessarily that all persons below the highest rank are in a state of potential revolt, as obviously persons of all intermediate positions depend for their *relatively* privileged status upon the very system that also requires their subordination to others. However, peers in relative authority obviously have much to share, and indeed the chief divisive elements are introduced by any tenure or promotional system which differentiates among them.

Since large productive organizations are likely to have numerous levels of authority, nominally clearly demarcated by chart and title, an interesting question arises. The question is whether sharp status divisions as a focus of common-status identification are less numerous than the potential number, and if so, where and why.

Received doctrine gives such a uniformly affirmative answer in terms of a dichotomous division as to make the question as posed appear to be pure pedantry. But this received doctrine is legitimately questionable.

Although Marx did not invent the dichotomization of industrial ranks, his position is a useful basis for discussion. The Marxian assumption of polarization was too restricted by historical stage (that is, early industrialization) and by particular property institutions. Early industrialization repeatedly exhibits radical differences between managers and men,[1] but later developments obscure and complicate the division rather than sharpen it. As to property conceptions, it is perhaps sufficient to note that by strict Marxian definition, the typical contemporary corporate executive is proletarian, possibly slightly contaminated by minority ownership of equity stocks given him as supplementary compensation.

It does appear, however, that sharp status divisions and correlative identifications are fewer than the potential number, and the questions where and why are relevant. Two rather general sources of division may be suggested: (1) discontinuities in the distribution of effective authority to decide policy, particularly as affecting employment, income, and career expectations; (2) discontinuities in career paths or "breaks in the skill hierarchy."[2] Now both of these sources of status division tend to intersect at or near conventional divisions between "management" and "labor." Neither is exclusively applicable to that division. All hierarchical discontinuities, such as that between staff subordinates and their managers, are in fact points of tension and strain, with or without formal organization around common status interests.

"Management" clearly has some common status interests in existing power relations and in the division of the rewards. The "outward" identification is complemented by identification with the interests of those in positions to which one may "reasonably" aspire. But this leaves many questions unsettled, including the apparent failure of the objectively "frozen" elements of the industrial middle classes to identify with proletarians or even perhaps with each other. The point of central interest here, however, is that general "employee" status is by no means preclusively the source of allegiance when confronted with multiple status differences and diverse occupational interests. This applies at all levels in the organization, not simply among managers.

Some Organizational Problems

If the four sources of cohesion (and therefore of division) comprise a fairly general array of alternatives, it does not follow that the problems of alternative bases of labor organization are thereby resolved. It is not possible to treat these sources of cohesion as a taxonomy of mutually exclusive bases of identification, for, to repeat, these are omnipresent principles. Any organization based on one primary principle has not thereby dispelled the others. Any attempt to combine the principles in a single organization incurs severe problems of clarity of collective goals amid multiple divisions of allegiance.

For example, a "management association" is either a common-status organization or a status-and-occupation organization. (In the latter case, however, many persons of managerial status—including most technical and professional personnel—would be excluded.) But the possible common interests with regard, say, to labor policies or attitudes toward government, and these are by no means sure or uniform, do not get rid of industry and firm divisions. Even at the level of the firm, managers are potentially divided by rank, by conflicts between line and staff, by competition among peers (individual or divisional), and by identification with diverse clienteles.

What, then, of the solidarity of labor? We have the historic dispute between craft and industrial principles of organization, and these clearly do not represent sin and virtue, respectively, despite liberal rhetoric. Either organizational principle is challenged by the other, in the form of rival unions or by internal division. Neither organizational basis dispels the firm or the industry as a focus of interest.

Strength of the Occupational Principle

The bonds of identification and allegiance that center on occupation appear more numerous than those surrounding competing principles. This appears to be true in static cross-section. It is given added weight by adding a dynamic perspective on the occupational structures of industrialized economies. The relative reduction of "unskilled" occupations, and the prospective upgrading of the "semiskilled" argue for an occupational orientation by a growing proportion of the gainfully occupied. This line of argument is consistent with the hardy survival of craft unions, with the proliferation of technical and professional associations, and with the increasingly explicit recognition of occupational and skill differences within industrial unions.

This line of argument is also consistent with a "coalition theory" of occupational groups. Such coalitions may certainly take place on the basis of status; the industrial union is such a coalition. Occupational groups may also form coalitions centering in employer or industry interests, or in a variety of more particular alignments such as line versus staff. Both because the recognized common interests giving rise to coalitions may be transitory and because of the intrinsic competition from other loyalties, there is reason to doubt the stability of particular coalitions.

Some Comments on Union Organization

A few supplementary notes on union organization are appropriate at this juncture.[3] They are concerned with the centralization of union power, the problem of power and responsibility, and the problem of participation and lethargy.

Union organizations, however democratic and decentralized in formal structure, exhibit a marked tendency to centralization.[4] This goes beyond the control of associations by organizationally dedicated minorities, which is a standard principle. The central administrative group is after all salaried, and therefore, not exactly comparable to the officers of local voluntary associations. If one reconstructs this historical development, at least in the United States, the top officials appear initially to serve as "staff" advisors to local unions and then gradually evolve into true line officers.

The basis of this evolution—and this no longer needs limitation to American experience—is the strategic power, including especially superior knowledge as well as possibly talent at central headquarters. Superior knowledge, in turn, eventually requires the addition of staff advisors at central headquarters. These staff specialists are likely to be used initially for various external relations (courts, legislatures, publicity on industrial disputes), but in performing these tasks, they inevitably gain some internal power.

Despite the tendency to centralization, national unions have many problems of internal compromise and uncertain solidarity, analogous to the political party in a one-party or two-party system.[5] Confederations of unions multiply these difficulties.

If union power is centralized, it is still formally legitimized by democratic accountability. If that accountability is vigorously enforced, the leadership is by definition internally "responsible." By the same token, external responsibility (as, for example, in relations with employers) may be impaired precisely because the electorate is capable of shifts in position, even of whimsical inconsistency. Stability of union operations may rest, therefore, in part upon emptying democratic forms of real content.

A vigorously democratic structure depends upon high participation in union activities by members. But for reasons that are general to associations and particular to the competing claims of the various loyalties of the worker, high, generalized, and continuous participation is unlikely. Union leaders can rarely be expected to encourage participation beyond particular purposes, such as an industrial dispute, since active political participation in union affairs breeds "factionalism" or at least instructions and queries to officers otherwise left to their own devices.

Most of the points raised here, in the specific context of union organization, can probably be generalized to other occupational groups, and especially to those that carefully avoid identification as unions and just as carefully pursue comparable goals with some equivalence in strategies.

Some Problems of Collective Relations

If the analysis of cohesion and division among the gainfully occupied is essentially accurate, it follows that collective "bargaining" relations are a pervasive potentiality within the labor force and even within the firm. Only one set of these relations, however, is formally institutionalized, and that not fully or similarly in all countries.

This section will deal primarily with "management-labor" relations,[6] but the warning must be repeated that this division should not be exaggerated by forgetting others. For example, other occupational groups develop employment standards, subject to negotiation with employers. And it must not be assumed, even with reference to an ordinary industrial dispute, that management is always as unified in its opposition to the union as the silence of dissidents would imply.

The Locus and Strategy of Bargaining

Labor organizations seem to achieve maximum effectiveness in pressing their members' common economic interests when they are able to effect control of a strategic process or service. Thus both skilled trades and professional groups have attempted, with greater or lesser success, to control not only training (and therefore both supply and quality) of practitioners, but also the terms on which their services will be performed. Where productive processes rely on considerable proportions of poorly skilled and thus easily interchangeable workers, some form of broader coalition like the industrial union may be the only effective substitute for the detailed control provided by the monopoly of strategic skills.

The reference to monopoly is in its common sense and not necessarily its legal meaning. The acrid dispute over the "labor monopoly" issue in the United States need not detain us. The plain circumstance is that all economic interest groups attempt to achieve comprehensive membership of all relevant persons, and then, to present a united front in representing the common interests in collective relations.

Although the potential client of professionals may have few ways of avoiding the latter's monopoly, this is not true to the same degree of the firm that faces a labor union. The union's short-run power is ultimately limited by the power of employers to change both the physical technology of production and the social organization of the appropriate "occupational mix." To make such decisions multilateral rather than unilateral is clearly a principal aim of union strategy and is certain to remain important in the future. Although the powers and procedures differ in a socialist economy, there is every reason to expect some form of representation of workers' interests in the technology of production.

The strategy of bargaining in enterprise economies includes a choice between the "whipsaw," with resulting pattern-setting, and industry-wide negotiation. (Since in the latter case both sides are actually coalitions, much of the determination of the outcome may be simply shifted from the public arena to the private caucus.) Union policy in industry-wide bargaining is likely to be directed toward "taking labor out of competition." Although this goal limits managerial power it should be noted that, in the extreme case of an employer group facing a single "vertical" union, the union may in a sense be "captured" by the industry to legitimize combinations and agreements not otherwise legal, and thus to enhance the entire industry's position in the interindustry competition for labor.

There are, as a general rule, management pressures to decentralize bargaining in order to avoid the effective collective power of the union, and union pressures to achieve common (at least firm-wide) bargains. But there are contrary tendencies on each side, and determining the locus of bargaining is itself an element in strategy. Management, for example, is under actuarial difficulties if fringe benefits, such as pension plans, are local. Even if issues are locally bargained, pattern-setting within the firm can scarcely be avoided. The normative and legal centralization of corporate responsibility, whatever the internally determined policies on "decentralization," clearly limits the possibility of diffusing that responsibility in labor negotiations.

Unions, while seeking uniform and thus centralized agreements, are subject to the diverse demands of locals, of various age groups, and in the industrial union, of various occupational groups. The normative and legal democracy of the union tends to add weight to these counter-pressures.

Where formal collective bargaining prevails, the required interaction within a framework of rules and precedents provides conditions for management-union coalitions. These may range from "sweetheart contracts" achieved by blackmail at the expense of union members, through effective coalition at the expense of consumers, to the use of the union as an advisory and disciplinary agency. Ideologists who view the true mission of the labor movement as revolutionary, that is, as fundamentally altering the institutional system, express alarm at the engulfment of the union by "the system." It does not require any ideological commitment, however, to note that there is a fundamental and intrinsic strain between any labor organization's ambition to increase its responsible influence on policies affecting its constituents and its function as an agent of protest for its constituents. This strain is maximally exhibited precisely in a nationalized industry under a labor party administration.

Economic Versus Political Activity

In standard treatises on labor movements, American labor unions are pictured as predominantly economic in orientation, others as highly political.* Surely this is a difference easily exaggerated. Any labor organization is political. The only question is the arena of power. The union's power may be used in a direct way against private employers, or in an indirect way through attempts to influence legislation and the course of judicial decisions. In the long run, straight "business unionism" with its corollary policy of "more and more" has revolutionary overtones.[7]

Nor are the direct and indirect attempts to exert influence or exercise power mutually exclusive alternatives in industrial societies. It appears, on the contrary, that *all* industrial systems, including the totalitarian ones, provide alternative avenues of pressure and protest. The selection of the arena of power is itself an element in strategy. (Mistakes are of course possible, as in the silly American corporate support of "right-to-work" laws, which manufactured a labor vote that might not otherwise have appeared.)

A directly political orientation of unions is likely to be a response to blockage in economic influence. Viewed historically, the publicly political activities of labor organizations appear to be closely related to the demand for political participation in the course of economic transition. If the suffrage has strong class (property) limitations—which were largely undermined in the United States prior to the full industrial revolution—direct and indeed violent political activity of workers may be expected.

Dynamics of Structural Change

If a general theory of labor organization is to be constructed, it must take into account orderly transformations as well as orderly relations among social structures. The final aggregate of notes accordingly presents some notions on dynamics.

A Natural-History Approach to Early Industrialization

Although it is quite clear that history does not precisely repeat itself, one function of the analytic social scientist is to abstract from the otherwise possibly important differences in details and identify recurrent sequences if they exist. There is a substantial basis for thinking that a

* Perlman's thesis was that American unions mainly eschew politics, whereas J. B. S. Hardman's thesis is that unions are "for" power accumulation. The two views are not inherently antithetical. See Perlman, *op. cit.*, especially pp. 169–176, 313; J. B. S. Hardman, "From 'Job Consciousness' to Power Accumulation," Industrial Relations Research Association, *Proceedings of the Third Annual Meeting* . . . 1950 (Madison: 1951), pp. 146–157.

generalized sequence exists in the historical and contemporary evolution of labor organizations and their relations with employers, and thus that various "early" stages of such evolution can be identified in areas now industrializing.

The sequence evident in "early" industrialization will be presented in terms of four stages, all prior to "advanced" industrialization and "mature" labor relations.

1. "Modern" or "patronal" management, with uncommitted workers, essentially reluctant refugees from the preindustrial economic sector.

2. "Modern" or "patronal" management with committed, loyal employees.

3. Both groups "modern," but with the rise of independent or quasi-independent unions of employees. Craft groups are likely to appear at first, because of their strategic position in production, either as exclusive unions or as the leadership of industrial (status-oriented) unions. The "élite" workers tend to be politically sophisticated, and the paradox that those who have fared best protest first is resolved by their "relative deprivation" in view of other rapid improvements in wealth and position.

4. The rise of status-conscious industrial unions, attempting a "labor monopoly," and exemplifying the radical disparity in wealth, power, education, and specific skills between managers and workers.

Now this sequence, if crudely correct, contains some morals. First, it is consistent with Marx, for his time, and for other places at equivalent stages. Note that at stage "2" there is probably an ideological asymmetry that is also consistent with Marx: namely, class-conscious managers (*Klass für sich*) and loyal employees (*Klass an sich*).

It appears, however, that a symmetrical status orientation (and consequent bipartite division) is likely to be a quite temporary phenomenon. At the "moment" that the preexisting managerial class-consciousness has been matched by a worker class-consciousness, both groups are already exhibiting internal divisions and strains that lead to confusing fractionation of solidarities. This fractionation has been explored here in terms of the simultaneous sources of cohesion and division among workers of all types. If this does not reduce industrial social evolution to a Marxist simplicity, neither does it leave the analyst helpless in the face of seemingly chaotic phenomena.

"Advanced" Industrialization

The dynamic forces in industrialized economies have been systematically underplayed in the contemporary literature of social science, and particularly in the discussion of "economic development" which tend to imply that history comes to an end with the completion of the industrial revolution.

The most important dynamic feature of industrialized societies, at least for present purposes, is the steady and assiduous change in the physical and social technology of production. This has several major implications for labor organization.

The "factor" costs in technical change are largely borne by employers, governments, or research institutions—except for the costs in skill dilution and obsolescence and possibly outright loss of livelihood, which are normally borne by the worker. This highlights the critical character of the control of technical change, particularly with regard to adversely affected groups. Labor organizations therefore attempt restraints on speed of change, various "cushioning" devices commonly known as "featherbedding," and rules regarding preferential rehiring, retraining at company expense, severance pay, and—now on the horizon —pension accounts that are "vested" in the worker and thus transferable to new employments.

Earlier combinations of physical and administrative techniques tended to replace men by machines for truly unskilled tasks, and also to "mechanize" production workers by fractionation of tasks into a multitude of jobs requiring short-cycle routine. This is the major category now affected by automation. If mechanization continues, as it surely will, then the principal clientele of industrial unions is likely to show a steady depletion of relative and probably even absolute size.[8] Meanwhile, other occupational groups of considerable skill have been created, including the perpetrators of technical change as well as the producers of rapidly increasing varieties of producers' and consumer's goods.

Now these two trends—reduction of the semiskilled and increase of all sorts of skilled, technical, and professional jobs—support the view that the occupational orientation will have a growing importance as the basis of labor organization. The number of such organizations is likely to multiply. In the case of white-collar workers in manufacturing and distribution, the prospective threat of displacement by the machine may end their historic resistance to overt union organization. Other groups will adopt names and postures of a professional or quasi-professional character.

The multiplication of occupational groups makes doubtful their concerted power, except possibly for some fairly large coalitions of an essentially transitory character.* With over four-fifths of the labor

* Mark Kahn's contrary position is not persuasive. He argues that there will be fewer and larger (and more multifunctional) national unions. He bases this forecast on predictions of craft union cooperation, craft autonomy in industrial unions, multi-

force consisting of wage and salary earners, there is nothing particularly distinctive in a common "employee" status to offset the multitude of occupational divisions. There will no doubt be some persistence of a division between "management" and "labor," with institutionalized arrangements for their collective relations. What remain to be seen are the patterns of collective relations affecting occupational groups that cannot clearly be classed as either management or labor, even within the firm. One high probability is the extension and strengthening of "professional" associations with various explicit codes regarding terms and conditions of employment. Such codes are normally enforced and binding on employers largely through the maintenance of professional discipline by individual members, but formal representation as a collectivity is always a possibility in case of an employer-employee dispute.

The growing interdependence of all economic groups and sectors within advanced industrialized societies will encourage private and public ingenuity to find equitable substitutes for the strike as a bargaining strategy. And since governments are perforce the residuary legatees of unsolved social problems, there is every reason to expect a growing legal control of economic relations even in countries with long traditions of limited action by the state.

Since a general theory should be predictive in an historic as well as in a simply cross-sectional sense, its final creators will need to refurbish our currently decadent performance of prophecy. Although the crystal ball may be clouded, it is not yet opaque.

References

1. See Arnold S. Feldman and Wilbert E. Moore, "The Society," *Labor Commitment and Social Change in Developing Areas* (New York: Social Science Research Council, 1960), Chapter 4.

2. See W. Lloyd Warner and J. O. Low, "The Break in the Skill Hierarchy," *The Social System of the Modern Factory; The Strike: A Social Analysis* (New Haven, Connecticut: Yale University Press, 1947), Chapter 5.

3. For a general review of recent literature on union organization, see Joel Seidman and Daisy L. Tagliacozzo, "Union Government and Union Leadership," *in* Neil W. Chamberlain and others, eds., *A Decade of Industrial Relations Research, 1946–1956* (New York: Harper, 1958), Chapter 1.

industrial organizations, the advantages of size, and the advantages of reduction of jurisdictional disputes. The latter part of the series is clearly discordant with the first part—a rather perfect non sequitur. Large status-oriented labor coalitions *may* appear, but their cohesive durability is extremely doubtful. All the evidence points in other directions. (See Mark L. Kahn, "Contemporary Structural Changes in Organized Labor," Industrial Relations Research Association, *Proceedings of the Tenth Annual Meeting . . . 1957* (Madison: 1958), pp. 171–179.

4. See Richard A. Lester, "The Changing Character of American Unionism," *As Unions Mature* (Princeton, New Jersey: Princeton University Press, 1958), Chapter 3; *Ibid.*, "The Theory of Union Development," Chapter 9.

5. *Ibid.*, Chapter 2, "The Essence of Unionism."

6. For a general review of recent literature, see Joseph Shister, "Collective Bargaining," Reference 3, Chapter 2.

7. See Will Herberg, "American Marxist Political Theory," *in* Donald Drew Egbert and Stow Persons, eds., *Socialism in American Life* (Princeton, New Jersey: Princeton University Press, 1952), Vol. I, Chapter 10, especially pp. 491–492.

8. See Robert L. Aronson, "Automation—Challenge to Collective Bargaining?" in Harold W. Davey and others, eds., *New Dimensions in Collective Bargaining* (New York: Harper, 1959), Chapter 3.

9
THE ADAPTATION OF AFRICAN
LABOR SYSTEMS TO SOCIAL CHANGE

Labor, we are commonly told, is more than so many warm bodies, trained muscles, or agile minds. It is people. We can rescue these homilies from the plateau of pious platitudes by rather precise specifications of what the laborer's role is or may be. The worker may be starved, coerced, or bribed into reluctant cooperation by a rather wide variety of events and techniques. He becomes a full-fledged participant in the productive process only when he becomes "committed." That is, he not only performs his allotted tasks, but he accepts the norms appropriate to the new productive organization. He accepts the legitimacy of the system of rewards and sanctions, while quite properly attempting to maximize the former and minimize the latter. He thinks, acts, and believes in terms of a market system and a system providing mobility by merit.

For reasons that will appear, if not already well known, this moral transformation of workers is in Africa nowhere far advanced. It is a little uncertain everywhere.

The Subsistence Sector

The premodern forms of economic production in Subsaharan Africa range from extremely "primitive" hunting and foodgathering to settled

SOURCE. Adapted from "The Adaptation of African Labor Systems to Social Change," in Melville J. Herskovits and Mitchell Harwitz, eds., Economic Transition in Africa (Evanston, Illinois: Northwestern University Press, 1964), Chapter 13, pp. 277–297; by permission of Professor Harwitz and of Northwestern University Press.
The preparation of this study was supported in part by the National Academy of Sciences—National Research Council, under Contract No. DA-19-129-AM-1309 with the Quartermaster Research and Engineering Command, U.S. Army. I do apologize, slightly, for the extensiveness of citations in this chapter; they were about double this length in the original, unpublished version. Being uncertain on facts poorly verified, I sought authentication.

agricultural systems of varying degrees of technical proficiency. Handicraft production, either utilitarian or esthetic, has been rather highly developed in some areas, minimally in others. The notion of a "subsistence" economy—that is, low levels of productive specialization and meager if any capital accumulation—does not necessarily imply the economic self-sufficiency of every family as the ultimate consuming unit. Considerable interdependence within and even between villages, mediated by various forms of trade, may modify the picture of an undifferentiated productive system.

It is characteristic of premodern social systems that most productive activities are carried out by units that are not specialized: in other words, by social units with "diffuse" functions. The primary family and often other elements of the kinship system have important economic functions. Larger units, such as villages or tribes, may provide the boundaries and network for specialization and exchange.

It follows from the primarily noneconomic basis of economic organization in such social systems that various productive and distributive activities are assigned less on grounds of efficiency than on the basis of other roles. The distinction is not precise, of course. For example, the division of productive tasks between men and women is to a large degree "arbitrary" from a technical point of view, but the recurrence of some patterns in widely scattered places suggests some quasi-rational basis for role assignments.

Women commonly perform the relatively light but routine and recurrent agricultural and household tasks.[1] Men do heavier work such as breaking up fields for new cultivation, cutting branches or trees for shifting forest cultivation, and commonly, hunting.[2] An interesting extension of the sexual division of labor is the greater probability that men will work in cooperative groups. This type of organization usually takes the form of mutual aid, with the farmer who benefits being responsible for food.[3] In Central and East Africa the beneficiary supplies beer, which is not regarded as payment to the working party, but as something to induce social conviviality,[4] since reciprocity of obligation still holds. One function of such work-cooperative parties in the "transitional" situation of labor migration of men is the maintenance of family agriculture even in the absence of the male.

The age-grading of labor, which may simply provide for nonworking infants and children, working youths and adults, and nonworking aged persons, can on occasion be quite complex. Thus the Adioukrou of the Ivory Coast, of former French West Africa, have an elaborate sevenfold age-grading of adult tasks in the cultivation and preparation of palm oil.[5]

Since technical efficiency has not been the primary criterion for productive organization, it is not surprising that levels of efficiency in indigenous agriculture are generally low. The International Labour Office has concluded that,

... the present basis of subsistence production represents one of the lowest levels of utilisation of human resources in the world and is at the root of the low standards of living in Africa. Until a greater quantity of food can be produced by a much smaller number of persons and a considerable portion of those engaged in subsistence production can be released for more productive activity, this situation is likely to remain unchanged . . .

Work . . . is dictated by the rhythm of the seasons . . . and all activities developed into a tradition sanctified by usage and surrounded by ritual . . . Work in the tribal setting requires neither foresight nor planning; it includes no notion of time, there is no specialization and no order other than that ordained by the seasons.[6]

Although the migratory system discussed in the first of the preceding excerpts provides at least the opportunity for greater efficiency of labor on the part of those remaining behind but continuing traditional production, the second part of the quotation indulges in gross, though poetic, exaggeration, since even in one of the most "primitive" modes of agricultural technology—that of the clearing, burning, shifting cultivation of forest lands—a cycle of several years is both planned and implemented.

There is a fairly standard doctrine that a "rational" organization of work is dependent on a monetary economy—a view maintained in the International Labour Office Survey.[7] Udy, however, has made a considerable case for the appearance of such organizations in many nonindustrial societies including some African ones.[8] As previously noted, there are some "technical" elements in the sexual division of labor— particularly the assignment of physically arduous tasks to males. The role of the male as hunter, warrior, and construction worker is common. But to this sexual division of labor must be added the difference in organization of work by sexes. The common appearance of the work group, despite the obvious note of conviviality introduced by beer drinking, can be assumed to rest upon a technical distinction between individual and group tasks. A major finding of Udy's comparative study which includes some twenty-six African tribal societies, is that "rational" work groups in nonindustrial societies are likely to be organized on a temporary basis, being employed for tasks that are not daily and routine.[9] Although this contrasts with the organization of work in commercialized economies, the evidence does suggest that transition to such economies may be somewhat less radical than is commonly supposed.

Transitional Adaptations

It is not ordinarily realized that Africa has been subjected to a great variety of external influences over a period of several centuries. The rapidity of contemporary change in political and economic structures, and the resulting heightened tensions, should not lead to the casual assumption that the continent remained in a stable *status quo ante* until the colonial period. The slave trade to North Africa, the New World, and Asia Minor, the introduction of "trade goods" by Europeans and Arab traders, the later political and religious imperialism that started more than a century ago, and the educational and economic transformations instituted by colonial governments—all have had their major and subtle effects on labor systems.

In the most general terms, the experience in Africa is a repetition of that in other technologically underdeveloped areas, although the details differ greatly. Workers have been induced to enter into new forms of activity by measures ranging from direct coercion to the indirect appeal of goods that only money will secure. They have been given training in varying degrees appropriate to new tasks and opportunities. They have been "pushed" out of traditional economic pursuits by contraction of the land available to them and by population growth as a by-product of increased sanitation.[10]

The details, however, are not inconsequential. The meeting of civilizations in Africa seems to have produced a richer variety of adjustments than exists in any other area of the world. Some of the adjustments considered here as "transitional" have proved remarkably stable and persistent, whether because of the underlying strength of the indigenous cultures, or because the policies of alien rulers have prevented more rapid and radical transformation.

Enterprisers in Africa seeking local labor commonly encountered a situation that was an extreme illustration of a type, namely, an indigenous population insensitive to financial inducements. In the absence of a monetary market in the traditions of many African societies, and with relatively inelastic demand schedules for products in any case, this behavior was inconvenient.

Slavery in various forms as well as many types of obligatory service at the instance of political rulers existed in many African areas prior to contact with Europe and America. Although in a sense providing a prior cultural base for new systems of forced labor, there were also negative consequences for new labor systems even of a noncoercive type. The International Labour Office *Survey* observed that "for many tribes any form of organized manual work for others has associations with slavery and is therefore despised . . ." [11]

There are at least three rather different situations in which forced labor has been sanctioned by governing authorities. First, there are personal services for recognized native chiefs, including agricultural work on the chief's land and the upkeep of his buildings. Second, there are various forms of the *corvée,* that is, obligatory work for public purposes such as porterage, road construction, and military service. Third, there have been types of essentially compulsory public recruiting for private economic activities, particularly in the earlier days of colonial rule, when local supplies of labor were inadequate and additional workers had to be sought at considerable distances.

The first form of compulsory labor, various services to native chiefs, has of course the superficial justification of preserving elements of the traditional social order. However, the combination of increasing legal restrictions and the evolution of the socioeconomic structure has operated to modify and transform such services. Thus, commuting of forced labor by cash payments is reported to have been possible in the Congo and Ruanda-Urundi.[12] Among the Alur of Uganda the service is viewed as a tax payment in cash, and actual performance is regarded as a penalty for default of payment rather than the normal method of fulfilling the obligation.[13]

The distinctions to be made among the three types of forced labor are not entirely clear-cut. For example, services to native chiefs in Portuguese Guinea are in part for the purpose of supporting orphans, the sick and infirm, and the destitute,[14] which in the light of modern views of welfare has a distinctly public flavor. On the other hand, forced labor "for the purpose of agricultural instruction" in the Congo, and compulsory agricultural work for the purpose of protecting against famine, recognized in Gambia and Tanganyika,[15] have a distinct flavor of public intervention for private economic interests.

Direct coercion of workers, even for public works, was scarcely consistent with the legal standards that prevailed in the metropolitan powers. This was particularly true if labor was uncompensated. A widely used form was the head or hut tax, payable only in cash, and thus in most areas payable only by the acceptance of employment for wages. "This coercion by indirection, which is more in keeping with European canons of law and ethics and conceptions of productive relationships, has been accomplished mainly by the power of taxation as a prerogative of constituted governmental authority." [16]

Under German administration in Tanganyika a variant of the cash tax was imposed. In one section of the colony every adult native male had to work 30 days within every four-month period for a private employer. If he failed to comply with this regulation he was conscripted for an equal amount of time on public roads.[17] Taxation, however, has lost its importance as a factor in labor recruitment. A considerable expansion of wage earning in the absence of indirect compulsion would seem to indicate that normal economic incentives have proved increasingly effective in inducing Africans to seek paid employment of their own accord.[18]

Certainly the outstanding feature of the contemporary system of employment in central and southern Africa is the pattern of relatively temporary employment of native workers who migrate to places of employment and then return to their villages. Like many migratory movements, this transfer of workers is compounded of various elements of "push" and "pull." Contraction of farm and grazing lands, coupled with population "pressure," results in a deteriorating relation of the indigenous population to the traditional means of subsistence.[19] The "pull" factors include the usual ones associated with urbanization everywhere—ranging from economic opportunity, real or imagined, through various social amenities, to the mere excitement of urban life.

The variant in the African scene is the temporary character of much labor migration, and the rather specific character of the economic goals. This latter characteristic had led to the concept of the "target worker." The targets may themselves be compulsory, as in the case of getting money for taxes. They may be derivatives of traditional patterns, as in the commutation of bride-price from cattle to money, the substitution of migration for more traditional and sometimes violent forms of activities calculated to gain prestige for young men, or the investment of money in improved agriculture. They may be specific consumer products, from clothes to bicycles.[20] As long as economic "wants" remain highly specific and inelastic, higher wages are likely to mean that the worker stops sooner, and nonfinancial incentives such as conditions of work must then be used in competition for workers.[21]

The "targets" of workers differ in both space and time. Where indigenous agriculture has become substantially commercialized, as in parts of both western and eastern Africa, there is not only a greater probability that temporary migratory workers will work for native employers, but also some probability that the income from such employment will be used to pay for capital improvements on the worker's own farm. In other areas, the temporary employee is much more likely to be oriented to current consumption.

Through time, it is understandable that just as some migration that seems to be temporary is in fact relatively permanent, so the targets of workers become generalized through their increasing incorporation in the market system of pecuniary, industrialized economies. The target, in effect, becomes money, for whatever it will buy. For the "target worker," strictly speaking, the rentention of village ties is unproblematical. It is his base of operations. Put in economic terms, his two sources of "income" are complementary. For the worker rather more fully incorporated into the labor and commodity markets, such ties may still be operative, and this requires some explanation. Commentators have emphasized the economic security based on rights in land, and the social security based on kinship reciprocities and traditional political structures.[22]

The sheer volume of labor migration would appear to have some impact at the places of origin as well as at the places of destination. Numbers of migrants in the tens and even hundreds of thousands, from relatively restricted geographical areas, repeatedly appear in the reports.[23] Perhaps more significant are the proportions of men absent from their villages, which various studies indicate may range from 25 to as high as 70% of the adult males.[24]

The effects of migratory patterns on traditional structures are, surely, a function at least of the volume and duration of migration, as well as the extent to which the "traditional" structures were, in fact, relatively integrated.

In Africa, the migratory labor system has taken on a quasi-permanent character. In the Republic of South Africa it has a legal status which stems from the restrictions laid on African urban residence and the attempt to "retribalize" all Africans. The official policy of *Apartheid* looks eventually to the near-cessation of the migratory system, however, by setting up separate geographical entities ("Bantustand") for Africans, and the substitution of European workers for the displaced Africans. Granting the sincerity of governments in attempting to avoid for the Europeans the fate of becoming a minority in a multiracial state, it is extremely doubtful that the extremely tense political situation will become less so, or that meanwhile *Apartheid* will mean anything except the most rigorous system of racial domination in the contemporary world.

In all of Subsaharan Africa the numerical magnitude of migratory labor appears to be increasing. Apart from the somewhat special, or at least extreme, situation in South Africa, the reasons for this rather peculiar adaptation have been summarized by the East African Royal Commission:

In the existing situation the migrant labour system appears to be the only one through which a considerable section of the African population can meet its needs, because the economic opportunities for more effective specialisation have either been absent or have been seriously circumscribed by legal and customary restrictions. For many Africans it is not now possible to attain a higher income level for the support of their families without working both on the land and in urban employment. This means that, given the present productivity of Africans over large parts of the rural and urban sector of the economy, the migrant labour system appears as the most economic choice which the African can make, however socially deleterious or otherwise undesirable it may be. Notwithstanding these disadvantages the system brings about an improvement in the economic condition of those who go out in search of paid employment. It follows that, if it is desired to curtail the system, it is necessary that the production opportunities in agriculture and in industry should be such that they can yield an income in cash and in kind that will be sufficient to enable the majority who work in either sphere to avoid working temporarily in the other. The replacement of the migrant labour system cannot be effectively accomplished merely by the introduction of special devices in the urban areas, but only as the result of a successfully long-term policy which includes both agricultural and non-agricultural improvement.[25]

A reasoned guess, however, is that the seeming stability of this structured compromise between divergent economic systems is spurious. "If this system provides a sort of statistical equilibrium it does not follow that it produces anything like a stable social equilibrium. Native labor migration serves as a bridge between rigid and otherwise incompatible types of social restraint . . . The restraints . . . appear to be subject to pressure that may lead to their collapse." [26]

Another type of migratory movement of workers, seasonal labor, is less peculiar to the African situation than is the longer-term contractual worker. Although the two types of migration seem to merge in some instances, and to spring from some of the same sources, the seasonal migrant is almost exclusively an agricultural worker.

The opportunity for seasonal wage employment stems in part from the relative underemployment of labor in the subsistence sector, making it possible for part of the labor force to aid in periods of peak demand for labor in commercialized agriculture. In part, the variations in climate, technology, and type of crop provide opportunities for farmers to work for other farmers during slack periods. The development of commercialized agriculture in West Africa has provided a considerable volume of employment for workers from neighboring regions.[27] An example of relatively long-distance seasonal migration is that of the migratory workers in the cotton fields of the Sudan. The bulk of the seasonal workers comes from French Equatorial Africa and

Nigeria, and consists of men who return annually to till their own crops.[28] The explanation of the uncommitted worker has been put succinctly in the International Labour Office *Survey*. If the worker

> . . . has ventured into the wage economy with the vague intention of remaining in it indefinitely, his native village or land unit remains in many areas an effective alternative to town life; no social or economic factors have yet arisen which link him and his fellows to industry and to town life . . . That he should try to retain such security as his rural background has to offer him is therefore normal. That his work in the wage economy should be conditioned by the complex of circumstances, largely unfavorable to him, which exist there is equally natural.[29]

In African multiracial territories, and to some extent throughout the Subsaharan area, some form or degree of the "color bar" has continued to exist. Official policy ranged from the denial of discrimination in French territories, through forms of "indirect rule" of predominantly African populations in some British territories, to open and legal racism in the Rhodesias and South Africa. African political ascendency in the newly independent states has not entirely ended the advantageous position held by the white merchant or employer.

Although much discontent incident upon racial discrimination arises from strictly social and political sources, its economic aspect cannot be set aside entirely. Two principal problems that affect the position of the African workers are the establishments of noncompeting occupational categories for African and European workers, giving the latter immunity from African competition for skilled, prestigious, and well-paid jobs, and discriminatory legislation or customary practices that not only bar any common European-African labor organization, but often prevent or sharply restrict the freedom of association of the African workers. The forms of the color bar have been modified in Rhodesia, with provisions for Africans to enter a wider range of "intermediate" occupations, and to present their views and grievances through union organization.[30] As one observer has noted, however, the ending of formal restrictions on access to occupations, whether imposed by law or by European workers, does not automatically produce Africans with the appropriate skills to claim the new opportunities.[31]

Secondary (manufacturing) industry has had little development in Africa. Where it has developed, the flexibility of occupational organization, in view of changing physical or administrative technology, has tended to give the employer a freer hand in opening positions to African workers, and thus avoiding the exceptionally high wages exacted by European workers who are firmly protected from native competition.

The International Labour Office *Survey* notes with reference to labor organization that,

... in some of the multiracial societies ... the policies and legal provisions relating to freedom of association, the right to organise and bargain collectively, and the settlement of trade disputes, are different for the various racial groups in the community. Such anomalies are generally stated to be justified because of the different stages of social evolution of the various elements of the societies concerned.[32]

One may note, with perhaps wry amusement, that the legislative imposition of racial inequality is itself a clear denial of the claimed justification, namely natural inequality, for if the latter prevented acquisition of higher skills, biology would need no help from politicians in keeping African workers "in their place."

The Stabilized Sector

The concept of a "stabilized sector" of African labor must be viewed in the special context of comparison with the clearly transitional adjustments between radically different socioeconomic systems. The stabilized sector refers to those portions of the economy (and particularly that portion of the labor force) that are fully and irretrievably bound up with the commodity- and labor-market systems. In view of the inherent dynamics of modern commercial and industrial systems, these segments are clearly not stabilized in any static sense.

The assessment of the extent and significance of relatively complete departure from traditional economic usages presents in the first instance a merely factual problem: what is its quantitative importance? Some detailed field studies indicate that the truly transformed or committed workers, even among the urban-born and long-term employees, represent a fairly small minority.[33] However, as Mitchell has pointed out,[34] the factual question is complicated by the conceptual one, and he rejects as synonymous the concepts of urbanization, detribalization, and stabilization. Even if stabilization is defined as "permanence" of residence in towns and participation in the labor markets, as a predictive measure it must have an attitudinal component—that is, intention and identification.

But it is precisely intention and identification that set the distinction between the "transitional" and "stabilized" forms of labor adopted in this discussion. Moreover, the very high turnover of African workers represents a mixture, in unknown proportions, of migratory labor in the distinctly African pattern and of workers simply changing employers. The latter may be somewhat whimsical or otherwise unreliable in their employment behavior, but they are acting *within* the modern labor-market system.

By implication, all or most forms of economic organizations and labor systems not in conformity with the norms and patterns of the older industrial economies are "transitional." This is a view that some scholars concerned with Africa would reject. They argue that the viable strength of indigenous social systems is such that the future forms of African economies will represent a mutual adaptation between the demands of the commercial-industrial system and the variable social systems found in premodern and contemporary African societies.[35]

The position may have both theoretical and factual support. It seems quite clear that the literature on economic development has fairly consistently underplayed the organizational flexibility and adaptability of the commercial-industrial system. At the same time, at least some students of contemporary Africa argue that such systems as that of migratory labor represent stable adaptations between divergent systems.[36] The very considerable development of wage-labor patterns, whether seasonal or settled, in the commercialized agricultural undertakings established by native farmers lends some further support to the view that the "stabilized sector" may not only include agriculture, but include it in ways somewhat alien to "Western" conceptions. It remains true that there is a labor market more or less corresponding to industrial economic patterns. Its exact dimensions are difficult to assess, and the significance of the deviations and their stability are disputed.

For those large proportions of native workers who intermix subsistence farming, cash cropping, petty commerce, and wage labor, the concepts of "labor force," "gainfully occupied," "occupation," and "industry," in the sense of sector of economic activity, do not neatly differentiate persons,[37] but rather have at best a temporary, cross-sectional utility.

> As the lack of specialisation in any one calling is a basic feature of the working population in Africa, employment statistics can only show the number of workers occupied at a given moment in definite occupations.[38]

Some approximate sense can be made of distributions of "workers" by major economic sector, distinguishing agriculture, "industry" (mining, manufacturing, construction) and "services" (commerce, professions, government, service, and the like). Even with this crude classification, however, the agricultural sector fails to distinguish among subsistence agriculture, cash cropping and various forms of farm tenancy, and agricultural wage labor. Thus, among wage earners as such, agriculture may provide relatively minor employment in areas where subsistence farming and small proprietorship prevail, and account for 40 to 50% of wage employment where commercial agriculture is on a larger scale, as in Southern Rhodesia, Kenya, and Tanganyika and South Africa.[39]

Mining accounts for almost one-fifth of the African wage-earners in South Africa, and a substantial proportion, from 8 to 13%, in Ghana, the Republic of the Congo, and the Rhodesias, but it must be noted that wage-earners in turn represent less than one-fifth of the economically active males in Ghana, and nearly one-half in the Rhodesias. Secondary industry, other than mining, is of small quantitative significance as an employer throughout Subsaharan Africa, ranging sharply downward from 20–25% among wage earners in South Africa and the former Belgian Congo.[40]

"Services" of all sorts generally represent a larger proportion of the employed population than does secondary industrial production. The statistical materials, unreliable at best, here encounter a further difficulty in that reliance on distribution of wage-earners excludes the self-employed. This category is of considerable importance in petty trade, whether the traders be the Asians of eastern and southern Africa or the Africans in the West. It should also be noted that governments are substantial employers of African labor, running as high as almost 30% of wage-earners in former French West Africa, where, however, the total of all wage-earners is very low, and over 20% in Kenya, where wage-earners are a substantial proportion of the gainfully occupied.[41]

However, except for a few detailed studies, occupational distributions strictly defined are essentially meaningless. The reason is that a majority of workers are unskilled, and accordingly have the widest possible transferability between occupations and between sectors of the economy. Various studies indicate that at least one-half to three-fourths of employed Africans are in this category.[42] Fawzi finds that even among governmental employees in the Sudan, who might be thought to comprise an especially select group, fully one-half are in the lowest category of skills.[43] Moreover, most of the employment and occupational data on African labor refers to males, for the rather simple reason that women are very little represented in the labor market. Women contribute an important and often even a major portion of the labor in subsistence agriculture and, in West Africa, in petty trade. With a few exceptions they are not commonly employed at wage labor.[44]

To the extent that a genuinely stable and committed African labor force develops, one would expect the appearance of occupational prestige patterns approximating those of older industrial countries. Two studies indicate that such is the case, though the inferential conclusions of their respective authors differ in one significant respect. Mitchell and Epstein [45] find little or no evidence of genuine class identification within the African group, the economic and political leaders tending to be spokesmen for Africans generally. Xydias, on the basis of some discontinuities in the prestige scale, concludes,

> Our theory is that social classes are coming into being and that their existence is already intuitively perceived by the Africans; although they are not yet sufficiently aware of these classes to speak of them or to classify them as we ourselves do.[46]

There is a remarkable paucity of descriptive materials relating to the organization of nonagricultural enterprises in Africa. The extensive *Survey of African Labour* by the International Labour Office says nothing on the subject apart from some comments on special problems of first-line labor supervision. One study of workers in Stanleyville contains a few data concerning the distribution of workers by size of enterprise. Approximately one-fourth of the wage-earners surveyed worked in undertakings employing 50 or fewer workers, one-half in enterprises employing 51 to 300 workers, and one-fourth in "large" undertakings with over 300 workers, of which approximately one-tenth was in two enterprises employing over 1000 workers each.[47] Except for large mining employers, the small to medium-sized enterprise seems most common.[48] The policies of mining employers have varied from those of the Copper Belt in Northern Rhodesia, with fairly impersonal management of unskilled, temporary employees, largely housed in bachelor barracks, to the more paternalistic management of the Compagnie de Haut-Kantanga, where it has been the policy to develop a stable labor force. Reports on fairly large-scale plantation and forestry projects indicate a variety of compromises between "modern" methods of organization, supervision, and remuneration, on the one hand, and an unskilled, uncommitted, and largely transitory labor force on the other.

Fairly pervasive organizational problems in African nonagricultural enterprises arise out of racial distinctions between workers and supervisors, with or without African "gang leaders" as intermediaries,[49] and the common tribal diversity of the African labor force itself, which may or may not be overridden by the new circumstances at the workplace.[50] Both the "color bar" and tribal diversity operate to maintain a distorted organization of the enterprises, and to provide a technically irrelevant complication in the modes of management and personnel administration.

One of the most remarkable features of economic change in Africa is the increased employment of Africans by Africans in commercialized agriculture. Some of the arrangements of tenancy and personal dependency have a distinctly archaic flavor.[51] Others strongly resemble a fully developed labor market in the agricultural sector of the several economies.[52]

It is not surprising, in view of the small numerical importance of "stabilized" workers in Africa, that labor organizations are relatively weak or nonexistent. The organizational weakness of unions of African workers, and their modest economic power, is complicated by two additional factors. The first circumstance, by no means uncommon in newly developing areas, is that unions tend to be highly political in their orientations and policies, partly as a consequence of the meager direct bargaining strength of unskilled and semiskilled workers. The second circumstance, which has a special significance in Africa, has to do with the official and unofficial restrictions on freedom of association and collective bargaining on the part of native workers—a manifestation of the "color bar." The extreme case here, again, is South Africa.

In situations where a high volume of employment by Africans has been coupled with the development of some stable workers and the emergence of some workers having more than minimum skills, unions of native workers have achieved some modest direct influence, as in Nigeria and Rhodesia. In Ghana unions have come under strong governmental control. But the "color bar" can discourage African unionization, and prevent the formation of multiracial unions. The African workers themselves are not immune to considerations of "cultural" differences, as shown by unions formed on tribal lines.[53] And though there is ample room for difference of view as to whether the "color bar," primarily political unionism, and the persistence of tribalism are temporary phenomena, a reasoned guess is that organizations based on common interests relating to status are likely to emerge, followed eventually by organizations deriving primarily from common occupational interests, as the occupational structure of the African labor force assumes a more "normal" shape.[54] *

Special Topics

The rationale for the organization of this report up to this point has been a simple three-stage model of social and economic transition. A

* See Chapter 8.

number of topics having a significant bearing on labor in Africa, however, do not fit this scheme.

Educational standards and achievements for African populations are relatively low throughout Subsaharan Africa. Only in the former Belgian Congo is the estimated adult literacy rate as high as 35–40%. The estimated literacy in Uganda is 25–30%. Ghana, Kenya, Northern Rhodesia, and Southern Rhodesia have literacy rates of 20–25%. The 5–10% category includes the Cameroons, Gambia, Liberia, Nyasaland, Ruanda-Urandi, Sierra Leone, Tanganyika, and Togoland. A census enumeration in Nigeria, 1952–53, indicated a slightly higher rate of 11.5. Finally, the large territories of former French Equatorial Africa and French West Africa, as well as Angola and Mozambique, have estimated adult literacy rates of 1–5%.[55] Data for South Africa are not available, but African literacy is probably under 10%.

The proportions of the total population in schools of any grade range from about 2% in former French West Africa and Gambia to about 12% in Ghana and Southern Rhodesia.[56] All of the countries and territories of Subsaharan Africa are in the lowest two categories of proportions of school-age children actually in school, those having 20 to 40% and those under 20%, with the single exception of Southern Rhodesia where 40 to 60% are so enrolled.[57]

This nonexistent or meager education does not seriously affect the economic potential of African labor as long as it is confined to strictly unskilled jobs. But the experience of industrialized countries indicates that the increased productivity of an economy requires the upgrading of labor, a steady reduction in the number and proportion of unskilled jobs, and the training of technical, managerial, and professional personnel. Such advanced training is not totally unknown among Africans,[58] but the numbers so trained are extremely small.

The African situation is of course only a relatively extreme instance of a phenomenon common in economically underdeveloped areas—an acute undersupply of indigenous workers trained for responsible positions, possibly coupled with some oversupply of certain categories of educated persons, either in view of the absolute demand or of the actual accessibility of positions to natives. It has been particularly the experience of colonial territories that the civil service has been especially attractive as an employer. The phenomenon of the unemployed or underemployed "intellectual" is not unknown in Africa, although it is less common than in some other areas of the world.

Education is of course promoted by modern states for reasons outside the merely technical advantages of literacy and trained skills for labor productivity. Aside from considerations of political and social partici-

pation, an especially acute problem where emerging African nationalism faces a variety of tribal and local allegiances in the same territory,
education is also looked to as a way of developing new economic wants
and aspirations.[59] On the other hand, some observers have noted the
limited impact of formal education as such, when set in a social environment providing strong negative or at least traditional pressures,
such as the opposition between individualistic educational achievement
and the strongly collectivistic values and norms of the tribal cultures.[60]

Another problem has to do with general or recurrent labor shortages
at the wages and under the conditions offered, coupled with extreme
underutilization of potential labor resources—that is, underemployment, of which Africa provides a classic case. Visible unemployment is
relatively rare, and confined to certain cities where immigrant workers
may exceed the labor demand. Nearby areas may at the same time
have shortages of labor for agricultural work.[61]

Subsistence agriculture of course had a chronic surplus of labor, in
the sense of "full" utilization, as partly demonstrated by the maintenance or near-maintenance of production, despite the absence of
large numbers of migratory laborers.

Estimates of underemployment or overstaffing in commercial farming, mining, and manufacturing are nonexistent. Such estimates would
in any case require a stipulation of the technological level to be used
as a base of calculations. Cheap, inefficient, and even "redundant"
labor may still be less costly than a more advanced technology, which
would require not only additional capitalization but probably also
more highly skilled and highly paid workers. Nothing resembling precise studies of productivity is available with regard to African labor.
This does not alter the unanimous conclusion that productivity is
extremely low. The factors are not difficult to identify. They range
from the environmental and physiological—climate, health, and nutrition—through inadequate technical organization and financial incentives, to the lack of coincidence in attitudes and values in the traditional
and induced social systems.

Climatic factors are probably less important than the prevalence of
various endemic diseases and low standards of diet and nutrition.[62]
Some employers have issued food rations to workers to assure the maintenance of adequate nutritional standards, although this is recognized
as paternalistic and distrustful of the employees' capacity to make
"sensible" budgetary decisions.

The most common assumption has been that African workers will
be used at unskilled jobs, requiring and justifying very low wages,
which in turn provide little incentive for conscientious productive

effort. The utilization of cheap, unskilled labor also has implications for the technical organization of production, including types of supervision. Wage scales are generally determined on the basis of minimum subsistence for the bachelor worker, with or without additional family allowances.[63] Such low wage scales are maintained in part by the racial differences in opportunities, and in part by the fact that the unskilled wage laborer can always be displaced by other rural migrants. Indeed, there are some indications that wages can be kept below the effective urban subsistence level because of the assumption that the worker gets additional support from his claims upon the products of his native village. Adjustment to a migratory labor system has still another consequence for productivity. This is the extremely high rate of labor turnover, with its inevitable costs in recruitment, payroll-record keeping, and instruction on the job. Changes of employers, which are also very frequent, have the same effect.[64]

Attempts to improve the productivity of African workers, apart from various incentive schemes, have centered on the development of criteria of selection, including psychological tests, and the provision of increased training, both at the job and in technical schools. Some limited success has been reported, under generally adverse social conditions.[65]

"Cultural" impediments to productivity are also difficult to assess precisely. The common lack of an individualistic competitive orientation on the part of the African was noted with reference to educational problems. It can be assumed that this also operates to restrict levels of aspiration in employment. The ILO *Survey* observes:

> Whatever the circumstances, there can be no doubt that the African is ill-adapted by any conditioning he has received through his economic and cultural background for assimilation as an effective element in a wage economy on the European pattern. It is equally certain, of course, that his aim in seeking wage-paid employment heavily influences his attitude to work and his response to incentives and makes it inevitable that his reactions will differ widely from those of the European worker, whose background and aims are so different.[66]

The social as well as economic security of the African may still largely depend upon his ties to the traditional social structure, as noted in the discussion of migratory labor. His feeling of insecurity in urban employment has been marked by observers in commenting on the lack of commitment, and attendant productivity among wage-earners.[67] The "feeling" of insecurity may very well be objectively justified.

The lack of commitment may stem in part from policies of employers, and even of governments, as they limit union organization and collective bargaining on the part of African workers. Apter emphasizes the positive attitudinal advantages to be gained from some participation in setting the terms and conditions of employment.[68]

Some factors related to low productivity of labor may now be summarized as a set of quasi-equations which may be metaphorically called "vicious circles."

Low wages, bad health and nutrition, poor performance.

Low wages, low incentives, poor performance.

Low wages, low skills, poor organization.

These "circles" require little further comment. They are not unique to Africa, although the system of migratory labor gives them an especially durable structural support there. When private and public discrimination are added, the circle grows a little larger, so that to those equations starting from low wages a fourth may be added:

Low wages, low income, poor demand.

Since the inconsistency of standards, attitudes, and values looms so large in problems of productivity, it is natural that attempts should be made to adjust policies and practices to take into account the workers' attitudes and experience. Thus a common practice in plantation agriculture has been task-payment rather than time-payment as more nearly fitting the experience of the subsistence farmer-turned-worker, including his lack of orientation to precision in matters involving time. Similarly, it is reported that with reference to the divergent tribal origins of workers, "The general consensus of opinion seems to be that on the whole, . . . homogeneous working groups give the best results.[69] Considerations of ethnic origin and individual status within the traditional structure also affect the selection of "headmen." These adaptations may be more effective in the short run than in the long, for they may prove to be barriers to the acceptance of more rational organization and criteria of selection and efficiency.

The great range of regulations that may be comprised by the term "labor legislation" and the multitude of political entities to be considered in this report make impracticable a detailed compilation of labor codes. Some general comments must suffice.

In common with many underdeveloped areas, African countries often have fairly "advanced" legislation regulating the terms and conditions of employment, union organizations, social security, and the like.[70] As is the case in other underdeveloped areas, these regulations may be poorly enforced, or in effect applicable to only a minority of workers, such as those employed in large enterprises.

The International Labour Organisation, through its draft Conventions and Recommendations, has had considerable influence on the course of labor legislation in Africa. Some of the Conventions, such as those relating to forced labor, regulation of recruitment, and abolition of the "penal sanction" in labor contracts, have had a special or even unique applicability to African practices. The summary of the situation by the International Labour Office is cautiously optimistic:

> In the majority of African countries there is already a substantial body of basic labour legislation based in large measure on Conventions and Recommendations adopted by the International Labour Conference. Indeed the extent to which such Conventions and Recommendations have already contributed . . . to the establishment of a framework of basic labour standards which are in force over extensive parts of the African Continent is one of the most striking features in the present situation . . .[71]

Summary and Conclusions

From the range of topics covered in this chapter, a few major points and issues may be noted for final emphasis.

1. The subsistence, or perhaps more properly the "traditional," sector of the economies of Subsaharan Africa demonstrates hardy survival powers in the face of modern economic, political, and other social pressures. They are by no means untouched, however. Some productive processes have been reorganized as a consequence of the periodical withdrawal of male laborers who leave to work in industrial projects, while cash from both labor and agricultural products exerts a growing influence. The absence of men has affected family relationships, and has tended to alter the position of women and children.

2. An outstanding feature of African labor is found in its pattern of temporary migration, predominantly by males, who neither fully abandon traditional modes of social organization, nor fully accept the norms and values of "modern" economic organization. It may be anticipated that the subsistence sector will increasingly be incorporated into national economies, and that the migratory labor system must be viewed as transitional, though this view is by no means universally accepted.

3. A small and not precisely determinable number of African workers is more or less fully incorporated into urban labor markets. The commercialized and industrialized portion of African economies have been identified as the "stabilized" sector, but only by contrast with such transitional adaptations as temporary labor migration. Even those workers who remain permanently in the labor market may not be genuinely committed to an urban-industrial way of life. Such commitment is strongly discouraged in the multiracial territories in the

degree to which the policy of *Apartheid* is implemented, but may be expected to grow in importance in the future.

4. Distinctions by color have been common, but African homogeneity is based more on anticolonial and racial grounds than on basic similarities in its highly diverse traditional cultures. The persistence of tribal, linguistic, and other cultural distinctions among Africans, even in the cities, impedes types of social organization adapted to new economic activities.

5. Though Africans must be assumed to be capable of learning the skills appropriate to a modern economy, given adequate incentive and opportunity, neither of these "givens" has been generally present. So rare indeed have been the opportunities for Africans to do skilled labor, except through governmental employment in British and French West Africa and Uganda, that the restraints of tradition cannot be judged against the restraints of discrimination.

6. As long as low-cost labor is available for positions requiring minimal skill, public or private employers must count on continued high turnover, low productivity, restrained expansion in effective consumer demand, and perhaps exceptionally high costs for technical and managerial personnel.

7. The strains inherent in industrialized societies are probably heightened by the various adaptive mechanisms developed in Subsaharan Africa that permit the partial persistence of traditional forms. Future labor systems may not precisely resemble those of the oldest industrial economies, but they will not resemble present African forms, either.

References

1. See International Labour Office, *African Labor Survey* (Geneva: ILO, 1958), pp. 13, 68, 88. This work will be cited hereafter as ILO.

2. Pierre de Schlippe, *Shifting Cultivation in Africa* (London: Routledge & Kegan Paul, 1956), pp. 140–148, with reference to the Azande of Sudan; P. H. Gulliver, *Labour Migration in a Rural Economy*, East African Studies No. 6 (Kampala: East African Institute of Social Research, 1955), pp. 33–41, with reference to the Ngoni of Tanganyika; Audrey I. Richards, "A Changing Pattern of Agriculture in East Africa: The Bemba of Northern Rhodesia," *Geographical Journal*, 124: 302–313, September 1958; Aldan W. Southall, *Alur Society* (Cambridge: W. Heffer and Sons, Ltd., for the East African Institute of Social Research, n.d.–1953?), pp. 271, 278–279, with reference to the Alur of Uganda; William Watson, *Tribal Cohesion in a Money Economy* (Manchester: Manchester University Press for Rhodes-Livingstone Institute, 1958), pp. 20–22, 33, with reference to the Mambwe of Northern Rhodesia.

3. See ILO, p. 66, with reference to Verubaland in Nigeria and to Sierra Leone. See also K. L. Little, "Land and Labour among the Mende" *African Affairs*, 47: January 1948, referring to a group in Sierra Leone.

4. Gulliver, *loc.cit.;* Southall, *loc.cit.;* Watson, *op.cit.,* pp. 106–110.

5. See Marguerite Dupire, "Organisation Sociale du Travail dans la Palmeraier Adioukrou (Basse Côte d'Ivoire)," *Revue de l'Institut de Sociologie,* II/III: 271–292, 1956.

6. ILO, pp. 32, 140.

7. *Ibid.,* pp. 66–68.

8. Stanley H. Udy, Jr., *Organization of Work* (New Haven, Connecticut: HRAF Press, 1959). See, however, the comments of Ombredano, who emphasized the lack of clear work plans and the coordination of work roles among some African groups in the former Belgian Congo. See André Ombredane, "Les Techniques de Fortune dans le Travail Coutumier das Noirs," *Présence Africaine,* 13: 58–68, 1952.

9. Udy, *op.cit.,* pp. 41–43, 49, 127, 128.

10. See Wilbert E. Moore, *Industrialization and Labor* (Ithaca, New York: Cornell University Press, 1951).

11. ILO, p. 140.

12. *Ibid.,* p. 298.

13. See Southall, work cited in Reference 2.

14. See Antonio Carriera, "Problemas do Trabalho Indigena no Colonia de Guine," *Boletim Geral das Colonias,* 24: 35–62, December 1948.

15. See ILO, pp. 297–299.

16. Wilbert E. Moore, "The Migration of Native Laborers in South Africa," *Milbank Memorial Fund Quarterly,* 24: 401–419, October 1946, quotation from p. 401.

17. See Charlotte Leubuscher, *Tanganyika Territory* (London: Oxford University Press for Royal Institute of International Affairs, 1944), pp. 64–66.

18. ILO, p. 295.

19. See Wilbert E. Moore, *Industrialization and Labor* (cited in Reference 10, pp. 48–55). With reference specifically to Africa, see Richard W. Stephens, *Population Pressure in Africa South of the Sahara* (Washington: Population Research Project, George Washington University, 1958); R. Delarozière, "Etude de la Stabilité de la Population de la Subdivision de Befoussam Pendant les Années 1946 et 1947," *Etudes Camerousaises,* 3: 137–187, September–December 1950; N. Gaurilov, "Labour Migration in West Africa," *Problemi Vostokovedenia* 3: 82–90, 1959 (in Russian, annotated in *African Abstracts,* 10: 482); P. H. Gulliver, *op.cit.* (Reference 2), pp. 16–32, and Gulliver, "Nyakyusa Labour Migration," *Human Problems in British Central Africa,* 21: 32–63, March 1957, with reference to Tanganyika; R. Mansell Prothero, "Migratory Labour from North-Western Nigeria," *Africa,* 27: 251–261, July 1957; Barbara Ward, "Some Notes on Migration from Togoland" *African Affairs,* 49: 129–135, April 1950. For a negative view of the importance of overpopulation for migration see G. N. Burden, "Labor Migration in Africa," *Corona,* 3: 55–58, 100–102, February and March 1951.

20. See, for example, J. R. Goody, *The Social Organisation of the Lowiili,* Colonial Research Studies No. 19 (London: H. M. Stationery Office, 1956), pp. 9–10, with reference to a group in the northern Gold Coast (Ghana); T. T. Steiger Hayler, "Wage Labour and the Desire for Wives Among the Lango," *Uganda Journal,* 8: 15–18, September 1940; A. H. M. Kirk-Greene, "Tax and Travel Among the Hill Tribes of Northern Adamadwa," *Africa,* 26: 369–379, October 1956, with reference to a group in the Cameroons; Aldan W. Southall, "Alur Migrants," *in* Audrey I. Richards, ed., *Economic Development and Tribal Change: A Study of Immigrant Labour in Buganda* (Cambridge: W. Heffer and Sons for the East African Institute of Social Research, 1954), Chap. VI.

21. See Eliot J. Berg, "Backward-Sloping Labor Supply Functions in Dual Econo-mies—The African Case," *Quarterly Journal of Economics*, 75: 468–492, 1961.

22. ILO, pp. 82–83, 138–141, Delarozière, *op.cit.* (Reference 19); B. E. C. Hop-wood, "The Place of Industrial Medicine in Uganda," *International Labour Review*, 78: 348–367, October 1958; William Watson, *op.cit.* (Reference 2); pp. 6–8, 134–136.

23. See ILO, pp. 137–144.

24. *Ibid.* See also Gulliver, *Labour Migration in a Rural Economy* (cited Refer-ence 2), pp. 1–15; Audrey I. Richards, "A Changing Pattern of Agriculture in East Africa . . . ," (cited Reference 2); Watson, *Tribal Cohesion in a Money Economy* (cited Reference 2), pp. 20–22.

25. East African Royal Commission, Cmd. 9475, *Report* (London: H. M. Station-ery Office, 1955), p. 154.

26. Moore, "The Migration of Native Laborers . . ." (cited Reference 16), p. 419.

27. See ILO, p. 79; Goody, *op.cit.* (note 20), pp. 9–10, with reference to the Lowiili of Ghana; H. Reginald Jarrett, "The Strange Farmers of the Gambia," *Geographical Review*, 39: 649–657, October 1959; Prothero, *op.cit.* (Reference 19), with reference to Nigeria; Jean Rouch, "Migrations au Ghana (Gold Coast)," *Journal de la Société des Africanistes*, 26: 33–196, 1956, with reference to migrants from French West Africa.

28. See Saad El Din Fawzi, *The Labour Movement in the Sudan 1946-1955* (Lon-don: Oxford University Press, 1957), pp. 4–7; Isam Ahmad Hassoun, "Western Migration and Settlement in the Gezira," *Sudan Notes and Records*, 35: 60–112, June 1952.

29. ILO, p. 142.

30. With reference to the earlier situation, see R. L. Prain, "The Problem of Afri-can Advancement on the Copperbelt of Northern Rhodesia," *African Affairs*, 53: 91–103, April 1954. With reference to more recent developments, see H. K. Hochs-child, "Labor Relations in Northern Rhodesia," *Annals of the American Academy of Political and Social Science*, 306: 43–49, July 1956; H. F. Oppenheimer, "Industrial Relations in a Multi-Racial Society," *African Affairs*, 55: 313–319, October 1956. Obviously, precise situations become quickly outdated, which little affects under-lying principles.

31. R. L. Prain, "The Stabilisation of Labour in the Rhodesian Copper Belt," *African Affairs*, 55: 305–312, October 1956.

32. ILO, p. 255.

33. See, for example, Godfrey Wilson, *An Essay in the Economics of Detribalisa-tion in Northern Rhodesia*, Rhodes-Livingstone Papers Nos. 5 and 6 (Lusaka: Rhodes-Livingstone Institute, 1940 and 1941); A. Daucy and P. Feldheim, "Some Effects of Industrialization in Two Districts of Equatoria Province," *in* International African Institute, *Social Implications of Industrialization and Urbanization in Africa South of the Sahara* (Paris: UNESCO, 1956), pp. 670–692; J. C. Mitchell, "Urbaniza-tion, Detribalization and Stabilization in Southern Africa: A Problem of Definition and Measurement," *ibid.*, pp. 693–711.

34. Mitchell, see Reference 33.

35. See Georges Balandier, "Problèmes du Développement Economique et Social de l'Afrique Noire," *Recherches et Debats du Centre Catholique des Intellectuels Francais*, 24: 117–125, September 1958; Jean L. Comhaire, "Economic Change and the Extended Family," *Annals of the American Academy of Political and Social Science*, 305: 45–52, May 1956; S. H. Frankel, "Economic and Social Evolution in Africa," *Times Survey of the British Colonies*, December 1950, pp. 12–13; Melville J.

Herskovits, "African Economic Development in Cross-Cultural Perspective," *American Economic Review*, **46**: 452–461, May 1956; Margaret Read, *Native Standards of Living and African Culture Change*, International Institute of African Languages and Cultures, Memorandum XVI (London: Oxford University Press for the Institute, 1938).

36. See, for example, Walter Elkan and Lloyd A. Fallers, "The Mobility of Labor," in Wilbert E. Moore and Arnold S. Feldman, eds., *Labor Commitment and Social Change in Developing Areas* (New York: Social Science Research Council, 1960), Chapter 13.

37. See ILO, pp. 110–116; Saad El Din Fawzi, "Labour Force of Sudan," in Philosophical Society of Sudan, *The Population of Sudan* (Khartoum: Philosophical Society of Sudan, 1958), pp. 40–47; United Nations, Department of Economic Affairs, *Enlargement of the Exchange Economy in Tropical Africa*, Supplement to the World Economic Report, 1952–53, (New York: United Nations, 1954).

38. ILO, p. 111.

39. United Nations, work cited in Reference 37; Stephens, work cited in Reference 19; Pierre Naville, "Données Statistiques sur la Structure de la Main-d'oeuvre Salariée et de l'Industrie en Afrique Noire," *Présence Africaine*, **13**: 279–314, 1952.

40. ILO, pp. 666–667.

41. *Ibid.*

42. *Ibid.* See also Georges Balandier, "Le Développement Industriel et la Proletarisation en Afrique Noire," *Afrique et Asie*, **20**: 45–53, 1952; A. Hauser, "Quelques Relations des Travailleurs de l'Industrie a Leur Travail en A.O.F. (Sénégal, Soudan, Guenée), *Bulletin de l'Institut Francais d'Afrique Noire*, **Ser. B.** 17: 129–141, January–April 1955; Nelly Xydias, "Labour: Conditions, Aptitudes, Training," in International African Institute, work cited in References 33, 275–367.

43. Fawzi, "Labour Force . . . ," see Reference 37.

44. See, for example, Walter Elkan, *An African Labour Force*, East African Studies, No. 7. (Kampala: East African Institute of Social Research, 1956); Elkan, "The Employment of Women in Uganda," *Inter-African Labour Bulletin*, **4**: 8–23, July 1957; Suzanne Comhaire-Sylvain, "Le Travail des Femmes à Lagos, Nigeria," *Zaire*, **5**: 169–178, 475–502, Feb.–May 1951.

45. J. Clyde Mitchell and A. L. Epstein, "Occupational Prestige and Social Status Among Urban Africans in Northern Rhodesia," *Africa*, XXIX, January 1959, pp. 22–40; Nelly Xydias, "Prestige of Occupations," in International African Institute, work cited in Reference 33, pp. 458–469. The paper by Mitchell and Epstein contains extensive references to other studies.

46. Xydias, see Reference 45, p. 468.

47. Xydias, "Labour: Conditions, Aptitudes, Training," see Reference 42, pp. 287–288.

48. See University of Natal, Department of Economics, *The African Factory Worker* (Cape Town: Geoffrey Cumberlege, Oxford University Press, 1950).

49. See, for example, Georges Balandier, "Le Main-d'oeuvre chez Firestone-Liberia, *Présence Africaine*, **13**: 347–354, 1952.

50. ILO, pp. 161–163; Cyril Sofer, "Working Groups in a Plural Society," *Industrial and Labor Relations Review*, **8**: 68–87, 1954; Elkan, *An African Labour Force*, see Reference 44, p. 26; P. Mercier, "An Experimental Investigation into Occupational and Social Categories in Dakar," in International African Institute, see Reference 33, pp. 510–535; Hauser, on the other hand, found familial and tribal affiliations giving way before common employee interests in enterprises in the Dakar

region. See A. Hauser, "Les Industries de Transformation de la Region Dakaroise," *Etudes Sénégalaises*, 5: 68–83, 1954.

51. ILO, pp. 67–68; Richards, *Economic Development* . . . , see Reference 20.

52. ILO, pp. 61–84; see Walter Elkan, "Introduction," in P. G. Powesland, *Economic Policy and Labour*, East African Studies No. 10 (Kampala: East African Institute of Social Research, 1957); Meyer Fortes, "The Ashanti Social Survey: A Preliminary Report," *Human Problems in British Central Africa*, 6: 1–36, 1948; L. P. Mair, *An African People in the Twentieth Century* (London: George Rutledge and Sons, 1934), pp. 122–128; Merram McCulloch, "The Social Impact of Economic Development on Rural Areas in East and Central Africa, *Information*, 14: 1–17, 1957.

53. Elkan, *An African Labor Force*, see Reference 44, pp. 49–59.

54. The first part of this position is supported by William H. Friedland. See his "African Trade Unions: From Bush to Copperbelt," *Information*, 22: 1–6, October 1959.

55. United Nations, *Report on the World Social Situation* (New York: 1957), pp. 80–81.

56. *Ibid.*

57. *Ibid.*, p. 67.

58. See J. E. Goldthorpe and M. McPherson, "Makerere College and Its Old Students," *Zaire*, 13: 349–363, 1958. A brief general synopsis of technical and higher education facilities is presented in ILO, pp. 34–39. See also A. Scohy, "Schools for the Children of Congo Workers," *Overseas Education*, 22: 62–66, January 1951.

59. See Elizabeth E. Hoyt, "Les Dépenses du Consommateur sous l'Influence du Changement Technique: Quelques Remarques de Politique Sociale," *Zaire*, 8: 115–122, February 1954; Hoyt, "The Needs of African Workers," *Human Organization*, 11: 27–29, Summer 1952.

60. See W. Hudson, "Observations on African Labour in East, Central and West Africa," *Journal of the National Institute of Personnel Research*, 6: 18–29, March 1955.

61. ILO, pp. 118–122.

62. *Ibid.*, pp. 147–150.

63. *Ibid.*, pp. 274–294.

64. ILO, pp. 144–145; see also United Kingdom Trade Commissioner, Board of Trade, *The African Native Market in the Federation of the Rhodesias and Nyasaland* (London: H. M. Stationery Office, 1954), pp. 1–4, 8; University of Natal, see Reference 48.

65. ILO, pp. 165–166, 212–215; C. A. Massa, "Notes sur les Conditions de Vie du Travailleur Africain en A.O.F., *Afrique et Asie*, 19: 37–45, 1952; William Top, "La Valeur du Travail des Salariés Africains," *Présence Africaine*, 13: 251–264, 1952.

66. ILO, p. 141. See also A. Serpas Tidjani, "L'Africain Face au Problème du Travail," *Présence Africaine*, 13: 108–115.

67. *Ibid.*; also P. DeBriey, "The Productivity of African Labour," *International Labour Review*, 62: 119–139, 1955.

68. David Apter, "Some Economic Factors in the Political Development of the Gold Coast," *Journal of Economic History*, 14: 409–427, October 1954.

69. ILO, p. 160.

70. For a discussion and summary of labor legislation, see *ibid.*, pp. 259–273, 322–441, 464–466, 521–522.

71. *Ibid.*, p. 521.

10

BACKGROUNDS OF SOCIAL CHANGE
IN LATIN AMERICA

The rediscovery of Latin American societies as a significant area for study by social scientists no doubt owes much to the practical concerns of foreign policy in the United States. The enduring shock of the nearby Castro Revolution in Cuba and the major impetus to technical assistance provided by the Alianza para Progreso combine to command the attention of the general public and that of students of Latin American culture and social organization. Yet the source of interest in any field of inquiry presumably has no bearing on the validity of the results yielded. Rather than adopting an attitude of protecting their esoteric specialty, scholars long interested in Latin American studies should perhaps welcome the signs of wider participation and the appearance of wider audiences for these studies.

My purpose here is to take a very broad view of social change in Latin America and to make generalizations that will require more detailed, specialized, and localized information before precise predictions can be made and knowledge can be used to shape a program of social policy. Indeed, the organization of my comments underscores the emphasis on backgrounds because my discussion has two introductions, not much middle, and a very short end.

First Introduction: A Bit of Theory

The social scientist's aim is to order and predict the phenomena of change in the rapid transformation of the type of societies encountered in Latin America. It is now commonplace to lament the absence of a

SOURCE. From *Industrial Relations and Social Change in Latin America*, William H. Form and Albert A. Blum, eds. Published by the University of Florida Press, 1965. Used by permission of the publisher and editors.

theory of social change. Yet this pessimism is scarcely justified if the demand for theory is made a bit less global than is usually implied.[1] Among the various approaches and propositions relating to social change, those focusing on societies undergoing modernization are perhaps superior to others, owing to the widespread interest in economic development and its social concomitants. Yet even in this more limited sphere it is necessary to clear away a pair of common conceptual fallacies before social theory can be utilized effectively.

Two Fallacies

Students of modernization rely on some assumptions and conceptual models that cannot survive even the test of the crude facts of social experience. One such assumption may be called the sociologistic fallacy, a term that perhaps exhibits my parochialism as a sociologist, for the fallacy is shared by practitioners in several other disciplines. In brief, and subject to further clarification later on, the sociologistic fallacy assumes that history began yesterday, if not this morning, at least as far as modernization is concerned. A second error, the functional equilibrium fallacy, views societies as normally existing in a steady state of balanced and interdependent actions and forces, exceptionally and temporarily disrupted by the intrusive influence of economic and related changes.

The works of students of economic development usually imply, if they do not explicitly state, that the leading element of modernization is economic change and that such change impinges directly on nonwestern societies which are typically changeless. Sociologists have been in close enough touch with anthropologists not to believe that all traditional societies are alike. Yet the perceived differences among societies have been, if anything, understated. Moreover, they have not generally paid much attention to the historic paths to the present, or, more specifically, to the ways these societies have been changing over considerable periods of time prior to modernization.

Fortunately, there are some exceptions to this fallacy of ignoring the past. De Vries,[2] for example, recounts the influences of political colonialism, economic exploitation, and missionary efforts in breaking the web of traditional relations. Blanksten,[3] attending primarily to political modernization and with special attention to Latin America, exhibits a commendable sense of history in tracing out contemporary difficulties.

The functional equilibrium fallacy is closely related to the neglect of history, for it too minimizes attention to long-term and continuous change. The perfectly legitimate detailed study of interdependent systems leads many social scientists to concentrate solely on cross-sectional or atemporal relationships. There is nothing wrong with this kind of scholarly approach. The mischief arises from an inadequate modification of the conceptual model of an interdependent system for use in the study of large-scale societal change.

What has happened, in effect, is that a three-stage model has been widely, though usually implicitly, used to characterize developing societies.[4] In keeping with the sociologistic fallacy, the preindustrial stage is seen as static. Industrialization (or other forms of modernization) is seen as providing a dynamic "transitional" stage, during which other elements of the social system must adjust or adapt to a major alteration of a basic component of the society. The consequences are usually depicted as a substantial homogeneity among "developed" societies, that is, they are becoming alike. And—though this is never made explicit, because to do so would immediately reveal the fallacy—societies on the far side of the industrial revolution are once more seen as in a steady state.

It is ridiculously easy and patently unfair to poke fun at these theoretical models. Despite their crudeness, they have produced many empirically tested "relational" propositions of great generality. But these are not enough. What is clearly needed is a conception of social systems that focuses on their changeful qualities and intrinsic strains while not sacrificing the useful and valid view that social behavior indeed does display interdependence, the essential characteristic of social systems.

Some Useful Theories

Although this introductory discussion of the kinds of theoretical baggage we need has postponed our Latin American visit, we may now make a positive selection of useful equipment. What follows can scarcely avoid resembling a shopping or packing list, as neither time nor the purpose at hand warrants extensive discussion.

The first and most general point to be noted is that social change is a universal feature of human societies, although the rate and breadth of change do vary through time and space. One major factor in this variation is the frequency and extensity of contact between societies. The assumption that traditional societies are static remains a fallacy, but the error is least where effective isolation has prevailed for considerable periods.

Change in the modern era is, however, characterized by two distinctive features: (1) Its magnitude has increased enormously. It is certainly more rapid in more places and more constantly than ever before. (2) By any crude measurement, most contemporary social change is either deliberate or is the secondary consequence of deliberate change.

Industrialization (or other forms of economic development) everywhere produces some characteristic changes in other aspects of social systems. Moreover, there are some social patterns that cannot survive economic modernization. Thus, to a certain degree, the position of functional determinism, which asserts that industrial development must everywhere produce societies which are very similar because industrialism is related to other parts of society in fixed ways, is partially exonerated. Yet, there are several major reasons for doubting that successful industrialization will everywhere produce societies that are functionally alike.[5] These reasons may be reduced to three: (1) Some features of the past are always relevant to the present, and the historical heritage persists in some form even in postrevolutionary regimes. (A specific application of this point to Latin America will be made in the following section.) (2) General world history also bears on the differentiation of societies. Countries now embarking on a course of rapid modernization need not repeat all of the contemporary content of advanced societies, and most conspicuously need not replicate either the rate or sequence of changes as they developed historically. (3) Arising from both the particular historical legacies and from what we may call the trajectory of modernization, the characteristic tensions are likely to differ from one society (or closely related group of countries) to another, and the way those tensions are managed is also likely to be different. Managing tensions is the state's special social responsibility. Without elaborating this argument further, this set of considerations serves to explain the grossly evident fact that industrialism is consistent with a wide variety of political regimes.

Second Introduction: The Heritage of Conquest[6]

The need for disposing the sociologistic fallacy is immediately apparent as our attention turns to social change in Latin America. Though the countries south of the Rio Grande (or the Rio Bravo as it is called by those who look north) qualify in varying degrees as traditional and underdeveloped, we must remember that they have been under western influence for four centuries or more. In some areas that influence has been so overwhelming that virtually no indigenous population has survived. In others, the resulting social order is based on both European and native customs, as well as on a mixture of the two.

Colonialism and its Aftermath

When Spain and Portugal conquered and colonized Latin America, they were behind northern Europe in the emergence from feudalism. For this reason many feudal-like patterns were transplanted and adapted in the New World. The Iberian governments were attentive both to the economic aspirations of their colonizers in exploiting the resources of the conquered territories and to the solicitude for native welfare voiced by at least some elements of the Roman Catholic clergy. Grants of land generally included the right to use native labor, whose spiritual and, to a degree, material welfare was entrusted to the new landlords. These grants established what might be loosely identified as a paternalistic system of labor. The clergy protested against outright enslavement of the Indians, although they did not voice similar objections to the importation of African slaves in the Caribbean, tropical Central America, and Brazil.

The colonial elites were composed essentially of three groups: the landlords, the clergy, and the military and civilian governors. More than most plural elites, these were all family-based and strongly interlocking—a characteristic of social stratification evident in Spain to this day.

Political independence early in the nineteenth century removed the power of Spain and Portugal and thus also reduced the ascendancy of immigrant rulers and other Iberian-born settlers—the *peninsulares*. Although political independence increased the authority of the descendants of colonists (the *criollos*), it did little to alter the shape of the social structure.

The nineteenth century saw considerable economic growth in the resources-rich "ABC countries" (Argentina, Brazil, and Chile), but in all of Latin America there prevailed a politically flavored economic colonialism and a kind of endemic and chronic political instability. The frequent revolutions were more commonly *coups d'état* than genuine alterations of the basic institutional order and often affected rural populations very little. This was, of course, not the situation with the genuine revolutions in Mexico, where actual civil war took place and where rural populations benefited from changed institutions. Bolivia, too, had such a revolution.

Why did Latin America on the whole stagnate throughout the last century, and, with notable exceptions, why does it continue to do so today? A precise set of historical generalizations, specifying the relevant conditions, is not feasible. We are thus thrown back on a multiple-causation explanation, which however inadequate is preferable to no explanation at all.

Throughout South America income distribution is highly uneven. Poverty and illiteracy are widespread. To a lesser degree, this is also true of Mexico, which has had its social revolution. Even in Mexico, the growth of a middle income group has been slow until recently. It is not far advanced in the ABC countries, and scarcely evident in the remaining Latin American countries. Remnants of feudal patterns persist in most rural areas, and full-fledged peonage (debt servitude), although nominally outlawed, flourishes in some of the Andean countries.

Commerce was never very widely accepted in Hispanic culture, and in Latin America it most often remains in the hands of ethnic minorities. The term *Turcos* (Turks) for the ubiquitous Levantines is ethnically erroneous, but as a term of opprobrium it sets the trader apart from social acceptability. Europeans and North Americans generally move in more elevated commercial and financial circles, and they do encounter some Latin counterparts, but the shortage of an indigenous merchant class is ever present.

The political instability noted above inhibits commercial growth to some degree. It is extremely inimical to industrial investment for long-term returns. Fixed capital installations are especially vulnerable to civil disorder or confiscation, but such hazards are perhaps not as severe as the less obvious ones of currency instability, unreliability of contractual agreements, and essentially whimsical changes of the rules of the entrepreneurial game.

Such economic modernization as has taken place often fits the model of the colonial economy. Exploitation of mineral and agricultural resources has yielded profits for investors. However, these profits have either gone back to the countries which put up the capital, been spent by local entrepreneurs, or been used to acquire additional land in order for owners to qualify for the time-honored privileges and prestige of the landed gentry. Today, some Latin American countries are clearly poorer in natural resources and perhaps in per capita income than they were a century ago.

Untapped and underutilized resources remain in Latin America, and the rich cultural heritage of the Old World and the New is by no means purely and entirely reactionary. Still it remains true that contemporary Latin America abounds with anachronisms and that potentials for improvement in the material conditions of life remain unfulfilled.

Some Cautions

Generalizations about Latin America often fall into the error earlier discussed, of assuming that preindustrial societies are alike. They clearly are not alike in many ways, and their differences are important both for precise prediction of future trends and for implementing appropriate social policies.

The Hispanic background provides a unifying factor; but geography, resources, and especially the historic heritage of Indian culture (in Middle American and the Andean countries) and Negro slavery (in the sugar islands and Brazil) make for very great differences. These differences falsify easy generalizations. It is also true that our information about social structure and change in Latin America is woefully inadequate. In the short sections that follow some educated guesses may provide a partial substitute for missing facts.

Management and Labor

Most of the countries of Latin America are at least nominally pluralistic in political structure, and thus permit a moderate to extensive degree of private enterprise in the production and distribution of goods and services. It is thus perfectly appropriate to examine the roles of management and labor in the present and future transformation of the institutional structures of those countries. Yet, still another caution is in order, for it is virtually inevitable that economic modernization will take on a political urgency that will reduce the pervasiveness of decentralized and market-oriented decisions characteristic in the classical forms of a liberal economy. One can expect that capital flow and international trade will come under governmental surveillance, and that there will be attempts to supervise prices and wages. Here and there state-owned enterprises may appear. Managers and workers there will be, and these productive segments of the population may have varying degrees of independence from political control and manipulation. But we should not expect that independence to be very complete.

Management

In most of Latin America the managers of industrial and commercial enterprises are still disproportionately composed of foreigners or persons of fairly recent Latin American settlement. Surprisingly, Spaniards figure prominently among these foreign managers, especially in textile production and particularly in Mexico and Peru. English enterprises were at earlier times important in Mexico (notably in railroad construction) and in Argentina (often in meat packing). They remain an important commercial element in Peru.

German migrants have had a major influence in Chile. Germans and Japanese have been very influential in São Paulo, which is the most rapidly developing area of Brazil. Buenos Aires in Argentina is virtually an Italian colony. And, of course, the Yankees, or *gringos,* are to be found everywhere. Substantial numbers of indigenous entrepreneurs in commerce and industry are to be found in the ABC countries and in Mexico, and a few elsewhere.

What can one say negatively of Latin American managers with respect to the problems of economic growth? The charges against them have some basis in fact and may as well be presented.

First, it is commonly noted that, whether in commerce or industry, the Latin American enterpriser emphasizes high unit profits—the "quick buck"—at the possible expense of higher volume with lower and more continuous, though slower, returns. Although subtle cultural or motivational elements may be involved here, one should not leap to those explanations without giving due credit to the foreshortened time horizons that political instability prompts. In addition, profits are more likely to be spent on luxuries or on land that yields low or negative returns, rather than in industrial reinvestments. Although cultural factors are difficult to deny, the uncertainty of the business environment must be reemphasized.

Second, the narrow and family-based circle of the elite inevitably influences the choice of entrepreneurial personnel and the relations among firms. The degree of nepotism and favoritism, when compared to advanced industrial societies, is scarcely surprising; nor is it automatically mischievous if indeed the social system limits education and other qualifications to a small segment of the population. The broadening opportunities for education will make such policies increasingly irrational, and in one way or another they are likely to disappear. That is, if the basis of recruitment is not broadened as a matter of sound business practice, the result will certainly be enforced by revolutionary regimes.

Third, and closely related to prevailing nepotism and the importance of personal contacts in personnel placement, is the culture of corruption. The establishment of an apolitical civil service is very incomplete in Latin American countries, and the laws are complex and often repressive as viewed by the businessman. Licenses, permission to operate in contravention of legal restrictions, as well as the more conventional quest for public contracts, all lead to a widespread payment of bribes. The *mordida*—the bite—is an expressive local term for the surreptitious support of public functionaries. This condition is again not peculiar to Latin America, or indeed to underdeveloped countries. The matter is one of degree, but the degree of corruption is sufficiently advanced that a highly rational and moral administration, public or private, is rare.

Finally, Latin American management stands sharply apart from the rank and file of workers.[7] The complex gradations of skill and authority, the highly-paid manual workers and the lower-paid clerical workers, are not nearly so common as in advanced industrial countries. This radical polarization of the work force is, again, not peculiar to Latin America. Rather it is typical of early industrialization everywhere, confirming in space the Marxian diagnosis which was so grievously wrong as a prognosis in the continuing course of industrialization. Yet it remains true that between the managers and the managed "there is a great gulf fixed," though certainly not fixed for all time.

Against this catalogue of disabilities, what is there to be said that is optimistic or favorable about the role of Latin American managers in economic development? In all honesty, not a great deal that is applicable to the present and immediate future can be said. Yet clearly some managers, whether educated at home or abroad, have a vision of the future and seek to break with the feudal past. The influence of governmental planners is, perforce, gaining, and some of them are strongly influenced by the able economists of the Economic Commission for Latin America (ECLA, or CEPAL in its Spanish version). If Latin American countries continue to provide any room for private enterprise, it should be expected that it will be in the context of a mixed economy. The rationalization of managerial selection and practices may not be decisive in determining the basic features of economic management, but continued ineptitude will certainly make private enterprise increasingly unlikely.

Labor

At first glance the older debates about labor availability for modern economic activity appear to have been tedious and tendentious. There is no numerical shortage of available workers in any developing country, if we set aside considerations of quality. Stationary or actually deteriorating conditions of life in rural areas, set against a pervasive quest for material improvement, have produced the overwhelmingly visible signs of surplus labor in the extremely rapid urbanization characteristic of Latin American cities. Explosive population growth in city and countryside alike—exceeding 3% a year in many countries—further expands the potential labor force. Despite this crude evidence of labor availability, both technical and motivational impediments stand in the way of a full-fledged and fully committed industrial labor force.[8]

Aspiration levels of workers are often very low. Simple regular manual employment is still beyond the reach of many. The universal public education provided everywhere by national laws is far short of attainment even where the greatest resources have been devoted to the goal, and in some countries it is a sham. Thus, acceptance of a kind of class position by workers and would-be workers is common.

Just as education is nominally universal, so is political democracy, but voting privileges are often dependent on the very education that the state has not provided. The effective denial of political participation to substantial segments of the population produces sporadic political disorders. The paradox observed elsewhere is confirmed in Latin America: abject poverty does not produce the leadership of protest. This comes from those who have fared relatively well, and particularly from union leaders and even from salaried employees in government and private enterprise.[9] The labor movements in Latin America appear to have a high revolutionary potential and perhaps a low potential for orderly reconstruction of archaic institutions. Unions, which with few exceptions are predominantly ideologically oriented, may in effect become the spokesmen for groups much broader than their own membership.[10]

One mitigating factor in the basic polarization of management and labor must be regarded as transitory, if not anachronistic. The paternalism of feudal patterns was after all not entirely harsh and exploitative. The industrial recruit may in fact seek the protection of a patron in the form of his employer or administrative superior, and become in a sense overcommitted to a particular employer. Rational impersonality in employment relations is more likely to prevail among managers than among workers. At least until higher skill levels are developed among workers and the bargaining power of labor shortage is added to the bargaining power of union representation, workers may be pathetically grateful for any employment.

On the other hand, the universal confidence in education as an avenue of personal and social improvement represents a possible route to orderly change both in individual life chances and in the transformation of the social order itself.

Social revolution of some form or degree is extremely likely in virtually every Latin American country except possibly Mexico, which experienced a genuine revolution over four decades ago. What will emerge in the postrevolutionary era is impossible to predict in detail, as science does not find itself comfortable with unique events. One can, however, be confident of certain structural changes.

There is likely to appear a great "Puritanism" in social recruitment and standards of performance. In particular, technical competence is likely to be emphasized, perhaps intermixed with political (rather than, say, familial) acceptability. Both public and private affairs are likely to be characterized by a strongly technological orientation, including a very pronounced emphasis on education as a channel of mobility. The social order is likely to undergo a gradual, but by no means rapid, reduction of the radical disparity between manager and the managed, innovators and reluctant followers, and the rich and the poor.

The outcome of modernization will certainly not be stable social orders in static equilibrium. Such stability cannot be predicted anywhere, and a society that embarks on a program of modernization has no fixed destination. The foregrounds of social change in Latin America are at least as complex as the backgrounds.

References

1. See Wilbert E. Moore, "A Reconsideration of Theories of Social Change," *American Sociological Review*, 25: 810–15, 1960. For a more extended discussion see Moore, *Social Change* (Englewood Cliffs, New Jersey: Prentice-Hall, 1963), especially Chapter 5, "Modernization."

2. Egbert de Vries, *Man in Rapid Social Change* (Garden City, N.Y.: Doubleday, 1961).

3. George I. Blanksten, "Transference of Social and Political Loyalties," Bert F. Hoselitz and Wilbert E. Moore, eds., *Industrialization and Society* (Paris and The Hague: UNESCO and Mouton, 1963), Chapter 9.

4. See Arnold S. Feldman and Wilbert E. Moore, "Industrialization and Industrialism: Convergence and Differentiation," *Transactions of the Fifth World Congress of Sociology*, Volume II (September, 1962), 151–69.

5. *Ibid.*

6. The title is borrowed from Sol Tax et al., *The Heritage of Conquest* (Glencoe, Illinois: Free Press, 1952).

7. See, for example, Charles A. Myers, "Management in Chile," Frederick Harbison and Charles A. Myers, *Management in the Industrial World* (New York: McGraw-Hill, 1959), Chapter 9.

8. See Wilbert E. Moore and Arnold S. Feldman, eds., *Labor Commitment and Social Change in Developing Areas* (New York: Social Science Research Council, 1960), particularly Chapters 1–4 by the editors.

9. See Clark Kerr et al., *Industrialism and Industrial Man* (Cambridge: Harvard University Press, 1960), especially Chapter 8, "The Workers: Impact and Response."

10. See George I. Blanksten, "The Politics of Latin America," Gabriel A. Almond and James S. Coleman, eds., *The Politics of the Developing Areas* (Princeton, New Jersey: Princeton University Press, 1960), p. 512.

PART **III**

SOCIAL STRUCTURE
AND THE INDIVIDUAL

11
SOCIAL STRUCTURE AND BEHAVIOR

The ordering of individual human lives in terms of a matrix of social expectations comprises part, or perhaps all, of the distinctively human qualities of behavior. Man is an inevitably social animal, and one whose social behavior is scarcely guided by instinct. He learns, well or poorly, social behavior of one sort or another. He invents values for himself and his collectivities, rules for his conduct, knowledge to aid him in predicting and controlling his environment, gods to reward and punish him, and other ingenious elements of the human condition. This wondrously inventive activity is itself, of course, behavior. Once its products are established in the human consciousness, they become in turn guides to further behavior.

There are several ways of making the relation between social structure and behavior no problem, as we shall note more fully later. Social structure, may, for example, be taken simply as behavior writ large or generalized, behavior itself being explained in some other way. Or, behavior may simply be regarded as the concrete manifestation of structural imperatives, those imperatives being explained in some other way.

The doctrine of equivalence will be rejected in this discussion, for reasons aside from the circumstance that to adopt either mode of arriving at equivalence would make extensive discussion unconscionable. No, our reasons are empirical and therefore theoretical: not only may the abstractions *social structure* and *behavior* be defined differently for

SOURCE. Adapted from "Social Structure and Behavior," in Gardner Lindzey and Elliot Aronson, eds., *Handbook of Social Psychology*, 2nd ed. (Reading, Massauchusetts: Addison-Wesley Publishing Co., Inc., in press); by permission of the editors and publishers.
I wish to acknowledge the extensive bibliographical assistance of Mr. Lawrence Hlad, who tried valiantly to keep me honest with respect to the research literature. I am also indebted to Dr. Orville G. Brim, Jr., for constructive criticism of the initial draft of this chapter.

analytical purposes, but also both show ranges of independent variability in their concrete manifestations. In examining the relations between structure and behavior we shall give scant attention to the psychodynamic processes that, through the concept of *personality,* link the acting individual to the social environment. By primary emphasis on the notion of structure as a framework for behavior we shall be taking a view of the relations between sociology and psychology rather different from that of Inkeles,[1] who highlights the concept of *normal personality* as the needful psychological input for social processes.

Our first task will be to explore the several alternative meanings of "social structure." We shall then treat the alternative views of behavior as an independent and dependent variable with respect to structure. We shall conclude with an examination of the behavioral correlates of various structural categories, with due regard for variability and deviance as manifestations, perhaps, of original sin, but certainly as confirming the problem of nonequivalence that provides the essential excuse for this discussion.

Social Structure: Alternative Minimum Definitions

It is perhaps an act of self-reassuring bravery on the part of social scientists to use so freely the concept of *social structure,* for it implies that there is something solid, indeed stable, out there to observe. The term *structure* invites architectural images, of edifices occupied or awaiting inhabitants. Yet the term is widely used in all analytic sciences as well as in some, such as geology, that are mainly taxonomic or descriptive. Like biology, the social sciences mainly straddle this distinction between the analytic and the descriptive, with consequent differences in the meaning of structure.

For a term that figures so prominently in the works of sociological theorists, social structure remains remarkably variable in its specifications, and some theorists are remarkably casual in their definitions and explications. Merton, for example, is a leading theorist whose concerns are mainly structural as compared, say, with those who emphasize motivational elements. Yet, in a long book, *Social Theory and Social Structure,*[2] one must search assiduously for a definition of social structure. This is the more remarkable as the term also figures in the titles of four chapters.[3] In one of them, the longest in the book, "Continuities in the Theory of Reference Groups and Social Structure" (Chapter IX), one does encounter, belatedly, a scanty definition of social structure, to which we shall turn presently. Earlier in this chapter some twenty pages are devoted to "clarifying the concept of reference group," but, with the exception of the few lines we are about to introduce, no pages to clarifying the concept of social structure.

Merton's particular definition is preceded by a discussion of three concepts: (1) role-sets, meaning the actions and relationships that flow from a social status; (2) status-sets, meaning the probable congruence of various positions occupied by an individual; (3) status-sequences, meaning the probable succession of positions occupied by an individual through time.[4] He then adds, "The patterned arrangements of role-sets, status-sets and status-sequences can be held to comprise the social structure."[5]

Now the initial difficulty with this particular formulation is that it necessarily starts with the unit *status,* which is defined as "a position in a social system," but we are not otherwise told what a social system is, nor how it is related to a social structure. Merton does recognize that he is in trouble, for he goes on to note, in a relatively rare fit of social anthropomorphism, that ". . . operating social structures must somehow manage to organize these sets and sequences of statuses and roles so that an appreciable degree of social order obtains. . . ."[6] Elsewhere, Merton provides some hints as to how this comes about. In his widely cited discussion of "Social Structure and Anomie"[7] social structure appears to comprise *cultural goals* (the more acceptable term is *values*) and *institutional norms* (which in accepted usage is a redundant phrase). It is the various forms of departure from these that constitute his types of *anomie.* In the following chapter on "Continuities in the Theory of Social Structure and Anomie" Merton is more explicit but no more helpful. He distinguishes cultural structure—". . . that organized set of normative values governing behavior which is common to members of a designated society or group"—and *social structure*—" . . . that organized set of social relationships in which members of the society or group are variously implicated."[8] The phrase "normative values" apparently comprises both the values and norms of the previous discussion, and social structure, though somehow "organized," is bereft of these elements. In Merton's discussion of the relation of science to "social structure"[9] values and norms are compressed into the term *ethos,* which seems to be the structure. We are thus left with some uncertainty as to what Merton or his readers are to understand by the term.

By contrast, Levy is very explicit in his use of the term *structure.* Though his most general definition of structure as a "pattern . . . of action or operation"[10] has a rather limited usefulness, as we shall note later, he goes on to distinguish "analytic structures" and "concrete structures."[11] By the former term he refers to *aspects* of the operation of a society (for example, role allocation, allocation of goods and services, allocation of power and responsibility); by the latter term he refers to *membership units* (or rather, the patterns that define the character of such units). Levy also makes other distinctions, such as the generality or partiality of a structure, its manifest or latent quality, and so on. By devoting most of his attention to the analytic structures of society, he asks how various functions get performed, which leads him to attend to the variety of concrete structures that comprise the principal *behavioral* basis for social action and interaction.

For Parsons, the term *social structure* seems most often to be used as equivalent to *social system,* which at the minimum comprises status-role units, integrated in terms of normative complexes and value-orientations.[12] But the term is no easier to tease out in Parsons' work than it is in Merton's. We note, at one point in Parsons' most comprehensive work in sociological theory, the following, passing comment: ". . . the integration of stable systems of social interaction, that is, of social structure . . . ,"[13] which can be made to mean a lot or very little. At another point there is a short discussion of ". . . differentiated social roles . . . , how they are distributed in the social system and how integrated with each other . . . This is what we mean by the social structure in the narrower sense of the term."[14] It has been given no explicit, wider sense, but values, normative complexes (which Parsons sometimes confuses with values) and actors, defined as status-role units, can be derived from the general tenor of the discussion. It must be said in fairness to Parsons that he understands the difference between analytic and concrete structures (like Levy, he prefers the former, and in both cases this is occasionally unfortunate), and, to a degree not true of our other witnesses, he seeks to integrate behavioral, including motivational, variables into his conception of the operation of the social systems.

Or let us take an even more extreme example. In *Human Behavior* by Berelson and Steiner,[15] which professes to be an "Inventory of Scientific Findings," there is no index reference—or, by inspection, textual usage—of the terms "structure" or "social structure." Now this either means that there are no scientific propositions about social structure—a position I am willing to affirm is patently false—or the authors do not like the term—and I cannot see inside their minds—or they have mainly neglected the structural characteristics of human behavior—a position I am willing to affirm is patently true. Their treatment of the individual characteristics of behavior in some social settings does indeed condone the term of "inventory," but their handling of strictly sociological concepts and variables is very uneven.

The bitterness that creeps into these comments on the use of the term "social structure" is partly a reflection of a sociologist's *mea culpa*. But it is also a plea for explicitness, and sweet reason in the use of a term and its explanatory possibilities, forthrightly, communicatively, and with a decent sense for the fine line between meaningless, analytical abstraction and a surfeit of poorly conceptualized descriptive details.

We shall be tolerantly eclectic and use the term in several distinct senses, for each poses different questions and problems for the relation between structure and behavior. We shall be able to distinguish five uses of the term *social structure:* (1) patterns of action, (2) social systems, (3) social differentiation, (4) statistical, distributive categories, and (5) orderly sequence.

Structure as Patterns of Action

Perhaps the most widely applicable definition of social structure and certainly the barest, is that of repeated patterns of action. "The term *structure* as used here means a pattern, i.e., an observable uniformity, of action or operation."[16] By this minimal definition one may properly speak of a subatomic, atomic, molecular, or cellular structure, if these are taken to signify interaction and not mere form, and indeed of a structure of ocean waves, pulsations of stellar light, sexual behavior of bees, or "bopping" between juvenile gangs. It is not proper by this definition however, if it is taken strictly, to speak of the structure of rock strata, of the grammar of an extinct language, or indeed of one of the manmade edifices of our original metaphor. Somewhat regularized (at least not unique) work exchanges among men on the assembly line in an automobile factory would thus constitute a structure, as would any similarly repeated meeting for lunch or for telling dirty stories around the drinking fountain. The formal administrative organization within which such patterned behavior displays itself would not constitute a structure by this usage, or, rather, would constitute a very extensive complex of such patterns, including those bound by formal rules of expectations as well as those that appear to be spontaneous.

Each of our other uses of the term social structure will be found to contain or subsume, this most elementary meaning of the term. It has the advantage of neutrality, of nonspecificity. It has the correlative analytic advantage of avoiding reification of groups and organizations by casting its net more broadly. The daily variations of traffic flows in the central business districts of cities thus turn out to be social structures as surely as do the actions of parishioners participating in an elaborate religious ritual.

The analytic neutrality of this use of the term social structure captures and in a sense equates the mate-selection practices of a nonliterate tribe, male primogeniture as a mode of selecting successors to kings, the propensity of American college students to riot in the spring, and the formally announced hours for opening and closing libraries.

As would necessarily be true of an analytic concept so devoid of particular content as to be applicable in a seemingly endless variety of particular contexts, this use of the term social structure has the deficiencies of its virtues. One question that is left entirely open is the explanation for, that is the etiology of, such patterned action. Is the observed uniformity to be explained in terms of common motivational propensities intrinsic to the actors? If so, are these instinctual or the product of a common learning? Can the patterns be interpreted in such nonhuman terms as *symbiosis,* an interdependence of species and their behaviors in a common ecological setting? Or are they explainable only in terms of other elements of social behavior, not yet specified, such as values, norms, role assignments, cognitive expectations, and rewards and penalties?

Now take a different set of problems. What do we mean by patterns or uniformities? If we take the epistemological position that all statements of relationship, in all scientific systems, are probability statements, then "uniformities" may not be invariant, and will still be significant. (This epistemological position is a very strategic one for social scientists to adopt. Whether because of the complexity of intersecting variables, the correlative difficulty of experimental controls, or the intrinsic randomness of the most elementary behavioral units, invariance in propositional form is rare.) Can we speak of a difference of ten percentage points in the labor-force participation rates of American women aged 35–39, as compared with their counterparts aged 45–49, as a uniformity? We shall return to problems of temporal patterns, which complicate matters. But even if we suppose the rates and their differences to be fairly durable, can either probability—both of which are far less than unity—be called a uniformity? Well, let us not get involved in semantic distinctions that may be trivial. What we seek to discount are the declared or implied claims to superiority of analytically bare concepts. Their utility is quickly exhausted.

The minimal utility of the view of social structure as patterns of action has a special poignancy in the present discussion. If that were all that could be meant by social structure, our mission would now be aborted, and indeed scarcely worth the effort to become pregnant. The definition of social structure in these terms is essentially behavioral, and thus inductive. Social structure *is* patterned behavior, and that leaves out only unpatterned behavior as a residual category. By suitable reference to conditions not themselves part of the definition of structure this approach permits generalizations about covariance: pattern A is predictably related to pattern B. It is even possible to state orderly sequences of patterns, such as Merton's reference to status-sequences, noted previously. But the mechanism of the relationship, to say nothing of it "explanation," is beyond the reach of the analyst, for these require reference to human actors, singly or in aggregates and probably reference to social values and norms or to their psychological counterparts as components of motivation. Without such additional "structural" elements, it is impossible to raise such questions as the relation of the individual to the group, or to distinguish normal from deviant patterns (save as a statistical distribution, which is not the same thing), or ideal and actual patterns.

The Social System Approach

The growing use of the term *system* in sociological discourse probably owes much to the influential theoretical work of Parsons.[17] In any event, it has served to highlight distinctly sociological levels of analysis of human behavior, by emphasizing the emergent properties of any order of phenomena which consists of elements *and their interaction*. In this general sense, social system is a concept no more restrictive or specific than social structure. However, there appears to be a considerable consensus that the term social system will comprise values and rules of conduct (both of which are sometimes regarded as *cultural* elements) as well as interacting individuals. "A social system requires that the units be persons—more properly *actors* or *role-players*—whose interaction is governed by rules or *norms*. Particular systems may be organized as groups, which then take on such additional characteristics as collective goals or *values*."[18]

The concept of social system can be made as elaborate as needed to suit analytical convenience or requirements. For example, the common values of a voluntary association may be few and simple. The "value system" of a large society may be very complex, and lacking in total consensus. Moreover, pluralism itself may be valued, which means that in some aspects of social life integration rests on tolerance rather than on substantive agreement. Similarly, any orderly interaction rests upon at least implicit rules of conduct. Yet when we view whole societies we can identify complex *systems* of rules relating to major social functions. These aggregations of related norms are conveniently called *institutions;* examples include marriage, property, and political authority. Like values, norms may be highly integrated (as a limiting case) or diversified and even inconsistent. Structural differentiation within a social system leads to questions of relations between structural units, whether or not these entail common or overlapping memberships. Where the individual has plural participation in a functionally differentiated system, concepts like role-sets and status-sets become highly relevant, not to mention role conflicts.

It is to be noted that the social-system approach to social structure is not defined in strictly behavioral terms. Acceptance and internalization of values and compliance with normative expectations (whether conscientiously or in response to current sanctions) are left open for determination and explanation. The actors have the attributes and actions demanded by the system as specified. If they uniformly have "no resemblance to real persons, living or dead," then the system is a mythical construct rather than an empirically-based model. Yet a complete matching is also not to be expected. Apart from the fact that no empirically-observed system is completely integrated, even in purely systemic terms, all rely on somewhat refractory human participants, whose biological variability interacts with variability in precise social experience to produce some measure of indeterminateness. The way and degree whereby the system determines behavior is subject to inspection, not made irrelevant by definition.

Structure as Social Differentiation

A few sociologists indulge in a use of the term social structure that is much more common among other social scientists: the uneven distribution of power and goods and services in a society; that is, social stratification. This is a curious usage. Of course, if social strata can be identified and ordered by clear criteria according to their relative status, the aggregate is in some sense a social structure. It resembles the geologists' or paleontologists' layering of strata, whence came the term. In no society does such ranking of segments of the population exhaust the significant ways that types and combinations of individuals are differentiated and subjected to prescriptions for their conduct. The extent to which the stratification is predictive of other forms of social organization is highly variable among societies, and the behavioral correlates of social position in this restrictive sense will occupy our attention rather extensively in a subsequent section.

If social stratification is defined, operationally, simply as the unequal rewards accorded to functionally differentiated positions,[19] then questions of the consistency of individuals' positions in various structures are appropriate, along with the extent that segments of the populations with approximately equal, generalized statuses can be said to constitute a *class* or other type of stratum.

It seems preferable, however, not to limit the term structure only to differentiated positions to which relative ranks can be assigned. Rather, the question of equality or varying degrees of inequality is a relevant attribute or dimension of *any* standardized role relationship. Social differentiation may be "lateral" as well as "vertical,"[20] and in either case an essential structural dimension is how complementarity or coordination is brought about among the specialized positional or behavioral units.

Structure as Statistical Categories

It has pleased social observers and agencies of the state to enumerate, catalogue, and classify various attributes and variable qualities of populations. The distribution of any characteristic, classified according to some useful criteria, may be said to constitute a "structure." We may thus properly refer to the age structure or age-sex structure of a population, its ethnic or linguistic structure, the occupational structure of the labor force, income structure, and so on.

In a sense, these structures are standardized ways for describing and indeed measuring social differentiation. Records repeated through time permit the measurement of trends in the absolute and relative magnitudes of the characteristics.

Since our concern is with social structure and behavior, we need to note some differences in the significance of statistical distributions of the sort we have been considering. Some of these categories may be viewed as orderly ways of using other structural approaches. Age, sex, nativity, and ethnicity are characteristics over which the individual has little or no control, but it is proper to ask what *ascriptive* relevance they have for social position and thus role allocation. Other categories represent summary measures of the operation of aggregated systems, such as nations or societies—for example, the distribution of population by place of residence (rural-urban, or size of community), educational attainment, income, or occupation. Still others represent summary measures of somehow-motivated actions: labor force participation, urban migration, consumer purchases, voting behavior, church membership.

The distinctions just noted are thin, and for many analytic purposes insignificant. The essential, methodological point is that for the last group of measures, the most convenient question is: "What accounts for . . . ?" For the first two groups, the most convenient question is, "What are the consequences of . . . ?" It is always permitted to transpose these questions, but it is not always easy. This is not to say that ascriptive categories, to say nothing of the outcomes of systemic operation, do not have social origins—they are not data in the sense of "givens" that must not be examined—but only to say that their relation to behavior is most readily seen in terms of consequences rather than antecedents.

Structure as Orderly Sequence

Structure commonly connotes rigidity, but this connotation is not intrinsic to the proper use of the concept. Social life abounds with predictable sequences as well as with coincidences and interconnections. Thus, for example, there is a temporal order of action and events.[21] Some of that temporal order is repetitively cyclical: days, weeks, months, seasons, years, and perhaps longer periods. The life cycle is clearly such a sequential order, which becomes social when rendered into terms of generations and their succession.[22] As earlier noted with reference to Merton's concept of "status-sequences,"[23] one may consider "normal" status transitions as a kind of *career pattern*.[24] Here we have a further choice of approach, intersecting previous distinctions. The career pattern may be identified on entirely inductive grounds, comparable to less intrinsically sequential *patterns of action*. Or, we may attend to idealized and normatively prescribed career patterns in a *social system*, and ask how the observed status sequences correspond to these normatively sanctioned expectations.

Still another example of sequential order is provided by Smelser's essentially stochastic approach to collective behavior.[25] For a number of distinct types of collective behavior he identifies the *sequence* of precipitating events. He thereby moves away from the usual approach of cross-sectional, multiple-factor analysis to one that offers promise of providing both necessary and sufficient conditions for specified outcomes. Since most types of so-called collective behavior run counter to the established and sanctioned norms of social systems, it is difficult to view them as social structures in the sense of systems. Thus Smelser's approach is essentially inductive, based on behavioral sequences. This is not a very damning criticism on ordinary scientific grounds, but we are left with no problems concerning the relation between these sequential structures and behavior.

Behavior: Independent and Dependent Variable

The conceptual exercise just completed was a necessary prelude to our central concerns with the individual and the aggregate, the behaving actor and the rather complex drama in which he plays his part.

Let us now be clear on an elementary point: individuals behave. They act, feel, think, react, believe, strive. They are born, mature, grow old, and die. It is important to state these simple verities, because sociologists and other social scientists are not always careful in their language. "The American Medical Association took a stand against any governmental support for medical research." General Electric announced a price increase in fractional horsepower motors." "France declared war against Liechtenstein, and was once more quickly defeated." "Harvard University granted honorary doctorates to five undergraduates on indefinite suspension for violation of the student honor code." "The Smith family regards itself as superior to its rather uncultured neighbors." Statements in this form, though not necessarily these statements, can be read in good newspapers and in otherwise good books on history and social science. For the most part, this is harmless ellipsis. Spokesmen for, representatives of, authorized officials or members of these organizations made known and otherwise acted upon the policies and practices indicated by the elliptical statements. Groups act through individuals, but it is equally true that individuals act on *behalf of groups,* or in conformity with other socially sanctioned expectations, such as those relevant to age, sex, occupational category, or educational attainment. Neglect of the first part of the preceding statement can lead to a kind of social anthropomorphism, or the "group mind fallacy."[26] But neglect of the second part of the statement can lead to a kind of atomistic view of human behavior that is equally fallacious. One position is as insane as the other.

Now this partial glimpse into the conceptual snares of dealing with individuals in collective situations has some further implications. If we attend to the nature of societies, or of lesser, organized social entities, it is clear that we are dealing with systems of social relationships. Those systems have a common feature of great consequence: they constitute an evaluative and normative order. Society is a moral phenomenon. Thus the operation and continuity of every social system in the exact sense depends upon a high (though not complete) degree of *moral conformity.* Put in proper, probabilistic terms: most people observe most of the social codes (or expectations) most of the time. Systems differ in their reliance on current sanctions rather than conscientious consent. A system exhibiting a very high degree of "complete conformity"—self-activated behavior by individuals who have internalized the appropriate values and norms—may still incorporate individuals who are responding to immediate rewards and penalties. But it is important to note that there are both empirical and logical limits to the extension of a kind of external, reactive, hedonic view of behavior. One individual's actions may be accounted for by reference to sanctioned expectations of others. But one cannot account for the expectations or the sanctions in these terms. Some portions of the collectivity, and influential portions at that, must believe in the goals and rules, for the system could not otherwise survive the discovery of its mythical character.

It is equally important to note the limits on terror as an instrument of social control. Terror is, indeed, somewhat effective. But aside from the question of what animates the terrorists—and who guards them?— there are prohibitive costs involved in a total regime of personal surveillance. Any social order depends upon at least apathetic compliance on the part of substantial segments of its participants, and conscientious compliance at least on the part of those exercising power.

It follows that all enduring social entities depend in some, and usually in high degree, on what I have been calling conscientious compliance. Translated into processual terms, *socialization*, in the full sense of internalization of values and norms as well as mere cognitive learning, can now be seen as a crucial link between the individual and the social structure. It is, we shall see, the uncertainties and ambiguities in that process that make this something less or something more than an endlessly replicating and endlessly redundant state of affairs.

The Sociological Extreme

We turn now to the substantive problems concerned with the intersection of the undeniably individual character of human action and the undeniably systemic character of most of its manifestations. For the moment, we shall treat this as a contest between the disciplines of sociology and psychology for the ownership of man, though of course joint and indeed multiple tenancy will have to be countenanced.

For the true-blue sociologist, individual behavior is a manifestation of the mandates of groups, or of other social categories. He starts, correctly, with the fact that *society is prior to the individual*. To make society a mere aggregative phenomenon, a summation of individuals or their contractual creation, is processual nonsense. That is not the way things operate, and they never did.

In this connection, a small aside relating to intellectual history is appropriate. Traditional political philosophy—a tradition from which classical economics derived, and from which the discipline of economics has yet to recover—dealt only with societies or polities or economies populated exclusively by adults, and mainly male adults at that. It thus did not occur to the theorists to inquire how individuals came to have their ideas of sensible order, or justice, or the material goals that would be maximized by self-seeking actors. Some of the silliness of the psychological and sociological assumptions displayed in these respected fields of learning could have been avoided by taking cognizance of the fact that societies replace themselves by biological reproduction and the unavoidable succession of individuals in social positions. Men and women are first boys and girls, from whom one cannot expect the creation of sovereign states or rationalized markets.

But we must push this argument further. The human infant at birth is quite unable to sustain life unaided. It is, moreover, remarkably badly equipped with instincts in the exact sense, that is, complex, unlearned patterns of behavior common to the species. These characteristics of biological man have compensations, which not only account for the survival of the species but also account for its ascendancy by ordinary tests of evolutionary theory. The principal biological compensation is a complex and relatively uncoded nervous system that, by its very "plasticity," permits *learning* and even *creativity*. But that biological capacity would be meaningless without the sociological compensation of relatively stable structures that afford support, tutelage, and orientations to goals and rules that do not exist in the untutored organism.

Let us pass over lightly questions of a strictly evolutionary character —how did the phenomenon of human society emerge?—for these questions can now be answered only by theoretical reconstruction and not by inductive generalization from observations now impossible. It does seem clear, however, that intelligence was a crucial evolutionary emergent, and that biological and social evolution have interacted from something like the beginning of man's differentiation as a species.[27] Evolutionary theory of variability and selective adaptation will also account for intersystem and intrasystem differentiation, but only retrospectively if environmental differences and changes are not independently subjected to a predictive order.

These questions of origins and changes do not figure largely in sociological discourse, where social systems and their distinctions are generally taken as given. This is a shortcoming,[28] but not one of crucial significance in the immediate context. Given the nature of biosocial man, and particularly his recruitment as an uncivilized infant, and given the existence of extant social systems, his behavioral characteristics are determined. National character, class, regional, ethnic, or occupational character become unproblematic. In the *explanatory* sense, individual behavior is accounted for by socialization and social control. That is how it comes to be that individuals act according to their positions in a system that provides a prior order for their lives. In the *predictive* sense, individual behavior and social patterns become an equation, which can be read in either direction.

In the extreme sociological position, only apathetic noncompliance and outright deviance spoil the equation, and for those, too, structural sources are sought. This simply requires a more complex and less neatly integrated model of a social system, by noting contradictory claims, value inconsistency, and outright conflict as realistic aspects of the social environment.

The Psychological Extreme

For the true-blue psychologist, or at least the one who deals with man at all, it is biological man that is fundamental. He attends to the unlearned characteristics and requirements for survival: to reflexes, drives, and various "needs."[29] These biological characteristics, if common to the species, or at least common to a separate and generative population, set limits on social variability, and thus in a sense "determine" structure.

To the common biological and psychic characteristics, which set limits to any enduring social system, the psychologist adds individual variability. He doubts the "cookie-cutter" notion of individual-role allocation, particularly in nominally ascriptive systems. His doubts arise both because of genetic differences, which imply less standardized raw material than sociological determinism assumes, and because of the complex interplay between these individual differences and the social settings that individuals encounter. Thus the social settings themselves are viewed as necessarily more adaptive than sociologists customarily admit.

There is an even more extreme view of individual ascendancy over social prescriptions. This is rarely stated, but it is implicit in various reductionist views to the effect that social behavior is, after all, individual behavior and can thus be understood properly by studying individuals. By this view, norms and values are mere instrumentalities of individual goal maximization, invented and discarded at will. A

somewhat modified view would admit the autonomy of socially sanctioned rules, but would regard them as setting conditions (of unex-
amined salience) within which psychological processes display themselves. The existence of the rules is of course not thereby explained,
except as they are assumed to suit the interests of unidentified others.

Some Sensible Positions

Let us now try to cut ourselves a path through the brambles of
intellectual disputes. At the very beginning we should acknowledge the
legitimacy of scientific specialization and differing modes of attempting
to reduce complex phenomena to understandable and predictable
order. Thus, there is nothing improper about dealing with human
personality as a system, whereby social prescriptions or social interaction become "inputs" to the system, or relevant conditions of action.
There is likewise nothing improper about dealing with organized or
patterned pluralities of actors as social systems, whereby actors and
actions are seen as either elements in the system, or possibly even as a
source of inputs to it. Now, all that is demanded of us is to examine
the relationship between these systems, and to that end we need to
establish some points of reference.

The Primacy of Society. Society *is* prior to the individual in the
temporal sense. It would be silly to deny this primacy, given the incapacity of the human infant at birth. But neither should its significance be exaggerated. Society is either a kind of abstraction, useful for
various analytical purposes, or more often than not, in terms of practical effects, it is the polity. In either case, the infant is scarcely born
into a society in the full meaning of the term, but into a decentralized
concrete structure—normally a family—which represents society only
imperfectly.[30] In childhood, the individual's encounter with society is
virtually always with such decentralized and sometimes rather specialized social units. His care, custody, socialization, and social participation are the functions of the family, the playgroup, the neighborhood, and occasionally such specific organizations or their representatives as the clinic and the police. These units of the great society are
not only structurally differentiated, but are also subject to chance
variability. There can be no assurance that each social unit that the
child encounters is an exact representative of society, or even of its
appropriate functional segment of it. Moreover, the child may be
orphaned or the familial unit broken by death, separation, or divorce.[31]
Thus we have to recognize the circumstance that the "agents" of society

are not themselves fully coordinated, a circumstance further underscored by the chance variability of any of these agents, even within
their approximate spheres of seemingly appropriate jurisdiction.

If we add into this set of partially indeterminate social influences the
undeniable fact of variability in the biological raw material to be
processed we come out with a looser set of social processes and products
than a pure systemic determinism would have us accept. We are thus
led to a recognition of some uncertainties in socialization, for absolute
standardization is unlikely.

By extension of this line of reasoning, we should not expect an exact
replication of social positions or social roles as individuals are replaced
in an ongoing social system. The combination of biological variability
with uncertainties in socialization adds up to necessary flexibilities in
social behavior. "Role requirements are thus likely to constitute ranges
of tolerable behavior rather than highly precise behavioral limitations."[32] It must be added that behavior exceeding the "tolerable"
limits is scarcely surprising under these conditions.

Social Differentiation and Individual Differentiation. We are perforce dealing with the interplay between two sets of principles both of
which are universal: the fact of social differentiation and the fact of
individual differentiation. No social system can ignore such basic
biological categories as age and sex, to say nothing of physique, genetic
intelligence, and perhaps differences in specific aptitudes that seem to
display themselves as unanticipated novelties. Aging, for example,
begins with conception, and constitutes both a continuous and discontinuous variable for individual participation in established social
orders. "The temporal order of social systems must somehow accommodate to the temporal order of biological man."[33]

In view of the dual principles of social differentiation and individual
differentiation, the match between them is always problematical. In
every ongoing human society the social analyst is faced with an intrinsic question: the relative operation and efficacy of *selectivity* and
socialization. The social solutions to this problem are variable, and
always partial. This gives rise both to real tensions and uncertainties
in the operation of groups and grander social systems, and, for the
analyst, real difficulties in discernment of how these principles operate.
The extremes of role theory emphasize only socialization. By this view,
any "normal" individual (which may be a way of begging the question) can be induced to perform the duties of the position to which he
is called, and indeed can be expected to internalize the goals and rules
that are appropriate. The extremes of stratification theory emphasize
only selectivity: the system so operates as to get individuals with

appropriate qualifications into the appropriate positions. (Davis and Moore come perilously close to that position by giving strong attention to the unequal supply of "talent" for positions of responsibility.[34]) It is not a great deal of help to assert, with undeniable validity, that both principles operate, for this even-handed solution evades empirical issues that remain unsolved: Under given standards of selectivity, how does socialization occur and what are its limits? Under given systems of socialization, how and where does selectivity occur? When these principles produce contradictions, what adjustments and systemic changes ensue?

The Individual and the Group. There is an unfailing lack of consistency between individual goals and the collective values attributable to and articulated by representatives of groups.[35] Part of the reasons for this incomplete conjuncture have been noted in previous paragraphs: particularly the probability of incomplete and somewhat erratic socialization, accentuated by variability in the qualities of human supplies to the processing system. There are, however, some additional considerations to be recorded here briefly, which will warrant subsequent, fuller explication.

Short of an unknown and theoretically improbable extreme of the "perfectly integrated" social system, the most compliant individual cannot accede to all demands, even if they are all legitimate, taken one by one. There are three universal scarcities: ". . . *time, treasure* (or material resources) and *troth* (loyalty or affective energy)."[36] Even in small, tribal societies, the integration and changeless stability of which have been consistently exaggerated in anthropological literature, there is no reason to suppose that the denizens lead lives troubled only by coping with the nonhuman environment. The human environment, even in seemingly simple societies, is wondrously complex and cannot fail to bear down on individuals with an uneven and, from time to time, impossibly peremptory hand. We should thus expect role conflict and status inconsistency to be intrinsic and endemic to sociay systems. The simple, unproblematical life of primitive people or of the historic past must be a fictitious, wishful reconstruction.[37]

There is, however, sound reason for supposing that problems of inconsistency grow with social differentiation. Where mutually exclusive segments of the population are put in differentiated and presumably complementary positions, problems of integration occur for the viability of the encompassing system, but that is not our present concern. That concern relates to functional differentiation of social demands as they bear on individuals: the family, the church, the polity, the work place, and a host of interest-oriented and expressive associations, which provide the person with a highly differentiated life-space and temporal spectrum. The more highly differentiated the social system in this sense, the more fractional the individual's segmental participation. This must necessarily increase the probability of role conflict, for the chance that all this works out neatly for each individual, taken one by one, is fairly remote. By the same token, these circumstances increase the chances of individual alienation in any particular action context, for the multiplication of positions reduces the probability of a uniform fit between the individual and the group, whether through selectivity or socialization.

Though it might be argued that a sufficiently wide variety of social patterns and social organizations would increase the chance of the individual's finding his particular niche in every instance (that is, an acceptable "status-set"), it must be noted that some of the demands on the individual are essentially ascriptive, such as age and sex norms, and for many others the individual's freedom of choice will be restricted in various ways and various degrees. Even if all choices were seemingly open, they could scarcely be also independent. "Tie-ins" will be common if there is anything at all to the notion of social system. Not all of these role requirements are likely to be equally and positively valued, so that some become "costs" attached to others. The man elected to an exclusive club may find that he is also expected to serve on the board of directors of a local charity. Membership in a fraternal order or service club may entail an unofficial and unspoken commitment to participate in recreational activities favored by a majority of members, or even to engage in partisan political activity though the association as such is nominally nonpolitical.

By this line of argument, part of the phenomena of alienation can be attributed to the attempt by individuals to reduce the cost of "tied-in" role demands. They seek to "accentuate the positive" and to minimize the negative. This assumes, of course, a kind of fixed quantum of commitment, and thus a kind of compensatory view of social allegiance. We shall later criticize this assumption as not uniformly valid.

From the point of view of the personality as a system, it thus becomes meaningful to inquire concerning the relative salience of various social involvements and commitments. This is at least as legitimate a personality inventory as are other character traits, though the two approaches are not mutually exclusive. From the point of view of any concrete social structure, it becomes meaningful to inquire concerning the distribution of members with respect to their reliability and apparent loyalty, since we have reason to suspect that it will not be uniform. But we also cannot assume that the "total social participation scores" of individuals—as measured, say, by man-hours of involvement—will be equal. There is accordingly no reason to suppose that the concrete social structures operate in a neat, complementary balance, one's loss being another's gain.

The Ideal and the Actual. Wherever there is a normative order—a set of rules and their sanctions—there is a high likelihood of some deviation. Norms are an intrinsic feature of structures in the sense of social systems, but it could be demonstrated that sanctioned expectations apply to each of the other concepts of structure. Important reasons for deviation have been indicated already. These lead, however, to a further social reality: the universal gap between the ideal and the actual. Ideal norms are standards for approximation, rarely if ever reached. Failure to achieve them does not make them irrelevant; for them to be irrelevant, the system should suffer no change were they simply removed, and such a situation would be rare indeed.

The gap between the ideal and the actual is a major and universal source of change I have previously argued.* Here the point is simply cautionary: if one starts from ideal prescriptions for behavior, one should not expect complete predictability. (This is a fairly common methodological failing of anthropological field studies, for the field methods are better designed to yield ideal patterns than they are to yield generalizations about actual patterns as related to those ideals.) Predictability of actual patterns will be enhanced, however, if attention is also given to such phenomena as "institutionalized evasions."[38] Divorce, for example, is an institutionalized evasion of the normative prescription for durable monagamous unions, and so, for that matter, is clerical celibacy. What Gouldner[39] calls "indulgency patterns" at the workplace—permissible tardiness, or a "second chance" following violation of an important and seemingly mandatory rule—are clear examples of actual norms. Note, however, that such practices make no sense without taking account of the ideal patterns. Emphasis on practical norms is not an argument for mindless behaviorism.

Some Methodological Traps. As one moves from the unit act through various intermediate levels—categories of acts typical of the individual, a syndrome of behavioral characteristics, a *personality type,* patterns of action attributable to a group, *group structure,* typical linking mechanisms among subsystems, the analytic components of a society, the *type of society,* and *all societies*—detailed information is lost in each successive stage of generalization. The succession of levels of generality just displayed implies a relatively low level of precise predictability from one end of the spectrum to the other. This is not to argue for

* See Chapter 1.

"getting back to the facts," or "bringing men back in,"[40] for such fundamentalist doctrines miss the point and the power of scientific generalization. To be able to say, as we can, that any society will have an orderly system of role differentiation is no trivial accomplishment, not to be undone by critics who do not understand the logic of analytic science. It remains true that the process of generalization is reversible only by adding back in the special information, the lower orders of generalization that were lost in the original endeavor. The unit act with which we started may well exemplify role differentiation, but to say more about it in a meaningful way is likely to require retracing the steps indicated, rescuing suppressed information along the way. This logical principle is so elementary that one can only be dismayed when it is ignored by what appear to be otherwise competent scholars. We cannot prevent the scholar operating at the level that he prefers, but we may properly object when he gets pious about it.

What we have been discussing is, in effect, a corollary of the *reductionist fallacy*, which is by no means unknown among psychologists, though mostly those of earlier vintage: Since social behavior is individual behavior—the argument goes—we can properly understand the former by exclusive attention to the latter. Nonsense. If social behavior is properly observed as organized into systems, as it clearly is, then analysis of such systems requires attention to the relevant elements *and their relationships*. The latter represents the emergent, systemic properties, and they are irreducible to the isolated elements. This is true of atomic, molecular, cellular, organic, and cosmic systems, and again one can only display impatience when it is ignored with respect to human behavior.

But of course reductionism goes on within the distinctively social sciences (that is, disciplines other than psychology) too. Economists commonly deal with motivated individuals, whose motivational structure is not acceptable to knowledgeable psychologists, and whose institutional environment is not acceptable to knowledgeable sociologists. Even anthropologists, who tend to prefer "holistic interpretations," commonly exhibit preferences for the small-scale system rather than the large. Oscar Lewis, for example, who has been a leading critic of foolish conceptions of "folk society"[41] permits himself to say, "Social life is not a mass phenomenon. It occurs for the most part in small groups . . ." and so on.[42] The problem is that the latter part of Lewis's assertion is demonstrably true as measured, say, by time-budgets and the former part of the assertion neither follows logically nor has any empirical warrant in the contemporary world. The existence of group and organizational involvements does not preclude social life as a mass phenomenon, which from time to time becomes a palpable reality and at other times a realistic generalization of and framework for more concretely organized social relationships. Again, the greater comfort that anthropologists feel with small collectivities (including small "cultures") is a preference we can neither properly forbid nor take very seriously. This is not to reject outright Lewis's contention[43] that large-system constructs—his concern is with cities in the discussion cited—may be too generalized for predicting personality; the question is empirical, and not to be settled by simply declaring that only smaller entities matter.

A third methodological problem has a special cogency in the present context. In no science can one predict unique attributes or events, though in some one may be able to "understand" them *a posteriori*.[44] When dealing with individual behavior, both psychologists and sociologists properly deal with a probability distribution of a class of attributes or events. The psychologist may attempt his prediction on the basis of a *personality type* (with some allowance for error because of individual variations) and the sociologist may attempt to proceed on the basis of institutionalized *role prescriptions* (at least equal allowances for error in actual performance being necessary). Neither can guarantee perfect success in the single case. And the juxtaposition of these predictive mechanisms is the recurrent, undercurrent theme of our present exercise.

The Intersection of Changing Individuals and Changing Structures. It has been conventional for sociologists and social psychologists, operating with models of stable structures and individual recruits to them, to view individual placement in differentiated positions as a kind of once-for-all process. Believers in fairly common socialization but unequal talents and other personality traits will opt for sorting mechanisms. Believers in the unchallenged priority of social systems over fairly plastic human raw materials will opt for differential socialization. Both of these positions miss essential points, and we must set them right. Several fundamental facts will be asserted here, their behavioral implications to be explored subsequently: (1) The human individual has a life cycle, which for any individual or across any aggregate of individuals is a combination of nature and nurture. We shall not dwell here on the structural determinants of variations in the length of life, but only insist that there is an inherent "developmental" process in the human organism and its capacities. Any notion of single sorting, or proceeding over a brief span from the savage infant to the civilized adult has to be false in all societies everywhere. It is not even a useful fiction; it is simply wrong.[45] (2) The intrinsic problem of succession in any enduring structure will inevitably introduce changes, even if minor ones, in the actual manner of role performance. (3) There are sources of change in structures in addition to the vacillation, drift, or evolution arising from mere succession. These include changing environmental adaptation, closer approximation to ideals, shifting balances of power arising from intrinsic conflicts, and deliberate changes instituted for progressive goals. The point of present relevance is to add a changing structure to changing individuals. Social placement and eliciting appropriate behavior thus turn out to be much more complex problems than appear in simple-minded formulations.

Current State: Structural and Behavioral Categories

We must now approach, even if hesitantly, the empirical questions: in what ways are social structure and behavior related? The long preliminaries seemed essential, if not exactly entertaining, but now we should be ready for the main event. We shall still have to deal with materials selectively. We shall, for example, have nothing to say about behavior in small groups, or so-called group dynamics—which, as I have elsewhere noted with respect to most of the research results, ". . . neither concerns groups as small-scale social systems nor changes in the significant dimensions of those systems."[46] In order to keep some semblance of order in a not very orderly array of established principles, we shall revert to the several meanings of social structure, earlier displayed, and examine their behavioral correlates or consequences.

Behavior Related to Patterns of Action

Since patterns of action are essentially derived by induction from behavior, we do not have a lot to examine by way of relationship. Nevertheless, the equivalence is not complete, and the lack of complete correspondence can be made modestly instructive. The first point to be noted is that precise uniformity of behavior is unlikely in any context of action. Thus, to speak of a "pattern of action" almost certainly entails a statistical norm—presumably a *mode,* as the most frequent value in a distribution. For any particular action pattern, some variant of the J-curve rule is likely to prevail.[47] If we are willing to accept a simple distinction between pattern-conformity and nonconformity, we shall not get the full shape of the deviations and certainly not its significance in explanatory terms. We may, for example, accept the notion that observed failure to follow the pattern is due to "chance" or "accident." This is a neutral and cautious way of expressing ignorance. If the same individuals show up on repeated observation among the "deviants," we may at least ask what makes them accident-prone.

If we recognize and record degrees of departure from pattern, we shall come closer to the proper shape of the J-curve. Most drivers, let us say, slow down for amber traffic signals, stopping if possible, and uniformly stop for red lights. A smaller proportion will stop for red lights but "run the yellow." A still smaller portion break the red light. But by now we have departed, surreptitiously, from a purely behavior interpretation, for we are recognizing the existence of norms—or at least of expectations, and degrees of their violation. Indeed, if one went about this study as a sort of natural history observation, it might take a while to detect the degrees of deviance. The explanation of these exceptional cases would be scarcely possible, and the explanation for the curious, color-coded regulation of the modal behavior could be recorded but scarcely accounted for without reference to administrative rules.

But let us carry this sort of behavioristic observation a step further. Suppose that we are dealing with a regularity of behavior that is not written into a rule-book somewhere. The daily and weekly flow of automobile traffic in a metropolitan area is guided by explicit rules of the road with respect to operation of the vehicle, but the temporal order of these flows requires reference to other normatively sanctioned practices relating to hours of work in clock time, length of the work week, holidays, vacations, and so on. The predictable temporal variations in mass and direction of traffic flows may be viewed as by-products of other structural patterns. Yet the traffic patterns have a kind of independent authenticity, leading to palliative measures on the part of traffic police, possibly to staggering of work hours on the part of employers, and to off-hours travel for those not normally constrained by the modal behavior. Thus traffic patterns exemplify "unintended but recognized structures."[48] The point of present interest is that pattern-recognition is likely to have normative consequences, and to elicit goal-oriented behavior to sustain or counteract the pattern.

Although it would be hard to find an action pattern at this level that could not be traced to one or more rules of conduct, let us imagine one that arises out of a coincidence of fairly independent events. Housewives may arrive at preferred grocery shopping days independently of each other and independently of predictable variations of supplies in the markets. The housewives' behavior may become a pattern in our current limited sense. However, the circumstance of repeated encounters with recognized coparticipants may well provide the minimum conditions for interactions and for attaching some slight normative value to expectations. Deviations from the pattern are then likely at least to call for expressed surprise, which may be taken as mild reproof. What is being suggested is that structures as patterns of action are likely to evolve into incipient social systems. They thereby cease to be mere generalizations of observed behavior, but rather become an authentic source of behavioral cues.

Behavior Related to Social Systems

When we inquire concerning the behavioral implications of social systems, we are at least dealing with two sets of phenomena that are analytically distinguishable. Because of the emergent properties of social systems with respect to collective values and norms that entail sanctions on behalf of the collectivity, social systems are not mere generalizations of patterned behavior. We are not here indulging in the "group mind fallacy," but neither are we willing to countenance the "reductionist fallacy." A social system commands the allegiance of at least part—and presumably a major part—of the participants that comprise its members or actors, and these loyal adherents "police" one another in the maintenance of virtue, but also impose expectations and sanctions on less-committed members or actual miscreants.

Social Control and Deviance. The old-fashioned sociological term, *social control,* seems appropriate to revive as representing the spectrum of modes whereby social systems induce or assure normal compliance on the part of members. Social control thus comprises Sumner's classic distinctions of degree of control and correlative degree of negative sanctions for violators: *folkways* (it is normally expected), *mores* (you ought to behave), and *laws* (you must comply).[49] But the term also comprises finer gradations and combinations of these external controls, and, importantly, the processes whereby individuals internalize the moral order through socialization.

Generally, the psychological interpretation of individual nonconformity has been to emphasize autonomous drives by the individual, which occasionally break through the restraints of civilization. In Freudian and some postFreudian interpretations, individual instinct is juxtaposed with social constraints, with emphasis on the tensions between the two.[50, 51] Sociologists, on the other hand, generally view deviant behavior as well as compliant behavior as socially produced, noting that the goals of human behavior are socially learned or socially conditioned and not properly instinctual.

Perhaps the most effective recent attempt to order the types and sources of social deviation has been Merton's analysis in his essay on "Social Structure and Anomie,"[52] and the subsequent amendments and refinements introduced by Merton in his second essay,[53] and by others.[54] By this view conforming behavior requires acceptance both of the values (cultural goals in Merton's language) and the norms (institutional means—later norms—in Merton's language). Deviant behavior may arise from adhering to goals while departing from approved means: *innovation;* from rejecting values while complying with standard rules: *ritualism;* or from rejecting both values and norms: *retreatism.* Merton adds one more deviant category, the rejection of extant values and norms but the espousal of others: *rebellion.*

The virtues of this approach are many. They prominently include the recognition of much of criminal behavior, such as that of the professional criminal and some amateur crimes against property, as complying with success values and being deviant only in the means pursued. It is also useful to recognize as deviant the compulsive following of the rules regardless of their current consistency with the values or mission of organized action. (Such actions commonly go unpunished, for it is generally the norms and not the values that carry sanctions. Whether oral rejection of values without other overt acts of rejection—for example, patriotism, belief in God, or the justice of corporate policy —is punishable behavior has been a troubled legal question for millennia.)

Merton, moreover, does not assume an almost-pefectly-integrated social system, which would make deviant behavior an *accident* of imperfect socialization. Rather, he attends primarily to inconsistency in values and in norms within observable concrete systems, and particularly in large and complex ones. It is to these inconsistencies that he attributes his several forms of deviation. This is not quite the position of moral man and immoral society, as Merton does not foolishly attempt to attribute any moral qualities to nonsocial man, who must remain a rather meaningless abstraction. This is, rather, ambivalent and ambiguous man in a society that is also inconsistent.

This approach to compliance and deviance warrants some extension, and also one or two critical comments. One extension that is partially implied but not quite reached in Merton's own second essay on the topic of "anomie" is that of *evasive innovation.* Merton's original formulation implied that there will exist a rule governing every conceivable, alternative means for achieving socially held values. This surely exaggerates the inventive ingenuity of past formulators of rules, and underestimates the ingenuity of current actors. Innovation involves, from time to time, not solely ". . . the use of institutionally proscribed means for attaining a culturally valued goal"[55] but also the use of behavior that is genuinely novel. This is one major source of the *principle of normative accumulation* that applies to all enduring social systems.[56] A still further extension of this amendment requires the recognition that in contemporary, modernized societies, change is institutionalized in many areas of social life, with positive values attached and procedures partially prescribed (for example, scientific research).[57] We are, note, still discussing the structural sources of behavior but the structure is getting more complicated.

The importance of evasive innovation is enhanced by attention to the importance of *ideal* values and norms, earlier noted. Some of Merton's discussion of his distinction between "cultural structure" and "social structure" in his second essay[58] implies ideal and actual practices, but he does not recognize the point and that adds to the confusion of his quite artificial distinction between the cultural and the social. The latter distinction is not the same as that between the ideal and the actual. Both are intrinsic to any social system, and thus help to account for such otherwise anomalous behavior as overconformity, which may aid in approximating ideal standards, though being undeniably troublesome in the particular context.

Still another complication is introduced if we take into account value differences applicable to different segments of a society. Cohen, for example, has argued that at least some behavior of (lower-class) juvenile delinquents is simply not oriented to what others have identified as dominant values, and by whom the behavior is regarded as deviant, but is rather in conformity with lower-class values, or at least with a "delinquent sub-culture."[59] The same might be said of beatniks, the "jet set," or other identifiable segments of the population with distinctive behavior patterns. This raises issues concerning the proper referent for the term "social system," for if by that is meant a large-scale and complex system such as, say, the United States, too much internal differentiation may be obscured relating to behavior that *is not primarily oriented to the system as a whole.* Some of this behavior we shall bring under inspection in ensuing paragraphs devoted to smaller and somewhat more coherent systems; other manifestations of the behavior within subsystems will turn up when we subsequently shift our attention to social structure in the special sense of social differentiation.

A final, conceptual note must be added on social control and deviance, for it has important implications for behavioral interpretations. The concept of *anomie* as used by Durkheim[60] refers to "normlessness." It is an attribute of a social system (or at least of a social situation) that in significant contexts simply does not provide guides to behavior. Merton, while referring to Durkheim's usage in his first essay[61] promptly extends the term to situations in which the regulatory system is by no means wanting. In the second essay Merton reaffirms his use of the term as referring to a quality of the social situation and not to subjective states of mind.[62] Yet he still misses Durkheim's special point, which is that certain objective social situations do not provide effective guides to behavior. The consequence is not one of Merton's types of what we might call "structured deviation," but rather is what Levy has identified as "individualism by default."[63] Such situations may be encountered where there has been a radical, discontinuous change in the polity or the economy, such as in devastating military defeat. It is not inconsistency in social control but its absence that is likely to produce, temporarily, a kind of law of the jungle, restraints arising only from prior habit and socialized conduct—now somewhat meaningless—and by purely hedonic acts and coalitions. Social control has literally broken down, and deviance is the "norm" in the sense of what one must expect. Such a situation is inimical to continued human existence, and will either be superseded by a measure of order, imposed in some manner, or a kind of Hobbesian state of nature in which few survive, and that precariously.

The Constraints of Groups. The extent to which groups exercise constraints over their members has long been recognized as a variable quality of group phenomena.[64] But here we must be cautious in use of the term "constraint." If by the term the connotation of involuntary compliance is admitted then it is probable that constraint is near its maximum in the administrative organization or bureaucracy—which, however, normally still allows at least the protection of alternative employments through operation of a labor market—and at its maximum in the dictatorial, totalitarian state. If, however, one means by constraint simply the range of the individual's energy and loyalty (and possibly time and treasure) caught up in group-relevant activities, then the small, multifaceted, so-called "primary" group must take precedence. There is nothing so stultifying to creativity as the highly formal, bureaucratic organization, except the tidy, little informal group.

Much of the research literature relating to group-determined behavior either refers to so-called small-group behavior, over which we have manifested a conspicuous impatience, or with partial individual involvement in a variety of functionally differentiated groups. For the latter, and often for the former, the concept of *role* figures prominently.

However, I believe some elementary distinctions are long overdue in the discussion of groups and individual behavior. Let us start with a limiting case, the truly totalitarian group, which comprises the *total* social participation not only of any individual, but also of all individuals in the encompassing system. (Its counterpart is a *pluralistic* system.) The leaders of contemporary totalitarian states in their fascist or communist variety aim at this comprehensiveness, and like all such efforts, they fail in varying degrees. But the social type, as a model, has a kind of gruesome interest. In principle, all internal differentiation involves a sort of balancing complementarity, and the totality is an "integrated structure." Where subsystems must be widely countenanced, as in the contemporary, complex, totalitarian state, each of those subsystems is bound to central organs of control by clear lines of accountability, but each individual owes also a direct allegiance to the central state and its leaders and professed ideologists. All this is planned and explicitly disciplined. It differs only in complexity and in formality of controls from the (similarly exaggerated) functionally integrated tribal society where the individual has mostly indirect but some direct linkages with the over-all system.

The concept of role behavior is permissible in such neatly integrated and tightly centralized social systems, but it will have primary significance where the system is actually not operating according to the ideal model.

We must now add some additional concepts relevant to group behavior: *complementary* (and its opposite, *independence*), and *preclusiveness* (and its opposite, *overlapping memberships*).

These distinctions are analytically separate; they are not simply redundant expressions of the same point. Either part of any of the dichotomous distinctions (which are almost certainly scales if examined closely) can be linked with either part of each other one. For example, complementarity may exist among preclusive groups, each of which is essentially totalitarian at least in the sense of claims on the loyalty of members. The type case here is the traditional Indian caste, membership in which is preclusive of other caste identification and defines the totality of socially relevant behavior. Yet the castes are themselves complementary in function and thus interdependent within some broader framework of social placement and social behavior.

Preclusive groups need not be totalitarian, but only mutually exclusive in a particular context of intergroup behavior. For example, physicians and nurses in a hospital, or managers and workers in an industrial organization have complementary positions, and membership in one group normally bars one from membership in the other.

But none of these groups is totalitarian in its claims on members, and so there is a determinable probability that persons participating in these complementary, preclusive groups will find themselves in the same social groups in other contexts of action.

Now the point with respect to the relations between specialized, complementary, but preclusive groups is that we are dealing with genuine intergroup relations, which cannot be reduced to merely individual terms. Of course, in these situations individuals enact roles, and indeed here the term tends to be used in its proper systemic sense: individuals are carrying out the prescription of the drama in which they find themselves, but the drama is the proper focus of attention, not the players. Concepts like role conflict and status consistency hardly apply in the particular context of preclusive groups. These problems get involved only as mutual exclusiveness of group membership breaks down in *other* functional contexts—when for example, occupational antagonists find themselves members of the same church or voluntary association.

Complementarity may not involve interdependence between preclusive groups but rather the organized differentiation across the spectrum of social functions. Thus labor-force participation or membership in a manufacturing corporation does not preclude family life, church membership, political participation, or a variety of other complementary activities. Some members of some groups will behave in a strictly group context, either because they are not involved in some parts of the spectrum of participation (for example, the nonworking housewife in her relations with her husband's company or her children's school), or because a particular group involvement has exceptionally high *salience* (housewives again, or company executives, clergymen, political officials). Yet multiple participation is scarcely to be avoided wherever organized functional differentiation of life activities has been established, and the relations between groups are likely to involve the plural-participating individual in role conflicts. Solutions such as temporal-spatial separation (role segmentation) and the determination of priorities in case of potential conflict provide common alternatives.[65] Actual role suppression, the simple abandonment of some functionally distinct obligations, is likely to be regarded as pathologically unbalanced behavior in the individual. If generalized in a uniform rather than offsetting manner—for example, if everyone pays attention to his occupation but not to his family or the conduct of political affairs—the consequence is *socially* pathological, prejudicing the continuity of a function requisite for the durability of the encompassing system. Tumin has argued this point at both social and individual levels with regard to the pervasive power of the economy in other nominally distinct functional contexts.[66]

We now move to the opposite extreme from the totalitarian system with only modest internal differentiation. This opposite comprises the social situation which is *pluralistic,* comprising *independent* groups, but with *overlapping memberships.* Such a social milieu is especially exemplified in the context of a myriad of voluntary associations, whether interest-oriented or primarily recreational and expressive in their announced values. Now interest groups may in fact be preclusive with reference to others representing hostile interests, and this may produce a kind of complementarity in the sense that the organization to promote one interest may make competing organizations representing other interests rationally necessary. Here, pure role behavior *in the intergroup context* is again to be expected. With other associations, however, such complementarity and interdependence as can be detected is likely to arise only when their quest for individual participants intersects with the scarce resources of potential candidates.

Role conflict is likely once more when voluntary associations compete with each other and with more structurally essential forms of social participation. The cross-pressured individual has not only segmentation and priority criteria at his disposal, but also the additional alternative of outright *role suppression.* If this alternative is generalized for any particular group, its consequences may be collectively fatal to the organizers' aspirations, but scarcely crucial for the total society.

Short of simple nonparticipation or group failure, it should be expected that the individual's behavior will be unequally constrained by the optional (and indeed by all) groups of which he is a part. Our interest here is not primarily with the relatively mandatory claims of organizations, such as corporations and other work organizations, but with behavior in relatively optional forms of social participation. Viewed in terms of the organized collectivity, the participation of members should be expected to be highly unequal, if for no other reason than the individually variable *salience* of various social involvements. This leads to the distinction from an organizational standpoint, between the active center and the passive periphery, or finer gradations in terms of some index of participation.[67] The immediate moral of this variable participation is that group membership will be unequally predictive of behavior, unless corrected for gradations of involvement.

We are, however, faced with a further complication, and that is that at the individual level we cannot count on compensatory behavior in various contexts of social action. Here is where "psychological" dimensions reenter, for *individuals have variable cumulative participation scores.* Feldman and Moore[68] suggested on theoretical grounds that participation and apathy are each self-reinforcing rather than compensatory (thus contradicting notions that frustration leads to diverted activity), and that view has been given partial, independent confirmation.[69] The immediate moral of this variable cumulative social participation by individuals is that group membership, even after correction for gradations of involvement, and after cumulation across all memberships, may not adequately predict individual behavior. Such prediction is likely to have special relevance, in appropriate contexts, for the high-participators and their near counterparts. For the low-participators and "non-joiners," formal group membership is a weak or worthless tool for detecting behavior. Here, one must revert to the individual in his successive life experiences, and hopefully to find in the cumulative encounter with frustration in socially sanctioned activities the predictive sources of current withdrawal.

The context of this discussion has been participation in organized social activities that are optional for any individual. But the point we have just been pursuing can be generalized further. If the activities are truly optional, the penalties to the individual for nonparticipation are fairly minor—though we suffer as social analysts. But such withdrawal is also likely to extend to all social contexts, and failure in some of them is no minor, optional matter. The nonparticipant in truly optional associations is likely also to have a minimal involvement with work, family, church, and community, or to have none at all. In these firmly institutionalized contexts of action, his withdrawal is plainly deviant.

We are dealing with the general failure of complex social systems to catch up some nominal members in an encompassing net. But let us not get carried away into a view of such resistant behavior as somehow individually self-assertive and heroic. Under extremely rare circumstances, it may be so regarded, though the constructive innovator or revolutionist finds it convenient not to fight the "system" on all fronts simultaneously. No, we are dealing with failures. Across social time and social space, publicly-held social theories have differed as to the individual or social responsibility for such failures. Indeed scientific and otherwise intellectual views vary as among a kind of biological or psychic inevitability (measures of inherent competence), a kind of moralistic view that (presumably competent) individuals exhibit unequal "strength of character," and a kind of sociologistic view that society dooms its failures and overt deviants to their dismal state. Social scientists have little to say on the second view and entertain an eminently sound position that no one does, but otherwise try to parcel out cases of failure and their causes, since no categorically general view is likely to encompass the range of carefully observed phenomena.

Representative Types of Groups. Groups are classifiable in as many ways as there are differences in attributes or dimensions of possible interest to analysts. It is also possible to distinguish, somewhat crudely, composite types. We shall deal with the behavioral correlates of three such types, to illustrate the degree of specificity that particular social systems involve.

The *family* is apparently a universal feature of human societies. It uniformly provides for regulated adult sexuality—though its monopoly on such behavior is unequally established—for legitimate procreation, initial social placement, and early socialization of the young. This means that there are certain required role-relationships: between adults, according to a sexual division of functions; between generations (with the responsibilities of parents also commonly differentiated by sex, and the socialization of the young similarly differentiated); between older and younger siblings, if for no other reason than the greater "maturity" of older children. Certain other types of behavior are also intrinsic to family structure. Given the universality of the incest taboo, sexual relationships in the narrow sense are limited to those involved in marital unions, and are forbidden between generations and among siblings. But the incest taboo also requires that separate lineages be joined in each marriage. Thus, whether the main way of tracing lineage is masculine, feminine, or both, each married person requires a set of rules for dealing with affinal "kinsmen," that is, "in-laws." This means further that there is always some strain between adult generations, regardless of the lineage system or other kinship variables.

The family or kinship is often called the "microcosm of society," but that is clearly an exaggeration. Again, given the incest taboo, the family cannot be a self-subsistent unit in terms of sexual recruitment, and it is commonly less than self-reliant in other respects also. Nevertheless, one can observe that the family performs political functions—the distribution of authority according to generation, sex, and relative age; economic functions—it is often a collaborative producing unit, with division of labor at least by age and sex, and always a unit for economic distribution; educational functions—particularly with regard to the untutored young; and affective functions—a relationship of stable intimacy upon which socialization depends, and, in modern societies, one of the few places where affectivity may be legitimately displayed.

The host of studies concerning family functioning and malfunctioning as they relate to individual behavior defy succinct summary. Certain points, however, warrant emphasis. They have been selected less randomly than may appear. First, the extent to which the family and more extended kinship relations govern behavior—the proportion of the individual's life space so involved—is quite variable. It is inversely related to the functional differentiation of social systems in other respects. Second, in no society will the family's claim on the individual be totalitarian, but in some the approximation will be close. Third, the uniformity or diversity of family structure and functioning—for example, with respect to child-rearing practices—is variable between societies. But cross-sectional diversity is to be expected in any society, partly for reasons of differential position of families in established social systems, partly because of essentially idiosyncratic variations. The range of variation from both sources is likely to be greater in highly differentiated societies.

The norm of family continuity, not only of the primary family through the period of child-rearing but also of the lineage through successive generations, is universal, and universally subject to evasion or violation. The sources of discontinuity include not only premature mortality, but also marital and intergenerational discord.

The contemporary Western family is buffeted by a host of strains, but to predict its demise from loss of functions is foolishness of an advanced order. The failure of some families to contain the behavior of some of their members indicates that families are given responsibilities of emotional satisfaction that are too great for some units to sustain.

In modern American society, the family remains an anchoring point for most members of the society. The proportion of adults who remain unmarried has always been small, and has been declining for some decades. Widowers tend to remarry though many widows "attach themselves" (if not physically, at least affectively) to children or, more rarely, siblings.

Males in late adolescence typically go through a period of several years when their familial ties are minimal in the extreme. Though this is consistent with the social separation of the generations, encouraged by our institutional structure relating to intergenerational mobility, the implication of this for social control is that these males are primarily oriented to age-peer groups and not to what must be called more "normal" behavioral supervision, which most societies have provided through the family.

The family, it should be noted finally, is a major and normally enduring component of the "significant others" who serve to reinforce norms earlier internalized, by exhibiting current expectations and sanctions. Where earlier socialization and the norms of the effective family differ, we encounter a variant of role conflict. We should expect such situations to result in some form of "behavioral disorder."

The claims of the family on the individual are prominently marked by affectivity, by demands on what we earlier called "troth." These claims may be made somewhat impersonal by strong institutional support, including legal principles, and thus the interest of "third parties," but reliance on such extrafamilial guides to conduct is indicative, in our society, that intrafamilial relationships are strained and in jeopardy.

The closest approximation to the family's claim on genuine loyalty is that of the *peer group*. Most of the studies specifically relating to peer groups are concerned with coalitions of age-peers among children and adolescents. In the type case these groups are informal and multifunctional. They are also "somewhat" equalitarian (thus justifying the term "peer"), but on closer inspection they may be differentiated according to various performance standards. It is because the valued attributes or abilities within such age-peer groups often have a low or negative value among parents, school officials, or public authorities that the groups have attracted attention as factors in both attitudes and institutionally expected performance.[70] Within the school situation, however—and thus largely leaving out such peer groups as juvenile gangs—Lavin's review of research findings indicates very little independent effect of peer groups on academic performance at elementary school levels.[71] The studies on high school and college performance yield more mixed results with respect to the particular criterion of Lavin's review—that is, academic performance. There is little basis for doubting that adolescent peer groups exert an independent influence on academic or other institutionally sanctioned behavior. But it cannot be assumed, cynically, that peer groups are uniformly antisocial in their prescribed attitudes.[72]

It should be noted that the peer group is not necessarily totalitarian in its claims on members, or even totalitarian with respect to spontaneous and effective allegiances as contrasted with officially sanctioned behavior. Lavin sounds a cautionary note: ". . . students are often members of several peer subgroups."[73] A comparable caution is applicable to the very large number of studies of "informal organization" in industrial settings and within other complex and highly formalized social systems. Such studies commonly assume, without examination, that an informal structure that arises in the ecological context of the work place is multifunctional—involving, for example, voluntary work exchanges, eating together, participation in illicit betting pools, visiting local bars out of hours, or exchange of entertainment among the families. It is much more probable that such informal activities are differentiated by membership as well as by function.[74]

Spontaneity of formation and informality of interaction do not necessarily lead to multifunctional operation. Indeed, if we examine such groups in terms of their operation with some turnover of membership, we should expect that for the new recruit both spontaneity and informality are seriously impaired.

There is no need to limit the term peer group to collectivities without formal organization. Children may form clubs, complete with club names and written constitutions. Adolescents may do likewise, or join clubs and fraternities already organized. Adults may join a myriad of clubs, associations, and occupational organizations, as well as participate in durable constellations of social relationships that are without names, officers, or written rules. And multiplicity again presents problems in predicting the behavioral consequences of group identification. Indeed, the predictive matrix may have to be extended to include groups to which the individual does not belong, but to which he aspires and thus takes as a behavioral guide through "anticipatory socialization."[75] The useful concept of "reference group" seems most appropriate with regard to just such segments of the individual's social constellation. In Merton's very extensive and valuable discussion of group influences on behavior[76] the term "reference group" seems to mean any group that matters, and thus to be a redundant phrase.

Complexity plagues us once more. Where multiple options exist in the individual's life-space, group identification alone may be said, in a kind of circular fashion, to be predictive of behavior. But since not all such identifications are preclusive, their implications for behavior are likely to require *both* a specification of the functional context *and* examination of individual attitudes or other indicators of relative salience. The social analysts' life becomes less hectic when he can find valid grounds for "overpredicting," that is, to identify the probability of high salience of a particular group identity, and thus to predict the influence of that group membership beyond the bare minimum evident from the group's functional position or apparent values. Thus, I have elsewhere argued that occupational identification will take precedence for workers (of any status) over competing allegiances in the work context—the alternatives being generalized status, the employer, the industry, or sector of the economy.* To this view I should now add another qualifying dimension: that the relative salience of occupational identity will be positively correlated with the prestige rating (or required training time) of the occupation. At some point along this continuum I should expect occupational identity to predict behavior beyond the limits of the work context. The occupational group would then become a peer group in the richer, multifunctional sense of the

* See Chapter 8.

term, a sense that the realities of organizational complexity forced us partially to abandon.

The most highly ordered form of organizational membership offered in contemporary life is that of employment in a *bureaucracy or administrative organization*. Such organizations seem to be manifestations of role theory carried to the limiting extreme. Specialization of functions is extreme. Coordination is accomplished by elaborately planned complementarity, supplemented by finely specified and graded authority. Impersonality and affective neutrality are prominent normative features. The job specifications and rules on relationships apply to offices, and not to individuals as such. The organization is thus equipped to endure extensive turnover and succession in positions, and such personnel changes are normal and frequent.[77] Only slight variations in these organizational features are introduced by different collective functions or missions; thus the army, civilian governmental agency, private business corporation, the university, or the hospital differ from one another in small details. Approximation to the "ideal-typical" bureaucratic specifications is correlated with organizational size, and conversely. A particular subtype is of special interest in the present context, namely what I should call a "custodial organization" and Goffman calls a "total institution."[78] The particular feature of this type is that part or all of the membership is subject to continuous surveillance; the organization, for these constituents, is thus not a functionally specialized segment of life's activities, but almost the boundary of life for the duration of their membership. Residential schools find themselves in the curious company of army reservations, prisons, and mental hospitals within this organizational category.

In principle, the plan of the administrative organization answers all questions relating to organizationally-relevant behavior of members. In fact, inquiry concerning the relation of the structure to behavior is still permissible. A number of sources of flexibility and uncertainty may be briefly noted.

First, perfection of planning is improbable. Thus, both overlapping role specifications and failure to provide for some essential functions are likely to occur.

Second, change in relevant conditions of operation, whether of internal or external origin, will make some positions obsolete, set up the need for new ones, and heighten the probability of jurisdictional conflict among continuing positions.

Third, bureaucratic organization is better fitted for placement by selectivity than by socialization, but is virtually certain to use both. Persons with the talents and training for established positions may not be available, or not available in response to the inducements actually offered. Filling higher positions by promotion—recruitment from within—is not required by the formal organizational model, but is customary. This implies at least cognitive socialization, based on "experience," but, more subtly, implies internalization of the normative expectations (role requirements) of new positions.

Fourth, organizational identification may be expected to vary among the personnel of the bureaucracy. Though some of this variance will be idiosyncratic from an organizational standpoint, it is still likely to have organizational relevance, which then has additional behavioral consequences. High identification may be given various organizational rewards, such as preference in promotions. Low identification may lead to actual severance, or to being passed by for a promotion otherwise in order. But variations in identification and its behavioral manifestations may also be partially predicted in structural terms. Commitment to the organization can be expected to be least among those who have fared least well in terms of relative position and income. It will normally be highest among those who have fared best, but especially among those who have wide coordinating (administrative) authority and responsibilities. The gradations of commitment will not exactly match the rank-order of formal position. Persons in relatively high positions may still be somewhat alienated, apart from idiosyncratic sources. They may have had what appeared to them as reasonable expectations for further advancement not fulfilled and thus have experienced "relative deprivation."[79] Another highly-placed segment of organizational personnel has primarily technical rather than administrative duties. These professional and technical (staff) people will normally display an occupational identification—the peer group again —greater than their commitment to a particular employer. One clear behavioral consequence, or demonstration, of this difference is the relatively high interemployer mobility of staff personnel.

Fifth, the necessary *succession* to positions, arising from retirement and death, if not from other, administrative sources of transfer, will necessarily alter actual role performance in some degree. The limits of tolerable variability must be narrow, but they must exist.

Sixth, and finally, deviance and evasion must also be expected. Excessive performance may be as troublesome as underperformance, and is often more mischievous because it is difficult to punish. Role ranges and gaps in the perfection of organizational integration permit other demonstrations of individual resistance to narrowly constricted conformity. I have elsewhere[80] identified several varieties of "useful troublemakers" who may be harbored within the awesome regularity of bureaucracies. These include: memory and conscience keepers, conscientious objectors, court jesters, creators, and (paradoxically) sinners —the last on the ground that occasional violations prompt righteous reactions, without which moral lethargy may set in.[81]

Again, it must be emphasized that these forms of "unexpected" behavior have part of their sources from the particular social system. They are not purely exemplary of the failure of organizations to guide or predict behavior, but rather indicative of the subtleties extant within social systems themselves.

Social Differentiation and Behavior

It sometimes appears that nonsociologists think that the most important sociological concept is that of "social class," and that many sociologists would concur. Certainly there has been a plethora of studies of class differences in behavior, ranging from differential fertility to differential participation in voluntary associations. I shall not attempt to go beyond a brief summary of the results of these studies here; a fairly adequate summary is provided by Berelson and Steiner.[82] More attention will be given to certain methodological and theoretical issues.

Indices of class status—particularly in the American context, in which most of the studies have been carried out—are positively correlated with educational performance, level of formal educational achievement (if not part of the index),[83] relative immunity to mental disorder,[84] participation in voluntary associations, formal rather than highly expressive religious participation,[85] and, less reliably, conservative voting behavior.

Through most of the Western world prior to World War II, class status and size of family were negatively correlated. Since that time class status has become a poor or negligible predictor of fertility behavior. Certain other relationships appear to be curvilinear: upper and lower segments of status distributions appear much more likely to indulge in gambling than does the extensive middle range, and the same parallelism of the extremes apparently applies, paradoxically, to emphasis on multigenerational and laterally extended kinship relations.

Of the multitude of studies that take "class" as an independent variable, those relating to differences in child rearing are especially interesting. There is some preponderance of evidence that (American) middle-class parents are more permissive with children than are lower-class parents.[86] Yet the behavioral consequences for the children themselves are uncertain: "In the preoccupation with demonstrating that children from different social classes have different patterns of family life, research designed to demonstrate the effects on young children of these patterns has been neglected."[87] On the other hand, Becker, citing a number of studies, indicates that permissiveness in a context of affective warmth (both more probable in the "middle class") has such consequences for the children as greater activity and creativity and ease in taking adult roles.[88]

We are now ready to introduce some qualifications and problems. The first relates to the concept of "class" itself. How real are the divisions into distinct strata? It is often asserted that European classes are more "real" than those of the United States, perhaps partly because intergenerational status mobility is lower—though this depends upon the reading of the evidence—and in any event by reliable self-identification which manifests itself further in distinct political identifications and even in one form or another of class conflict. In the American context, it has been customary for investigators to use some combinations of status indicators, and arbitrarily to mark off three segments of the resulting distribution as upper, middle, and lower classes. The refinement of using some multiple of three—exemplified by Warner's work[89]—does not change the arbitrariness of the procedure.

In American survey studies, an overwhelming proportion of respondents identify themselves as "middle class." A standard stance of interpreters has been to account for the popular "myth" by reference to the predominance of middle-class standards as ideals that secure "inappropriate" class identification. Now I strongly suggest that the respondents are approximately correct and that it is the interpreters who are attempting to perpetuate a myth. The income distribution of American families is distinctly diamond-shaped, with a wide middle, a narrow upper point, and a not very wide lower one. The distribution of educational achievements has a similar shape. To the extent that occupations can be reliably rated in terms of relative prestige—and that is easily exaggerated—the populous middle ranges are again evident. The implication of all this is that if class is taken to be tripartite and is taken seriously as a structural feature of social life, it provides no substantial basis for differentiating the behavior of the bulk of the population, which forms what Wilensky has called the "middle mass."[90]

In view of this difficulty and the related problem of arbitrary boundaries, some scholars have abandoned the frequently meaningless charade of grouping distributions into strata, and use instead some index of "socioeconomic status" (SES). Income and education almost always figure in such indexes, and the prestige rating of occupations not uncommonly. Now here the methodological question needs to be raised: does the construction of a combined SES index improve prediction as compared with the use of separate components? It is widely assumed that additional variables will improve the prediction ("or account for more of the variance") of the dependent variable. Perhaps, but the assumption warrants empirical examination. For example, education or occupation will be found to be a better predictor of family budgetary behavior or "styles of life" over rather broad ranges of income than will actual income differences. Miller and Swanson suggest that the distinction between "bureaucratic" and "entrepreneurial" occupations is more predictive of differences in child-rearing practices than are conventional "class" distinctions.[91] Brown concludes that ". . . the style of life of the family unit in this country (United States) depends chiefly on the occupation of the father." He adds "There seems to be nothing in the prestige ratings given occupations to suggest a class structure . . ."[92]

Income, on the other hand, is certainly the best single indicator of savings-behavior; additional predictive power could probably be added by taking note of occupational differentials (not necessarily ranked), but probably little by educational levels held independent of occupation and income. Simplification, again, may cost too much as a research strategy.

The preceding cautionary note is given added point by the many forms of social differentiation not commonly included in SES or definitions of class. Family, lineage, ethnic origin, and "race" may be irrelevant in some social contexts, crucially relevant in others. Performance (note: behavioral) criteria are often taken into account as modifications in formal status by way of addition or subtraction, and may occasionally supersede formal status. (In an evil world this seems to happen much more often as a way of losing effective status rather than of enhancing it.)

We are in fact raising a problem that is far reaching. The question of equality or inequality of participants is appropriate in *every* social context. Even where nominal equality is the norm, it is very likely to be shaded, by evaluations of differential performance.[93] But the critical question for concepts of class or even generalized social status is whether these highly specific and segmental ranks can be transferred or converted into a more general currency, a kind of cumulative and amply founded status. The probability of consistency and cumulation of status in an extremely diversified social order appears low on statistical grounds, and it is improper to assume the result without empirical examination. But turn the problem around. The implications of the insistent doubt just raised would also damage the deductively predictive power of generalized class or status indicators. The high-status executive or outstanding professional may *not* be a leader in his community, an officer in his club, a vestryman in his church, to say nothing of being excellent at his hobbies, an ornament to his neighborhood, or the executive in charge of his own household. He may get no extra kudos for his family lineage, but the probabilities *are* good that he is a "Wasp" (White-Anglo-Saxon Protestant).[94] Not everything is independent. On scientific, though not necessarily on policy grounds, one may be thankful for small favors.

Our tribulations are not quite done. The point of reference in the preceding paragraphs has been the multifaceted or at least multiroled individual. But we must also take into account preclusive groups. Here also we encounter social differentiation, but a reliable ranking of the groups may not be possible. We encounter Baptists and Methodists, Republicans and Democrats, Masons and Odd Fellows, Lions and Rotarians, families who acquire things and those who acquire experiences, urban dwellers and (a few) rural dwellers, Easterners and Westerners, and so on. Now by the sheer numerical distribution of such identifications in a community one may be able to get a plurality vote in a popularity rating or a preferential scale. (Note that despite our use of pairs, the distinctions are not commonly dichotomous.) One may even be able to link some differentials to nominally independent status indicators such as income. But it is extremely unlikely that one could secure a *consensual* basis for any ranking, or even for the criteria to be used. Modern society, or at least American society, abounds with distinctions without a difference, if by difference is meant a reliable, relative rank. More than incidentally, it is the very pluralism of American society that not only reduces the consistency of commonly used status indicators, but also reduces the relevance of so-called general status for a variety of other, optional forms of social participation. If social scientists think that this is more than slightly unfair to their search for reliable order, they may recall that it is only in such social settings that they are likely to be accorded much tolerance, or even permitted at all.

There is still another, and related, problem of interpretation. It is, in essence, whether certain segments of the "class system"—for example, the hereditary poor or various racial or ethnic minorities—are to be viewed as differential participants in a common system, or as constituting "subcultures." By the latter view, such groups would essentially constitute enclaves, in a society but not of it. This is in part an empirical question, the answer to which is not clear from available evidence. Merton answers critics who suggested that his "cultural goals" were not truly common by presenting evidence that *some* portions of the alleged subcultures share the values of the dominant majority, and arguing that uniformity should not be expected and that its partial absence is not damaging.[95] Incidentally, one does not have to be very sophisticated in psychological theory to be suspicious of oral (and perhaps real) rejection of a goal that the respondent has notably failed to achieve. This does not mean that the goal was never shared, would not be shared if the opportunity-structure were different, or indeed may not be currently held in some real sense. In this case, though the evidence, to repeat, is mixed, it seems preferable to opt for simplicity. To take a simple point: income is such a crucial mechanism for transfer of goods and services in contemporary society that a genuine rejection of income-aspirations cannot be interpreted as a preference for a different set of cultural values; it is simply insane.

Neither the structure of social differentiation nor the individual's place in it is immutable. Let us here attend primarily to individual change (that is, mobility), though the probability of mobility is notably affected by structural change. Of the many kinds of mobility (geographical, occupational, interemployer, and so on) we shall limit our brief inspection to general status changes, and distinguish only intergenerational changes and movement within a career.

The first point to be noted is that any general system of social inequality (or social stratification) tends to be self-perpetuating between generations, since the family is a primary agent of initial social placement and socialization, and thus offers differential advantages to its offspring. In no society could this hereditary replication be complete, because of the reality of genetic differences and because demographic replication is extremely unlikely and in fact unknown. The situation in modern societies provides further sources of intergenerational mobility. For a variety of causes that include rapid technological change, changes in international politics, and the organization of deliberate change in a great variety of social contexts, the nature and distribution of the positions to be filled are subject to major change, and mere intergenerational replication is inappropriate or impossible. Many of the sources of change in the "demand" side of the social structure also affect the supply side: the quest for talent that leads to the liberalization if not the equalization of educational opportunities as a major sorting and allocative mechanism.

Let there be no mistake. Parental social status is partially predictive of the aspiration levels and achievements of children. But, as usual, the differences are clearest at the extremes and less easily detected in the wide middle ranges. Moreover, as long as the structural changes just noted continue, anything resembling precise inheritance of status must decline.

Educational achievement may be taken as a kind of precareer mobility, and an extremely influential one at that. Changes in the demand for talents or skills during a breadwinner's life will also affect his career chances. Though the over-all trend in the occupational structure is that of upgrading, some participants do not in fact "make the grade," so that the structural changes are depressing or disastrous. Remarkably little more is known about the interplay between structural and motivational elements in career mobility. One can be sure that chance and "connections" have some significance, and presumably demonstrated merit has some. I have elsewhere speculated on the interplay among aspirations, expectations, and achievements in administrative careers, but I had nothing but impressions to rely on.[96] We can, however, note two additional points meriting further inquiry: What are the "coping mechanisms" for unexpected success as well as unexpected failure? What are the costs of success, not only in terms of probably increased responsibility but also in terms of life patterns and possibly relatives and friends left behind?[97] It may seem needlessly solicitous to point to the problems of the successful, but if we retain our impartiality they merit attention along with our inquiry into the problems of the downtrodden.

Behavior in Terms of Analytical, Statistical Categories

We shall have little to say about the behavioral counterparts of social structure viewed as a statistical distribution of personal attributes or achievements. Of those that generalize or aggregate differential behavioral characteristics, one may ask for explanation in either motivational or structural terms. The two sorts of explanation should have, hopefully, some mode of relationship. Let us take two examples, rather than running through a tedious list.

Fertility behavior for a long time in the Western world was, in a rather perverse way, largely determined by social status. It was perverse in that those who could best afford large families had the smallest, and conversely. The historic explanation of the inverse relation between social status and fertility can be put most reliably in terms of the differential distribution of access to knowledge about contraceptives and of mobility-oriented aspirations favorable to their use. On reexamination of the evidence, urbanization and industrialization, commonly identified structural changes, were extremely crude and unreliable predictors of fertility limitation, but educational levels a rather good one. We have then a structural change, which is implemented by a partly constant and partly variable motivational constellation, to produce a significant behavioral result as displayed in statistically significant differentials. This example may be pushed further, for the change in the inverse relationship between status and fertility can be attributed to completion of a process of structural change.* A greater equalization of formal knowledge, and presumably of attitudes favorable to deliberate choice, largely wiped out the previous structural sources of differential behavior. Indeed, with increasing frequency, the relationship between social status and fertility turned positive; children were no longer conspicuous evidence of ignorance and error, but could be taken as evidence of deliberate choice, and therefore comparable to other symbols of conspicuous consumption.

Incidentally, the age structure of a population, itself chiefly a consequence of past fertility trends, will be a principal determinant of current birth rates, apart from all other general and differential factors.

A similar mixture of structural and motivational elements is involved in differential labor-force participation rates. For adult males, labor-force participation is normal, and the exceptions of some small interest, since some involve physiological and psychological disabilities, and others represent structural pathologies. Age-at-entrance, and age-at-exit for the male worker are strongly structural (including institutional) in their determination. Female labor-force participation rates are subject to the same institutional and some of the same structural conditions as those of males. For many females, however, and particularly those married, labor-force participation must be regarded as essentially optional. Though such "structural" elements as educational attainments are variable, and such "motivational" elements as quest for additional income might be assumed to be inversely related to the income levels of husbands, the best single predictor of labor-force participation of mature married women is the absence of dependent small children from the household. Thus a particular structural change in the family (a conspicuously motivated change), the early cessation of childbearing, has behavioral consequences that can be generalized as the age-structure of female labor-force participation.

We have already noted, in passing, some consequences of changes in occupational structure, and similar linkages could be traced to income or residential distributions. The important point to be underscored is that a "purely structural" analysis is difficult to maintain. At times,

* See Chapter 14.

it is much too coarse-grained. The kind of brief structural analysis used with reference to age differences in female labor-force participation will not account for many of the exceptions: the married women who enter the labor market, though they have minor children, modest education, and husbands with relatively good incomes, and the married women who remain safely feminine in their social participation though they have no children in the household, are well educated, and have husbands with extremely modest incomes. Finer structural distinctions may account for part of this variance, but reliance on motivational variables is likely to prove convenient at an early point.

In other instances, structural explanations of behavior may prove highly reliable, but still leave a sense of incompleteness. The analyst seeks *instrumental closure,* that is, motivational elements that may not be directly observed but are rather posited as intervening variables in order to turn a bare prediction into an "explanation." The structural explanation of statistically expressed resultants of behavior may be rather elaborate and sophisticated. Witness Davis on social factors in mortality differentials[98] or Davis and Blake on fertility determinants.[99] On the other hand, the "proximate" explanations for various participation rates—college attendance, urban migration, voting—may adduce very simple, summary structural and motivational variables. In no case is it quite possible to dispense with some kind of motivated actor.

Sequential Structures and Behavior

There are many situations, we have argued previously, where the structural ordering of behavior is not simply cross-sectional and allocative, but involves a temporal order of expected behavior. We have glanced briefly at our extremely modest knowledge relating to careers, and commented even more briefly on the structural changes inevitably introduced by positional succession. I have elsewhere noted the universal importance of marking off major stages in a normal life cycle by public rituals, *rites de passage.* Indeed, any standardized temporal ordering of activities is a sequential social structure. The process of aging provides an excellent example of the ways that the inevitable aging and mortality of biological man intersect with continuing social systems. As that is the topic of Chapter 13, it need not be discussed here.

We have paid little attention here to the effects of *changing* structures on behavior, as that is dealt with in other essays, particularly in Chapter 13. We have traversed a lot of thorny terrain concerning social structures and their complexity, much of our journey being an attempt to differentiate and bring a measure of order out of a welter of social phenomena. When we get appropriately, but somewhat preciously, precise about the structuring of individual behavior by something called social structure, doubts and uncertainties abound. When we deal with more massive, but cruder, relationships a theoretical order once more serves to organize volatile and unstable behavioral phenomena.

References

1. Alex Inkeles, "Sociology and Psychology," in Sigmund Koch, ed., *Psychology: A Study of a Science* (New York: McGraw-Hill, 1959–63, 6 vols.), vol. 6, 1963, pp. 317–387.

2. Robert K. Merton, *Social Theory and Social Structure,* revised and enlarged ed. (Glencoe, Illinois: Free Press, 1957).

3. *Ibid.,* Chapters IV, V, IX, and XVI.

4. *Ibid.,* pp. 368–370.

5. *Ibid.,* p. 370.

6. *Ibid.*

7. *Ibid.,* Chapter IV.

8. *Ibid.,* p. 162.

9. *Ibid.,* Chapter XVI.

10. Marion J. Levy, Jr., *The Structure of Society* (Princeton, New Jersey: Princeton University Press, 1952), p. 57.

11. *Ibid.,* pp. 88–98.

12. Talcott Parsons, *The Social System* (Glencoe, Illinois: Free Press, 1951).

13. *Ibid.,* p. 36.

14. *Ibid.,* p. 114.

15. Bernard Berelson and Gary A. Steiner, *Human Behavior: An Inventory of Scientific Findings* (New York: Harcourt, Brace and World, 1964).

16. Levy, *op.cit.,* p. 57.

17. See, for example, Parsons, *op.cit.*

18. Wilbert E. Moore, *Social Change* (Englewood Cliffs, New Jersey: Prentice-Hall, 1963), p. 6.

19. See Kingsley Davis and Wilbert E. Moore, "Some Principles of Stratification," *American Sociological Review,* 10: 242–249, 1945.

20. See Paul K. Hatt, "Occupations and Social Stratification," *American Journal of Sociology,* 55: 533–543, 1950.

21. See Wilbert E. Moore, *Man, Time, and Society* (New York: John Wiley and Sons, 1963).

22. See S. N. Eisenstadt, *From Generation to Generation: Age Groups and Social Structure* (Glencoe, Illinois: Free Press, 1956).

23. Merton, *op.cit.;* see Reference 2.

24. See Harold L. Wilensky, "Orderly Careers and Social Participation: The Impact of Work History on Social Integration in the Middle Mass," *American Sociological Review,* 26: 521–539, 1961; Delbert C. Miller and William H. Form, "Occupational Career Patterns as a Sociological Instrument," *American Journal of Sociology,* 54: 317–329, 1949.

25. Neil J. Smelser, *Theory of Collective Behavior* (New York: Free Press of Glencoe, 1963).

26. See Floyd H. Allport, "The Group Fallacy in Relation to Social Science," *Journal of Abnormal and Social Psychology,* 19: 60–73, 1924.

27. See T. G. Dobzhansky, *Mankind Evolving: The Evolution of the Human Species* (New Haven, Connecticut: Yale University Press, 1962).

28. See Moore, *Social Change*, Reference 18.

29. For example, see H. J. Eysenck, *The Structure of Human Personality* (New York: John Wiley and Sons, 1953); Neal E. Miller and John Dollard, *Social Learning and Imitation* (New Haven, Connecticut: Yale University Press, 1941; Silvan S. Tomkins, *Affect, Imagery, Consciousness* (New York: Springer, 1962), Vol. 1, *The Positive Affects*, pp. 243–271.

30. On the meaning of society, see Parsons, *The Social System* (cited in Reference 12), p. 19, and Levy, *The Structure of Society* (cited in Reference 10), pp. 112–113.

31. For a review of studies on effects of children's separation from parents, see Leon J. Yarrow, "Separation from Parents during Early Childhood," in Martin L. Hoffman. and Lois Wladis Hoffman, eds., *Review of Child Development*, Vol. I (New York: Russell Sage Foundation, 1964), pp. 89–136.

32. Moore, *Social Change* (cited in Reference 18), p. 13.

33. Wilbert E. Moore, "Aging and the Social System," *in* John C. McKinney and Frank T. DeVyver, eds., *Aging and Social Policy* (New York: Appleton-Century-Crofts, 1966).

34. Davis and Moore, "Some Principles of Stratification," cited in Reference 19.

35. See, for example, Chris Argyris, *Personality and Organization* (New York: Harper, 1957).

36. Moore, *Social Change* (see Reference 18), p. 62.

37. See Oscar Lewis, *Life in a Mexican Village: Tepoztlan Restudied* (Urbana, Illinois: University of Illinois Press, 1951).

38. See Merton, *Social Theory and Social Structure* (Reference 2), p. 318.

39. Alvin W. Gouldner, *Wildcat Strike* (Yellow Springs, Ohio: Antioch Press, 1954).

40. See George C. Homans, "Bringing Men Back In," *American Sociological Review*, 29: 809–818, 1964.

41. Lewis, see Reference note 37.

42. Lewis, "Further Observations on the Folk-Urban Continuum and Urbanization with Special Reference to Mexico City," *in* Philip M. Hauser and Leo F. Schnore, eds., *The Study of Urbanization* (New York: John Wiley and Sons, 1965), pp. 491–503, quotation from p. 497.

43. *Ibid.*, pp. 496–498.

44. See B. F. Skinner, *Science and Human Behavior* (New York: Macmillan Co., 1953).

45. For rectification of this error, see Orville G. Brim, Jr. "Socialization through the Life Cycle," in Orville G. Brim, Jr. and Stanton Wheeler, *Socialization after Childhood: Two Essays* (New York: John Wiley and Sons, 1965).

46. Moore, *Social Change* (see Reference 18), p. 55.

47. See Floyd H. Allport, "The J-Curve Hypothesis of Conforming Behavior," *Journal of Social Psychology*, 5: 141–183, 1934.

48. Levy, *The Structure of Society* (see Reference 10), pp. 87–88.

49. William Graham Sumner, *Folkways: A Study of the Sociological Importance of Usages, Manners, Customs, Mores, and Morals* (Boston: Ginn and Co., 1907).

50. See Sigmund Freud, *Civilization and Its Discontents* (New York: Jonathan Cape and Harrison Smith, 1930).

51. August Aichorn, *Wayward Youth* (New York: Viking Press, 1935); (paperback ed., 1965).

52. In Merton, *Social Theory and Social Structure*, see Reference 2.

53. *Ibid.*

54. See Robert Dubin, "Deviant Behavior and Social Structure," *American Sociological Review*, 24: 147–164, 1959; Richard A. Cloward, "Illegitimate Means, Anomie, and Deviant Behavior," *American Sociological Review*, 24: 164–176, 1959.

55. Merton, *Social Theory and Social Structure* (see Reference 2), p. 181.

56. See Moore, *Social Change* (Reference 18), pp. 26–27.

57. *Ibid.*, pp. 58, 68.

58. Merton, *Social Theory and Social Structure* (see Reference 2), p. 162.

59. Albert K. Cohen, *Delinquent Boys: The Culture of the Gang* (Glencoe, Illinois: Free Press, 1955).

60. See especially Emile Durkheim, *Suicide*, translated by J. Spaulding and G. Simpson (Glencoe, Illinois: Free Press, 1951).

61. Merton, *op.cit.*, in Reference 2, p. 135.

62. *Ibid.*, p. 162.

63. Marion J. Levy, Jr., "Patterns (Structures) of Modernization and Political Development," *Annals of the American Academy of Political and Social Science*, 358: 29–40, 1965.

64. See Pitirim A. Sorokin, *Society, Culture, and Personality* (New York: Harper, 1947).

65. See William J. Goode, "A Theory of Role Strain," *American Sociological Review*, 25: 483–496, 1960.

66. Melvin M. Tumin, "Some Disfunctions of Institutional Imbalances," *Behavioral Science*, 1: 218–223, 1956.

67. See Moore, *Man, Time, and Society* (Reference 21), pp. 106–114.

68. Arnold S. Feldman and Wilbert E. Moore, "The Society," *in* Moore and Feldman, eds., *Labor Commitment and Social Change in Developing Areas* (New York: Social Science Research Council, 1960), p. 64.

69. See Wilensky, as cited in Reference 24.

70. See John D. Campbell, "Peer Relations in Childhood," *in* Hoffman and Hoffman, eds., cited in Reference 31, pp. 289–322.

71. David E. Lavin, *The Prediction of Academic Performance* (New York: Russell Sage Foundation, 1965).

72. *Ibid.*, pp. 134–138.

73. *Ibid.*, p. 138.

74. See Delbert C. Miller and William H. Form, *Industrial Sociology: The Sociology of Work Organizations*, revised ed. (New York: Harper, 1964), pp. 223–287.

75. See Merton, *Social Theory and Social Structure* (Reference 2), pp. 265–268.

76. *Ibid.*, pp. 225–368.

77. See Wilbert E. Moore, *The Conduct of the Corporation* (New York: Random House, 1962), pp. 21–46, 79–90.

78. Erving Goffman, *Asylums* (New York: Doubleday and Co., 1961).

79. See Samuel A. Stouffer and others, *The American Soldier: Adjustment During Army Life* (Princeton, New Jersey: Princeton University Press, 1949), Vol. I, pp. 124–130.

80. Moore, *The Conduct of the Corporation* (see Reference 77), pp. 163–166.

81. See Emile Durkheim, *The Division of Labor in Society*, translated by George Simpson (New York: The Macmillan Co., 1933), pp. 70–110.

82. Berelson and Steiner (see Reference 15), pp. 476–490.

83. See Ernest Havemann and Patricia S. West, *They Went to College* (New York: Harcourt, Brace, 1952).

84. See August B. Hollingshead and Fritz C. Redlich, *Social Class and Mental Illness: A Community Study* (New York: John Wiley and Sons, 1958).

85. See Liston Pope, "Religion and the Class Structure," *Annals of the American Academy of Political and Social Science*, March, 1948, pp. 84–91; E. T. Clark, *The Small Sects in America* (New York: Abingdon Press, 1949).

86. For an extensive review of relevant research, see Bettye M. Caldwell, "The Effects of Infant Care," *in* Hoffman and Hoffman, eds., cited in Reference 31, pp. 9–87; also Urie Bronfenbrenner, "Socialization and Social Class through Time and Space," *in* Eleanor E. Macoby, Theodore M. Newcomb, and E. L. Hartley, eds., *Readings in Social Psychology* (New York: Henry Holt, 1958), pp. 400–425.

87. Caldwell, *op.cit.*, p. 81.

88. W. C. Becker, "Consequences of Different Types of Parental Discipline," *in* Hoffman and Hoffman, eds., cited in Reference 31, pp. 169–208.

89. See W. Lloyd Warner and P. S. Lunt, *The Social Life of a Modern Community* (New Haven, Connecticut: Yale University Press, 1941).

90. Wilensky, see Reference 24.

91. Daniel R. Miller and Guy E. Swanson, *The Changing American Parent: A Study in the Detroit Area* (New York: John Wiley and Sons, 1958).

92. Roger Brown, *Social Psychology* (New York: Free Press of Glencoe, 1965), p. 113.

93. See Wilbert E. Moore, "But Some Are More Equal Than Others," *American Sociological Review*, 28: 13–18, 1963.

94. See E. Digby Baltzell, *The Protestant Establishment: Aristocracy and Caste in America* (New York: Random House, 1964); Vance Packard, *The Pyramid Climbers* (New York: McGraw-Hill Book Co., 1962).

95. Merton, *Social Theory and Social Structure* (cited in Reference 2), pp. 170–184.

96. Moore, *The Conduct of the Corporation* (see Reference 77), pp. 173–179.

97. See Melvin M. Tumin, "Some Unapplauded Consequences of Social Mobility in a Mass Society," *Social Forces*, 36: 32–37, 1957.

98. Kingsley Davis, *Human Society* (New York: The Macmillan Co., 1949), pp. 562–586.

99. Kingsley Davis and Judith Blake, "Social Structure and Fertility: An Analytic Framework," *Economic Development and Cultural Change*, 4: 211–235, 1956.

12
THE INDIVIDUAL IN AN
ORGANIZATIONAL SOCIETY

I believe that the field of "industrial relations" as we have understood the subject in the last three decades does not have much of a future. I think most of the subject matter of the field has been misunderstood, misconstrued, and misrepresented by both the academic community and the staff representatives of industrial relations in business and industry. The academics and the practicing professionals have shared in a kind of conspiracy. The conspiracy consists in a mutually reinforced will to believe in a myth: the notion that the concept of industrial relations is precisely definitive of a singular and crucial division of the industrial labor force. The argument goes: Between management and labor there is a great gulf fixed. Each party is homogeneous, organized, and articulate. And since these parties are caught in a condition of coerced cooperation, they have *relations*. But I suggest that this gulf has not been very firm or very fixed since the latter part of the Nineteenth Century, when the corporate structure started to emerge, and has been ever more fluid ever since.

While most management men and the newly emergent spokesmen for labor interests were accepting the Marxist notion that there was a fundamental division between property owners and the people in their employ, the bases of proprietorship were shifting. Managers have become proletarians by strict Marxist definition. Workers have been steadily upgraded rather than downgraded in average educational and

SOURCE. Adapted from "The Individual in an Organizational Society," *in* John H. G. Crispo, ed., *Industrial Relations: Challenge and Response* (Toronto: University of Toronto Press, 1966); by permission of the editor and publisher.
I owe the term "organizational society" to Professor John William Ward, now of Amherst, who several years ago conducted a Princeton University Conference on the theme.

skill levels. A growing proportion of white-collar workers could not be called managers, nor production workers, nor clerical record keepers and communicators, but rather technical, scientific, and professional workers.

The whole traditional fabric of industrial relations has come apart at the seams, and indeed has shredded into tangled strands. Specialized occupational interests, division by rank, function, and bureaucratic subdivision, highly individual preoccupations abound in the contemporary work organization. The industrial relations man for management is also a professional, and thus already in a role-conflict situation. He also is supposed to deal with hard-bargaining unions, whose united front is increasingly rare. Life is now complicated, and it will not get simpler. *Au contraire.* And he may find himself bargaining *for* himself and his peers almost at the same time that he is bargaining *against* other representative, collective interests. If we mean to take the term, and the scholarly mission, of "industrial relations" seriously, we must surely attend to contemporary organizational complexities, and not assume that we are dealing with two well-organized antagonists. I shall return to the industrial setting in due course, but first I want to complicate life even further, by taking a somewhat broader view of what organized life means to the individual participant in contemporary civilization.

Paradoxes abound in contemporary society. We are becoming simultaneously more specialized and differentiated in our ways of making a living and in our life styles and more homogeneous in our basic consumer standards and in our participation in the national culture. We are becoming increasingly committed to the nuclear family, consisting of parents and their immature children, and with the generations and adult siblings socially and spatially separated, and increasingly reliant on communications and informal transfers of services among the nominally separate units.

I offer here another paradox, though its character is partially semantic. We are both disorganized and highly organized, and indexes of both would undoubtedly show an upward slope through time.

Let me turn to the concept of disorganization, for it will be lurking just offstage in the subsequent low-keyed drama, after we have permitted it a central place in the plot.

Many of the phenomena of daily life in the United States and other contemporary societies that are identified in the popular press or in sociological texts as examples of social disorganization are genuinely pathological. That is, the conditions or actions so identified reveal failures of the society to fulfill stated aims, or threaten its capacity for continuous operation, or at the least demonstrate that some segments of the population enclosed in the society's political boundaries have somehow not performed according to normal expectations. Despite some tedious attempts of occasional sociologists to identify every action or social manifestation as subtly beneficial to the social order, I think it should be said plainly that some social behavior is clearly sinful or otherwise disruptive. Most of crime and delinquency and of various indicators of alienation such as alcoholism and drug addiction can be taken as displaying the failures of social organization. On a grander scale occasional manifestations of discord merit the designation of disorganization. I refer, for example, to truculent polarization in political allegiances, such as the unconscionable pretensions to virtue on the part of persons who have unmerited privileges, or the dismaying displays of discontent among those who have succeeded beyond their dreams as well as, plainly, beyond their merits. The radical left when it had some significance often offered a certain appeal to equity, while offering silly or iniquitous schemes for its achievement. The radical right does not even offer equity, but only the restoration of a mythical, heroic past when people "knew their place."

Yet there are certain examples of disorganization that are such only by comparison with an abstract—I will not say ideal—model of a perfectly integrated system. By this view, we may look at a society cross-sectionally—that is, at a moment of time—and observe widespread differences in custom and cuisine, in residence and religion, in economic interest and political intent, in belief and behavior. Competition and discord meet the eye, and the elementary facts are not changed by calling the system pluralistic. With a little more trouble, we can also observe unequal rates of change in various aspects of social phenomena. If they all fitted together neatly once upon a time, that has not been true lately, and will not be so in any future that matters to mortal men.

Though some of the disorder, both persistent and changeful, that meets the observer's eye is truly random or aberrant, a great deal of it is organized. And that brings me back to the paradox that while the indexes of disorganization increase, so do the indexes of organization. In terms of concrete aggregations of individuals with common goals and regular procedures, of collective forms of working and playing, of disciplined procedures for pursuing the production of goods or the exchange of information or the governing of men, human concerns do get organized. Not to join the group is to be a social isolate, and that is social death.

In the real world of experience, the closest approximation to the *integrated* complex society must necessarily be the totalitarian structure, where inconsistency, competition, and choice are at least nominally forbidden, and where all change is nominally planned and directed according to a grand scheme of temporal priorities and necessary functional counterparts.

If, therefore, I here adopt the position of the social critic as well as that of the social analyst, it is within the context of preserving pluralism, with all the untidiness that is the cost of permitting a measure of liberty and therefore choice, and not that of suggesting an insufferably tidy system.

Before dealing with such grand themes as the position of the modern American corporation, and problems of responsibility and power in big business or big government, I want to ease into the subject by looking at some of the other organized features of contemporary society.

"Let's Get Organized"

"Now is the time for all good men to come to the aid of their party." Untold millions of student typists have printed out these words, most often thoughtlessly. Since women comprised the great majority of typists until recently, there may have been some ambiguity as to what party the men were meant to aid. But the call to organize, to join in collective efforts, is heard throughout the land, and it seems that it grows louder as competing voices contribute to the din.

Freedom of organization and assembly is a cherished political right in Anglo-American legal systems. Though the legal environment is more restrictive where codified law prevails, as in Western Europe, and associations are highly manipulated in communist countries, all modern societies display a plethora of organizations. Many of these associations have little to do with the work place or the residential community, though some may have their primary locus and rationale in occupational and community life.

For convenience, associations may be divided into two categories: interest-oriented and expressive.[1] Interest groups are organized to do good or at least to combat evil. The common interests of their members may be occupational—labor unions and professional societies come to mind—or otherwise economic. Thus, local merchants banded together as a Chamber of Commerce may seek new industry for the community, causing a counterorganization of residential property owners adjacent to the proposed industrial site. Incidentally, since American political parties represent coalitions of heterogeneous interests, the issues that divide local communities rarely cut along party lines; the constituted political machinery accordingly proves inadequate for resolving the

problems and new, essentially political, organizations are created
ad hoc.

Interest groups often represent the narrowly selfish concerns of the
members. Such groups tend to preclusive membership: ". . . only a spy
or a pretty silly joiner would become identified with two or more
contestants."[2] The group is likely to be viewed by its members as a
mere instrumentality for making common cause among those with like
concerns, though some organizers and high participators may indeed
become committed to the collective identity as such.

Of course not all interests are selfish in the ordinary sense. Charitable
and welfare associations also appear, and make their claims to allegiance. They compete with amateur sporting clubs, groups devoted to the
more passive recreation offered by bridge or poker, and a host of literary
and collectors' societies. These expressive associations are not commonly and overtly divisive, as are the narrowly constituted interest
groups, but in the United States the array of associations of both types
offers ample testimony to the intrusion of racial and ethnic distinctions
into matters ranging from technical occupations to butterfly collecting
that appear to have little relevance to ethnicity.[3]

The association may be defined residually as a formally constituted
organization representing the like or common interests of members, for
whom membership does not constitute a livelihood. Of course some
large associations do afford paid staffs, but this administrative detail
scarcely affects the fact that associations are essentially nonwork organizations. Indeed I have argued in a recent book[4] that associations are to
be found primarily in modern industrial societies whose work organizations are also highly specialized and where there is a fairly sharp
demarcation between mandatory time—represented by the school and
the job—and discretionary time.

The groups we have been discussing are often called voluntary associations, for in the pure case—which may be closely approximated only
in the Anglo-American institutional system—the individual has the
option of which associations he will join, and in fact whether he will
join any. Now occupational associations commonly attempt to achieve
mandatory monopolies over practitioners, with varying degrees of
success, and even organized charity can be pretty compulsory if it uses
the evil offices of employers to extract participation. But there is also a
subtler problem of freedom in a highly organized world. Does one any
longer have the rational right not to join? Self-help may be inadequate
in pursuit or protection of one's interest if those with adverse interests
gain strength through collective action. Another typing exercise goes,
"The quick brown fox jumped over the lazy dog," and its moral in this
connection is that the right to apathy may have been lost irretrievably.

The Perils of Pluralism

The performance of everything from the world's work to the world's play by functionally specialized organizations presents the individual with problems that are usually discussed in terms of status and role. There are problems of *status consistency* when the individual is a participant in many distinct contexts of action, in each of which he is subject to formal ranking or at least to evaluation of performance. There are problems of *role conflict* when organizations enter competing claims on time, treasure, or emotional allegiance on the fractionated individual, who must still somehow attempt to act as an integrated entity.

But functional specialization may also be viewed in terms of intergroup relations. Specialization, we have seen, by no means insures against competition for scarce resources. Even where there is clear complementarity among the specialized units—the family and the factory, the service club and the church, the union and the bowling team—there are ample opportunities for conflict, especially in terms of power and jurisdiction. It is merely tedious to note that groups as such do not feel, plan, or act; individuals do these things on behalf of collectivities. Intergroup conflict cannot be understood at the individual level.

The necessity of dealing with groups becomes self-evident when they do not share a common membership, when in fact membership is preclusive. Even when there is complementarity between the preclusive units—for example, physicians and nurses, business management and labor unions, manufacturers and retailers—the opportunities for conflict remain. Indeed, they may be heightened by struggles for power and jurisdiction in carrying out their interdependent functions.

Other preclusive groups may attempt to become "totalitarian," to establish separate and largely self-contained communities. Historically the communitarian sects tried to set themselves apart from the world. And in the urban setting settlements of recent immigrants maintained a separate identity that was a joint product of poverty, discrimination, and choice. Both types of separateness were subject to the intrusive effects of larger forces: the commodity market, the labor market, the state, and its perhaps most devastating instrument, the compulsory public school.

Though various sectarian and ethnic groups have become "assimilated" in varying degrees and at varying speeds, assimilation cannot be understood solely in terms of the sacrificing of old beliefs and customs in favor of a unified and dominant culture. The dominant culture has incorporated the traits of ethnic minorities while incorporating their carriers into the social life of American society.

Yet ethnicity is by no means a thing of the past, and in the conspicuous case of the American Negro is very much with us indeed. Yet despite the exceptionally submerged status of the Negro, the dominant culture itself is strongly marked and enriched by elements of Negro origin.

The American language, polity, and economy have evolved while mainly retaining their course with relatively minor effects from the diversity of religious and ethnic elements. Religious diversity persists and is an outstanding feature of American pluralism. Political diversity persists and incorporates ethnic interests, but ethnic and racial interests are rarely decisive at the national level. On all these scores the Canadian situation is more complex.

To counter the homogeneity feared by critics of mass culture, we have been considering some strongly competitive and even divisive elements in the contemporary scene. Cuisine, art styles, and religious beliefs have become matters of preference, tolerable differences rarely leading to organized hostilities. Ethnic conflict now involves only Negroes and Puerto Ricans. Economic interests and political views command the capacity to stir passions and occasionally to imperil public order and the interests of third parties. But perhaps the greatest perils of pluralism come not so much from frontal oppositions but from such a degree of discretionary specialization that a common identity or a common culture is lost to a host of diverse organizational interests. The other side of tolerance is indifference, and that may go to the point of disengagement.

Bureaucracy Rampant

We have so far avoided the workaday world, which now deserves our attention. Here especially we are organized, possibly to a fault. The economy of individual farmers, craftsmen, and traders was in good part fictional when it was made the model for classical economics early in the Nineteenth Century. The magnitude of the myth has increased ever since, as larger and larger proportions of the labor force are coordinated, not primarily by the market but by the authority of owners and managers. A simple measure of bureaucratization is the proportion of the labor force comprised by wage and salary earners— leaving out independent farmers, individual proprietors, and those professionals and craftsmen in what we may call private practice. This proportion is highly correlated with indexes of economic development as countries are compared at a particular time, and has grown more or less steadily in the older industrial countries.* In the United States, over four-fifths of the labor force is bureaucratized by our definition, and farming is no more immune to the process than is urban manufacturing or governmental service.

The problems posed by bureaucratization are generally so well known as to require no more than brief recapitulation. The solutions to the problems are less easily called to mind, for some of them do not exist.

One of the first problems to be noted is that despite our cherished ideology of individualism, most members of the labor force have bosses. The realization that most of the bosses have bosses in turn may soften the subordination by sharing it, but that is not likely to help much. The employed individual is constrained by authority but also by a complex division of labor that requires highly specialized performance. Though the narrowness of specialization may decrease as one moves to higher levels of skill and authority, the progression is neither regular nor certain. Many relatively well-paid bureaucrats, public and private, are almost as completely "boxed in" as is the man whose actions are paced by a machine.

By organizing work—the producing of goods, managing money, providing public services, healing the sick, or educating the young— through complex and interdependent administrative structures, we gain the benefits of specialization in higher productivity, and pay certain costs. We separate work in time and place from most other meaningful activities of life, and at the workplace itself we threaten man's initiative and occasionally even his dignity.

The "organization man"[5] is depicted, with partial accuracy, as subjected to demands for conformity, to stultification of creativity. For many, a stable career consists of relatively passive rides on upbound escalators rather than climbing the ladder,[6] though at higher altitudes an occasional executive finds himself airborne in an ejection seat.

I do not want to paint too dark or too monochromatic a picture. For many factory workers, technology has passed beyond the phase of human subordination to mechanical requirements and pacing. The remaining workmen manipulate and monitor machines, or else diagnose their ills and apply therapy. Some managers have opportunities for being venturesome, if their prior experience has not systematically suppressed their creative abilities. And a rapidly growing, though still small, proportion of organizational positions demand truly professional qualifications and perforce offer indulgence of the professional's typical

* See Chapter 7.

commitment to creative problem-solving. In fact, it is the increase in the demand for specialized and rapidly updated knowledge and the use of that knowledge for rational decision that prevents bureaucracies from being too rigidly authoritarian. The manager often knows less than his subordinates, each in his own field, and that situation has a moderating influence on the exercise of power.

The individual has some other protections against the massive power or massive inertia of organizations, but all of them in combination may still be an inadequate foundation of freedom. First, though the individual employed by an organization thereby submits himself to terms and conditions of work that are in the first instance administratively determined, he has not, in most instances, totally abandoned the protection of the market. Where the individual is not free to change employers, as he is not in totalitarian regimes or in military service, his subordination to the system lacks this elementary protection. An employers' association blacklist has a similar consequence. And it sometimes happens that the individual's accumulated experience is so peculiar to a single employer's operations that there is no effective external market; he can move only by losing some of his skill and therefore market value.

Second, the individual may have collective protection through labor unions or other occupational associations. The effectiveness of such organized protection depends upon the capacity of the employee's organization to hold an effective monopoly on the services in question and thus to prevent the employer from substituting more amenable workers for the recalcitrant objectors. Such a capacity in turn necessarily rests upon political protection of employee organizations; the state becomes an invisible third party to disputes if it does not actually become a visible one. It should be underscored that it is not only manual laborers or department store clerks who have such organized protection. Professions commonly seek licensing from the state as a way of maintaining standards, and many make actual membership in the professional association an additional condition for practice. But this means that the salaried professional is always protected by his brethren, at least implicitly, particularly against demands that he perform contrary to the established codes of his calling. Note also the irony that the individual gains some independence from the employing organization by submitting himself to the discipline of another organization. The union or professional association, however, offers at least the nominal forms of democratic determination, and that is clearly not the case with administrative regulations set by bureaucracies.

A third, and rarer protection, is provided by an independent judiciary for the adjudication of disputes in such private polities as corporations or universities. We may note that judicial processes are built into military organizations, where the individual lacks the protection of the market, and many civil service systems have orderly bases of appeal. Though civil service appeals often involve job security, the military court offers one way of dealing with another problem intrinsic to bureaucracies: the abuse of power. How does the subordinate avoid compliance with an "illegal" order, that is, one contrary to the established rules and precedents of the organization? Union contracts often provide for a multistage grievance procedure, which is essentially judicial. But the managerial employee commonly lacks such protection, except as a one-stage appeal to the boss's boss may prevail as a more or less formal right. Until business management becomes truly professional in both technical and ethical standards, and that is some considerable way into the future, there is a fairly strong case to be made for judicial procedures in private bureaucracies.

There is, fourth, another alternative to the internal judiciary, and that is the legislative and judicial protection of the state itself. We have now established fairly extensive precedents for legislative action on wages, hours, safety, and workman's compensation, the rights and powers of unions, and so on. There is also some precedent, but less firmly established, for review by the regular courts of the abuse of administrative power. One way of doing this in our legal system is to view the announced administrative regulations of private organizations as constituting contractual conditions for all employees. This is the principal basis in law and equity for firing the subordinate who fails to do his job or violates various rules. But what happens when principal officers violate rules, or middle managers violate rules out of sight of their superiors but at the expense of their subordinates? Who guards the guardians? In most private corporations, they guard themselves, a notoriously flimsy restraint on the abuse of power. It is in this area where I think we may expect to see a rise of external review if private organizations do not take steps to provide their own restraints.

The Untidy Society

Although everywhere we look we encounter multiplying organizations, some of which are growing in size and power, the total result is remarkably disorderly. Now of course the meaning of freedom is choice and the cost of choice is uncertainty, but we cannot so glibly gloss over some glaring defects of the contemporary disorder.

Take first, the giant corporation.[7] It is by no means free of restraints, but it retains substantial power of irresponsible action. The market offers some discipline, but consumers may have at least as great a dependence on one of a strictly limited number of suppliers as the converse; and if those suppliers act in concert, even if implicitly and without illegal conspiracy, the consumer has little protection. The corporation also has other clienteles: stockholders and other investors, suppliers of materials and components, employees, local plant communities, the state in its multiform activities, and the public not elsewhere classified. But the restraints and interests bearing on the corporation often work at cross-purposes, and require balancing, placating, or even manipulating. These and other duties fall on the chief executives, and the very confusion of interests and uncertainties about goals warns us that we cannot be sure how all this chaos gets organized. Stockholders are treated as another clientele, neither irrelevant nor clearly primary. The quest for position in the market appears to account for corporate behavior better than the quest for profits. And there are strong signs that the organization itself, and particularly its managerial inhabitants, take top priority among the interests that corporations serve.

Now self-interest is not despicable in our traditions, particularly in economic activities, as long as there are counterbalancing restraints to protect the interests of others. And that is where the contemporary conduct of the corporation appears to me to be weakest. In sociological language, the large corporation with diversified equity ownership is incompletely institutionalized, as the older restraints of private property and competitive markets have not been replaced by more relevant responsibilities.

To say that corporate managers have now become trustees of their organizations to assure their continuity and their current service to clienteles is to substitute one uncertainty for another. The responsibilities of trusteeship are also poorly defined in law. But one qualification of the trustee is firmly institutionalized, and that is that his service be disinterested. The richly rewarded corporate executives clearly fail that crucial test.

To say that corporate managers are becoming professionalized, with what that implies by way of intellectual and ethical standards, represents a small measure of truth, but the process is very incomplete and its completion still would not resolve the issues regarding the priorities among clienteles—or, to put it another way, the answer to the question, what is the corporation for?

Having turned over one batch of uncertainties, let me consider another aspect of pluralistic organization. Though we speak of self-service—which is essentially passing on part of distribution labor to the consumer—man is irretrievably social and most services are rendered for others. In fact, viewed precisely, all labor consists of services, but so do other acts for the benefit of others. If we ask, how do services get performed and allocated in human societies, the most frequent answer would be in terms of kinship and related structures and various informal but traditional reciprocities within communities. Within modernized societies there are two other modes of getting services performed, and in some still a third. One of the major marks of modernization is the development of a labor market, which means in effect that services are rewarded with wages, salaries, or fees. Some of these services are devoted to producing and distributing physical goods, true, but others are devoted to administration, to education, and indeed to ministering to all man's concerns from the religious through physical and psychological health, relations to the law, and to such mundane matters of traditional concern as care of those too young, too feeble, or too old to care for themselves.

In all modernized societies the market mechanism for getting such services performed is supplemented, and in some virtually supplanted, by the intervention of the state. Rather than various benefits being contingent on ability to pay, these are rendered on the basis of "need" by public agencies. Thus the "fisc" is substituted for the market, with taxation based on ability to pay, but no guarantee of a *quid pro quo*. Indeed, the mechanism is precisely that of a "transfer" from those who pay taxes to those who need services—with virtually every adult in both categories in one respect or another. It is a mode of distribution that has received remarkably little intelligent analysis from the scholarly community, as economists are rather uneasy outside the market mechanism, and other social scientists have lacked the skills, or the interest in dealing with the ways welfare benefits are handled. While their hearts bleed, their minds lack the vital juices for thought.

We have in the United States, not uniquely but to an unparalleled degree, another alternative to informal, market, and fiscal modes of providing services. That way is private philanthropy. I should like to call this a "fourth force." This is not the time or the place to drag out numbers and balance sheets, but it is evident that both the charitable organization dependent on current contributions and the endowed charitable trust play extremely important roles in scientific research, health, education, and miscellaneous welfare activities—including the fine arts along with nursery schools as examples of welfare.

In this area, once more, we encounter the problem of trusteeship, but not terribly tainted with the crude calculus of self-interest. Not that we can assume that all chairmen of community fund drives or workers in voluntary social work agencies or the professional staffs in endowed foundations are self-abnegating saints, but rather that they are under more severe lawful restraints and not subject to such ambiguous definitions of their situation as being possible beneficiaries of rewards for having a good year in the market. About the only external review of the responsibilities of foundations comes from an examination of their tax exemption, but it is surely high time that some more dispassionate scrutiny be given to their appropriate functions in an organizational society that provides alternative mechanisms for private benefits and public well-being.

I have considered that my mission is to point to some unmistakable trends in the shape of our modern era, with several sharp glances at uncertainties that call for mature consideration and possible action. I do not plead for a system that is tidy, for that way lies total constraint and possibly collective disaster. But I do think that it is not too much to ask that some social scientists develop a sense of relevance that need not destroy their claims to objectivity. The relevance I have in mind includes examination of the alternative ways of solving life's dilemmas and the intrinsic problems of organized existence—some of which grow in urgency and all of which change in their realistic manifestations. We have increasingly turned to government, and national government at that, for resolving conflicts and curing glaring inequities. Most of the alternatives so far offered are plainly reactionary: a nostalgic reconstruction of a mythical past which was in fact unmistakably evil. The powers now at our command are greater, along with the problems they pose. Organize we must and legislate we must, and adjudicate we must—for these are standard mechanisms for problem-solving and tension-management. But underlying these is the necessity to understand, to identify, and, let it be said plainly, to set goals and preferences. It is just possible that an organizational society that is pluralistic can survive. But not without good sense along with good will.

References

1. See Wilbert E. Moore, *Man, Time, and Society* (New York: Wiley and Sons, 1963), Chapter 6, "Voluntary Associations."

2. *Ibid.*, p. 107.

3. See Frederick G. Ruffner, Jr., and others, eds., *Encyclopedia of Associations*, 4th ed., Vol. I, *National Organizations of the United States* (Detroit: Gale Research Co., 1964).

4. Wilbert E. Moore, see Reference 1.

5. See William H. Whyte, Jr., *The Organization Man* (New York: Simon and Schuster, 1956).

6. See Wilbert E. Moore, *The Conduct of the Corporation* (New York: Random House, 1962), Chapter XII, "Climbers, Riders, Treaders."

7. The paragraphs on corporate responsibility are based on Reference 6, especially Chapter I, "Management in Moral Crisis," and Chapter XXI, "Public: Political and Profane."

13
AGING AND THE SOCIAL SYSTEM

Man, in his quest for intellectual distinctiveness and spiritual exclusiveness, has often minimized or neglected his biological nature. In that he has been abetted by many social scientists, for by attempting to evade biological determinism and avoid having human behavior become merely a special branch of mammalian zoology, the social scientists have tended to deal with cultural man more than biological man. The two of course can scarcely be distinguished analytically, and certainly not concretely.

Human evolution is a complex biosocial process. There is no reason to suppose that biological adaptation ceased with the emergence of "culture,"[1] which, after all, is coextensive with the human species in time and space. And as long as man does not control the meteorological and geophysical forces around him, and remains subject to the discipline of his own mortality, he cannot be said to have mastered the nonhuman environment in order to live in one solely of his own creation.

The social scientists' neglect of biological man has been selective rather than total. Human sexuality has not been left to the exclusive attention of poets and novelists; it figures in not a few scholarly treatises—especially those of psychologists and sociologists. And children enter the picture in those disciplines also. They almost never appear in economics or political science. And in all of these disciplines, most of the more abstract analytical and theoretical systems of the social scientists appear to deal exclusively, if implicitly, with normal adults. Even if attention is paid to the implications of biological recruitment in the continuing necessity for incorporating the recruits into an ongoing system, this process of *socialization* is most commonly

SOURCE. Adapted from "Aging and the Social System," *in* John C. McKinney and Frank deVyver, eds., *Aging and Social Policy* (New York: Appleton-Century-Crofts, 1966); by permission of the editors and publisher.

treated as of short duration in early childhood, leading to a one-by-one and nearly instantaneous conversion from savagery to civilization.

A rather different perspective on social organization and social process results from dealing with the entire human life cycle as a necessary biological dimension of continuing social systems. Indeed, age as a kind of neutral and continuous variable, which manifests itself in both continuous and discontinuous changes in behavior, is relevant for most forms of social discourse and social structure. Our task here is to examine the interplay between this unavoidable basis for individual change and the social system that comprises the ordering of behavior according to values and norms, and allocates activities to actors in terms of positions and roles.

The conception of social system entails the notion of interdependence among constituent elements. The concept does not require the assumption that "everything fits together." Within the temporal and spatial boundaries of any social system identified and specified, there may be acts that are discordant and acts that are simply indeterminate. These become empirically determinable dimensions or characteristics of systems, neither impossible by definition nor necessarily destructive of other systemic qualities if discovered. The concept also does not require the assumption that systems remain static. At the minimum, functional relations are rarely instantaneous. But the relations among elements may be sequential as well as merely reciprocal, and how systems change is as legitimate a query as how they persist.

The title of this essay will be taken seriously in the following discussion, in that we shall deal in part with life-cycle phenomena and not solely with those persons at later parts of the cycle, the aged. The ultimate cause of death is birth, and aging is a process that starts at conception. This elementary biological fact is intrinsic to social systems, though it may be neglected for various analytic purposes. It can scarcely be left out of account if we wish to attend to the facts of systemic change, or to inquire about the way life-cycle phenomena affect the operation of the social order. Our procedure will be to deal first with the implications of the fact that immortal systems are inhabited by mortal men. We shall then examine continuities and discontinuities in the life cycle. Since culture and social organization in large part flow between generations and along age lines, we shall attend to the differences between true reciprocities and what we shall call "serial service." Finally, in an era when the pace of many social changes is accelerating, we shall note the additional strains that arise between the cumulative experience of the aging individual and the collective experience of social systems.

Role Relationships

A society as a whole or any continuing social organization is perforce faced with a succession of actors or role-players. Man's mortality assures the necessity of recruitment. Ultimately that recruitment rests on biological reproduction, but various positions require prior socialization or at least the achievement of some testable or arbitrary degree of "maturity." Typically, various social positions have some kind of age-specificity, though the age grade may be rather broad and not always defined in precise, chronological time: for example, infancy, childhood, youth, adulthood, and, perhaps, old age. Transition from one broad age grade to another thus entails some discontinuity in the life cycle, a subject to which we turn in the following section. But it also entails replacement as individuals leave an age grade, whether they leave by "graduating," or, sooner or later, by death.

In all societies there may be considerable periods in the life cycle when aging is gradual and expected role relationships essentially constant. During these periods, cumulative experience or even physical vigor may count for little in differentiating younger and older members of the category, so that there is little sense of either progression or retrogression. This appears to be most often true of the broad age grade of adulthood, and even in a highly graded society such as our own, many of the powers and responsibilities of adults have little variability according to either exact chronological age or social seniority in the position.

Yet the succession problem remains. And for any social role, that is, any role beyond the passive one of the newborn infant, there are two interacting sources of variability among recruits: biological competence and aptitudes, and differences in exact socialization experience. I have accordingly argued elsewhere[2] that vagaries and uncertainties in the socialization process must introduce flexibilities and change potentials in any continuing system, and that these potentials are increased by the associated necessity for adult role requirements to constitute tolerable ranges rather than highly precise specifications. The replacement of those who move through and out of a system by recruits moving in will introduce some changes in the system itself, however small that change may be. Obviously the rate of replacement should be correlated with the rate of systemic change, apart from all other considerations.

We thus encounter the paradox that life expectancies are low and social succession high precisely in the underdeveloped areas of the world where the social order is commonly supposed to be traditional and relatively unchanging. Though the latter assumption no doubt has been exaggerated, two countervailing sources of stability may be noted. First, the risks of mortality do not bear equally on all ages. The average expectation of life is greatly affected by the mortality of the very young. Adults may not have death rates radically higher than those in more economically advanced societies.

There is a second source of stability in "traditional" societies despite somewhat higher turnover through adult mortality. For those who reach adulthood, the social structure is generally much less finely differentiated than that of modernized societies. This lack of detailed differentiation is especially true of the system as it bears on the individual, though, for the structure as a whole, status and other distinctions may be rather extensive. The Indian structure of castes and subcastes, for example, is wondrously complex, but the individual is not subject to their distinct demands either simultaneously or *seriatim* through a career. Once the individual is placed in the system, the role-demands and skills may be relatively simple, standardized, and easily acquired. Mortality that is merely "high" but that does not literally wipe out a standardized segment of the system may have little gross impact on the way the survivors play out their roles. (Differential mortality between status segments would of course have consequence for their relative positions.)

We are dealing, then, with mortal men occupying and passing through positions in a system that is in principle immortal. The magnitude of the succession problem depends on the way age-specific mortality rates intersect with the age-grading characteristic of a society and its various subsystems.

Let us assume, probably correctly, that age-specific mortality actually has the greatest relevance for succession and accompanying structural change where many people move through a somewhat graded career —and that would be primarily the situation in modernized societies. Let us also assume that the structure is more or less adapted to relatively stable or slowly changing mortality conditions within and among the various age grades. Then we should expect the greatest structural dislocation by sharp changes in mortality conditions. As a concrete illustration, substantial war losses among young men in military service leave gaps in the "recruitment cohorts" for subsequent civilian employment, improve the competitive career chances of the survivors and those just younger and incidentally damage the marital chances of their female contemporaries. Conversely, to take a hypothetical situation, a substantial reduction of mortality rates of men over, say, 50 years of age, would impair the promotional prospects of younger men and postpone the demise of persons in lifetime positions. (One cannot avoid noting the parallel at the individual level of the impatient heirs of a wealthy but long-lived ascendant or the watchful suspense created by an over-age hereditary ruler.)

Different age cohorts in a population represent different "environmental histories," including differing mortality conditions. When we add structural changes that are at least somewhat independent of current age-compositions—for example, variations in employment opportunities for new entrants to the labor force—it is clear that age cohorts have differential "life chances" as they move through a social order. It goes without saying that life chances are also differentiated by sex, by "class," and by other variables, but our focus here is on the intersection of age and social patterns.

In general, changes in proportional age distributions are much more a reflection of changes in fertility than of changes in mortality. After a careful examination of the evidence, Coale concludes that ". . . the rising fraction of the aged in western countries has not resulted from lowered death rates but almost wholly from a long history of declining fertility."[3] He also notes[4] that the substantial variations in fertility in the United States over recent decades has produced a highly irregular age distribution.

Persons now (in 1965) aged 65 and over are of course the survivors of birth cohorts before the turn of the century, when fertility rates had not gone far in their downward slope. The growing proportions of aged persons in the population and the prospect for those proportions to go on increasing is largely a function of subsequent fertility declines prior to World War II. Persons now in their early 30's are the survivors of small birth cohorts during the Depression and the smallest proportional increase over the period of 1960–1985 will be the "mature" segment of the population, 20–65. A little before the end of the century, in the absence of major declines in mortality rates at older ages, American society will have a temporary respite from the swelling number of oldsters as the Depression babies finally reach retirement age.

Since we are dealing with succession to social positions as individuals age, that is, move through the life cycle, and since we are concentrating for the moment on the demographic components of succession, we need to note two other points. One relates to the lack of what we may call "demographic replication," and the other relates to the average length of generations.

With regard to demographic replication I have previously noted that

. . . a precise total and differential control of fertility and mortality is extremely unlikely. Thus the exact size of a population cannot be expected to remain stationary through time, and it is even less likely that births and deaths will exactly maintain existing distributions among various social categories.[5]

What this means is that the social system must permit some mobility between generations, even if placement is nominally hereditary. That implication leads to another, namely, that socialization into prospective future roles in the life cycle must be uncertain or improper for some people in any society. These problems are of course much more severe in modernized societies, where mobility is the necessary norm and where the future is cloudy and uncertain because of rapid structural changes. To these points I shall return in another context.

The rapidity of "demographic turnover" (with its implications for social succession) is also affected by the length of generations. If we define generational length as the average age of parents at the birth of their children, it is almost certainly higher in underdeveloped than in modernized societies. This holds true despite the practice of very early marriages and childbearing in many societies, for in the absence of contraception mothers who remain alive and fertile continue childbearing until menopause. The present and recent situation in modernized societies, even during the "baby boom" is characterized by relatively early marriage, early childbearing, *and early termination of childbearing.* In the United States relatively few babies are born to mothers over the age of 30. If these shortened generations continue—and there is every reason to suppose that they will—the multigenerational lineage will be increasingly common with most children having all their grandparents alive until the children themselves reach maturity.

We have been examining the demographic flow of recruits to social positions relative to age. The succession problem of course is somewhat more than the flow of birth cohorts through age-distribution tables or life tables. We must also bear in mind variations in time and space of the social significance of age and aging. Various systems set minimum and maximum ages for types of social participation: labor market entry, marriage, voting, holding office, or—later in the cycle, compulsory retirement. Other rights and privileges or their termination are made functions of time rather than age as such: years of qualifying experience, terms of office, length and thus seniority of service. When coupled with age minima these temporal patterns may be viewed as a further aspect of succession.

It is a commonplace that different social systems place differing values on various stages of the life cycle and allocate differing privileges and responsibilities to the older age groups. Yet whether most individuals experience a gradual and steady rise in relative position as they age until the time that they die or become unmistakably senile, or go through an ascent and descent only partially parallel to their physiological capacities, the age curve of social participation is irretrievably cyclical in view of man's mortality. The temporal order of social systems[6] must somehow accommodate to the temporal order of biological man.

Age Grading and Life Cycles

Let us examine age grading and life cycles in a little more detail and narrow our field of vision to modernized societies and particularly to the contemporary United States.[7]

With the growth of a highly standardized educational system which is compulsory to ages ranging from 14 to 18, most of the children and youths of the society are caught up in a system involving rather precise age grading. This grading involves orderly progression from year to year, interspersed by somewhat sharper transitions between broad types of schools: for example, primary, secondary, college, and postgraduate. Though some individuals may be advanced or retarded according to the age-grade norms, there is a marked tendency in educational organization to accommodate individual differences *within* grades. Thus an individual's place in this formal organization can be inferred with high probability from knowledge of his age alone. When membership in the system becomes competitive and optional, as is generally true at higher levels, cohorts become depleted and age-grading tends to become looser for those remaining.

The adult breadwinner is also subject to age grading, though of a somewhat looser sort. Particularly for those in administrative careers in the military, civil service, or large private bureaucracies such as universities and corporations, there are always norms or standards for advancement with age. Careers will of course be affected by market demands for levels and types of skills—witness the ambivalence of today's senior professors when they compare their own slow advancement with the quick achievement of full professorial rank by men a few years beyond their doctoral studies.

Careers are also affected by the inconsistency between permanent tenure until formal retirement and the pyramidal shape of administrative hierarchies. Even if age—or its organizational equivalent in seniority—is a major requirement for promotion, it cannot be an exclusive one, for some members of an age cohort must be left behind when the positions thin out faster than the ranks of eligibles.

The adjustment problems of aging clearly are not confined to persons in retirement. The age grading of achievement, even if loose, presents adjustment problems throughout adulthood, particularly for regular members of the labor force. Keeping up with, falling behind, or forging ahead of one's age peers provides a constant or periodically recurrent opportunity for comparison.

A somewhat different problem is presented by the interrupted career. Married women who enter or reenter the labor force after the youngest child has reached adolescence have dual careers in the sociological sense, with a temporal ordering in their respective primacy. Their adjustment problems include loss of time (and its experiential equivalents) as compared with potential competitors with singular careers. They also find themselves in competition with current or recent labor-force entrants among the young. Apart from the preferences of employers for youths, which may be nonrational, the young may have a distinct and sensible advantage in this competition: they may have both a superior basis of knowledge and skills, either because of secular improvements in educational levels and standards or because the housewives' former competence has deteriorated, and the young may have superior habits conducive to continuous learning and adaptation.

Remarkably little is known of career patterns, or of the forms of career building in later maturity. There is a good deal of folk wisdom, of untested reliability, concerning crucial periods in age and achievement. Some organizations such as the military fomalize age-grade relationships, with the man who falls behind his contemporaries ("overage for rank") required to retire early or resign. In other careers the competitive system encourages occasional reappraisals—for example, when a man is passed over for promotion, thus closing his last opportunity for access to very high positions. I have elsewhere[8] discussed speculatively the complex interplay among aspirations, expectations, and achievements in graded careers. The frustration intrinsic to career competition is commonly commented on, though again we have little exact knowledge on the levels or significance of such frustration and the relative success of various coping mechanisms. Yet the man who exceeds his own earlier expectations, if not his wilder dreams, is also worthy of note, for he too has adjustment problems: living up to his unexpected success, and quieting his misgivings concerning his own relative merit.

Not much progress is going to be made in our understanding of aging in later maturity until we develop the underlying data on career sequences, and analyze those data in terms suitable to their complexity. The model is that of the Markov chain, whereby reaching certain points (due regard being taken of age or rate of prior movement) establishes probabilities for reaching later points in the chain. Unfortunately, few social scientists are methodologically equipped to handle this kind of analysis.

Despite ample examples of somewhat regularized age grading, some of it annual, there are discontinuities in the pace of aging. Some of these are formally marked off and honored by passage rituals. Others are more subjective, and still real and important. MacIver[9] notes that adults experience "indifferent intervals," often whole decades, interrupted by sharp realizations of aging as the ages of 30, 40, 50, 60, and so on, are reached.

The past when matters were better synchronized and coordinated may be largely mythical, but it is certainly true that the unequal rate of contemporary changes adds new degrees of problems if not new kinds. The shortened generation that derives from earlier cessation of childbearing does not correspond to the lengthened expectation of life and its implications for living to and beyond retirement age. Thus mothers tend to "retire" from their major role some 20 years before their husbands retire from work. The mothers whose youngest child has reached secondary school have the alternatives of entry or reentry into the labor force or of some form of leisure-time activity. They also comprise the bulk of what may be called the "volunteer labor force," upon which many community and welfare programs depend for services. If they choose economic activity, they must somehow make adjustments to their lack of continuous activity and accumulated experience. They may need to join technologically displaced males in adult retraining. If the women do not enter the labor market they must find a use for unaccustomed leisure. They may be in effect in early retirement, and the rising rate of female alcoholism attests to some failures in adjustment.

Women then tend to "retire" much earlier than men, despite their greater life expectancy. They may in fact have nearly half their lives in which they are not performing their "primary" female role, though in a sense they may continue to play an "integrative" role, both within the family system and in the neighborhood and community. Alienation is less surprising than its comparatively low incidence. And by the time their husbands retire, the wives have had considerable practice in filling up time in some sort of secondary roles. There is no assurance at all that the wife thus becomes an appropriate role-model for the retired male, as leisure may be as sex-differentiated as are primary adult roles.

The extended experience that many women have in use of leisure before they reach old age may stand them in good stead, as they may be unwittingly preparing for widowhood, which is probably their eventual lot. The off-phase cycle deriving from higher female life expectancy is exacerbated by the conventional practice of marrying men a year or two older than they—or if a remarriage, the age differential is likely to be considerably greater. The aged population thus comprises a disproportionate number of widows, who are not only cut off from children and grandchildren in varying degrees, but also have lost the marital companionship that may have previously substituted for maternal responsibilities.

Serial Services and Sequential Flow

Most human populations are recruited biologically. The exceptions, such as migratory resettlement or celibate religious orders, are either temporary or parasitic. The truism about biological recruitment takes on significance with the additional fact that the human infant at birth is quite unable to sustain life unaided. There is thus an intrinsic flow of "services" from older to younger members of a population, at least until the younger ones are able to fend for themselves. In all societies the overwhelmingly predominant structure for assuring the support and primary socialization of the young is the family. Though the family is rarely the exclusive agency of socialization, it is temporally primary and always important even where other formal and informal mechanisms operate.

Now the usual view is that the services between the generations in premodern societies begin to balance into complementarity as children take on various tasks, and finally change directions as parents who have lost productive vigor are supported by their mature offspring. Children thus become economic assets for the family as a productive unit by their added labor and then become old-age insurance for the parents. When things work out according to the model, there is a kind of balanced reciprocity which achieves balance only after several decades.

Such intergenerational reciprocity assumes that the young actually survive to add substantial effort to common activities and to become the primary source of economic support. With high infant- and child-mortality rates prevalent in premodern societies, the initial support by the parents often must be unrepaid. The reciprocity also assumes that parents live to an unproductive old age requiring support by their children, and that too, somewhat less often, is not the case. Nevertheless, the long-term reciprocity exists frequently enough to constitute a kind of standard.

The usual view of the family in modernized societies and particularly in the United States is that the social separation of the generations (and of siblings) at the maturity of the children cuts off the repayment. Services then run in one direction only, and from the point of view of a kind of hedonic calculus, parenthood becomes sacrificial.[10]

It is clearly true that the social mobility requisite to an industrialized society requires a separation of the generations in terms of social function and status, and is most consistent with a nuclear, conjugal family system that permits adult siblings also to find their ways separately in competitive placement. But I believe that the scattered evidence now at hand is consistent with a somewhat different view, by adding a temporal perspective to structural arrangements. It appears that the *initial* impact of economic modernization is the most damaging to laterally and vertically extended kinship reciprocities. The traditional patterns are commonly undermined not only by the residential separation of new recruits who leave the countryside or village to find new opportunities in modernizing cities, but also by the fact that the new recruits (typically youths and young adults) operate in radically novel structural and institutional settings. Between the old ways and the new there may be very little basis for mutual understanding, to say nothing of uniformity of social position.

As most of the population gets caught up into a modernized socioeconomic system, the separation of the generations and siblings in terms of the *kinds* of systems they participate in is partially reduced, though continuing rapid change means that some generational differences in social experience are intrinsic and an enduring feature of modernized societies.[11]

It appears, then, that the contemporary American kinship system has been able to survive the social inequality of its constituent primary families. Many kinship duties have become optional rather than mandatory, with consequent strains in attempting to honor competing claims. In most American legal jurisdictions, mature children are not responsible for the support of indigent parents, though this does not of course remove the claims of conscience.

If one asks, "Where does the American family turn first in time of trouble?" the modal answer is almost certainly, "To kinsmen." One might have to except rather standardized professional services available from physicians, school teachers, and clergymen. But illness that requires home nursing and family care, many types of financial emergencies, and bereavement, certainly, commonly call for use of kinship bonds. If residential propinquity permits, even such services as shopping and baby-sitting may be rendered unilaterally, traded in kind, or traded with crude complementarity. Of course, the reestablishment of kinship ties has been aided by improved transportation and communication.

From the scattered evidence, services and simple visiting are most likely to link the female kindred, financial assistance to link the males (except for financial help to widows, which may be regarded as the primary duty of sons.)

In the broad perspectives of comparative social change, the partial restoration of kinship ties after the shock of modernization is one of a somewhat limited range of instances of structural continuities in modified form after a substantial and discontinuous structural change. Such instances occur only once in each system, but recur in social space (time being incidental) as successive systems undergo a somewhat standardized transformation.

More to the present point, the strains in the modernized kinship system are intrinsic. (Since in every kinship system separate lineages are linked by marriage, there are always intrinsic strains between primary families and other kinsmen, but that is another matter.) Given the intimacy of intrafamilial relations and the primary functions of affectivity and normative socialization directed at the young, it would be unlikely that adults emerging from this structure should treat one another as strangers. The links between generations are likely to endure, apart from all considerations of property transfers or other economic attributes of lineage.

If a society is viewed as a system that not only persists through time but also accumulates physical capital and "cultural heritage," it is clear that the young can scarcely repay their inheritance. There is therefore a kind of unilateral flow of goods and services from generation to generation, or at least from predecessors to successors. In addition to true reciprocities, there is a kind of *serial service,* the initial beneficiaries "passing it on" rather than "passing it back."

The occurrence of serial service is by no means unique to the temporal order of generations. Much of the division of labor in modern manufacturing, though complementary in the grand design of the organizational plan seen in cross-section, is not strictly reciprocal. The workman at later stages in continuous assembly does not reciprocate the prior services of his fellows; his duty is to render services for those still later in the sequential pattern. An even closer parallel is offered by Whyte[12] in his description of suburban communities inhabited more or less briefly by young corporate executives subject to administrative transfers. Residents render all sorts of initial services to newcomers, passing along thereby benefits earlier received from *their* predecessors. Again, the obligation incurred by the newcomers is not to repay their benefactors, but to render like services to later arrivals. It is probably because sociologists have been exclusively preoccupied with models of self-balancing systems that so little attention has been given to serialization.

One aspect of serial service from generation to generation that was briefly alluded to above deserves some comment: namely, patterns of property inheritance.[13] The widespread practice of some form of inheritance in kinship lineages usually has been neglected by those who viewed traditional obligations between generations solely in terms of delayed reciprocities. At least for those prosperous enough to accumulate some kind of an estate beyond their own needs for support—which in some places become a kind of *quid pro quo* for their old-age support by heirs[14]—the sequential flow is clear.

In contemporary society, however, we encounter some further dislocations of what had previously seemed to be normal patterns. The increased longevity of the old may substantially reduce the size of the prospective inheritance by the needs for current support, and in any event postpones the transfer. (The ambivalence of heirs may be rather acute, but they can scarcely admit, let alone express, their impatience.) The effects of increased longevity are reinforced by those of shortened generations. Thus, by the time the last surviving parent (usually a widow) dies, the heirs are probably well beyond the middle of their own careers, that is, at a time much too late for their life chances to be greatly affected. In this situation, expenses for higher education of the young may be taken as a kind of "hidden capital transfer" or preinheritance, and more or less nominal loans for home purchase serve a similar function. Though I know of no evidence on this, it seems probable that lifetime distributions to immediate heirs are increasingly common, with posthumous transfers skipping a generation and running to grandchildren, who are at a more propitious stage of the life cycle to benefit from an inheritance.

Lest we get carried away, however, by the not very gripping problems of very well-to-do families, we should return to more statistically normal patterns. Here there is little question that most parents make genuine sacrifices for their children, both for current levels of support and especially for providing educational and similar bases for competitive opportunity. And these sacrifices are, I believe, not made with an eye toward future, reciprocal benefits. Rather, the parents precisely expect serialization, that is, that the children will behave similarly to provide services and opportunities to the following generation. To be alliterative, serial service becomes sacrifice *seriatim*. And the rewards, if mundane at all, must be satisfaction in conscientious performance, not the expectation of reciprocal return. This may not be tragedy, as I once characterized it,[15] but it will serve until the real thing comes along.

The sacrificial elements in the flow of services between generations are not completely unrequited. Some financial support and various services are provided by children for aged parents directly. And since support of the aged on the basis of need or one the quasi-insurance principles of Old Age and Survivors Insurance has become a matter of public policy, the young *do* support the old. This is a nice example of the "loss of family functions," but the function of old-age support, I have argued, often has been either irrelevant or poorly performed within the world's range of kinship systems.

The adjustment problems of aging in contemporary society would be severe enough if we attended only to the demographic changes that have increased the proportions of the aged and the basic structural changes associated with economic modernization. But a simple before-and-after comparison is inadequate for appraising current and prospective problems. A society does not become quiescent once it achieves a modern demographic balance and modern forms of structural differentiation. On the contrary.

It is particularly to the problems posed by the pace of continuous change that this concluding section attends. The procedure will be to compare individual change in the course of experience during a life cycle and collective change as wrought by a multiplicity of individuals in a social system. We shall examine briefly four typological cases of the interplay between aging individuals and social systems.

First, let us take the situation, typical of so-called traditional societies, where most structural changes are relatively minor, and aggregate change relatively slow. In these circumstances the view of the individual "passing through" a system is approximately accurate. The individual in the course of his life may essentially replicate the lives of his predecessors. And since generations properly go by lineages and cannot be applied cross-sectionally to entire populations, all ages coexist. Thus, even in the improbable event of very fine age grading, prior role models are constantly at hand. The inevitable slippage in training between true generations may thus be partially offset by the existence of "collateral intermediaries" who serve to smooth out the generational gap. The frequency with which this situation occurs in the contemporary world should not be exaggerated, in view of the universality of radical structural changes, but it has some interest as a kind of limiting case with extensive historical importance.

If structural change is somewhat more rapid, the adjustive individual may be able to keep current—the microcosm in effect replicating the macrocosm. The individual in the course of aging adds experience at about the pace that events are taking place. As a small example of this, an artisan or other technically trained producer may be able to "keep up" with developments as they are introduced by the aggregate of practitioners.

A third situation is one widely prevalent in newly modernizing societies. Structural change may be so rapid and so radical that it is essentially discontinuous with precedent. Here both the innovators and the adherents are likely to be young, with role models that are doctrinal and borrowed from other social systems. The aging person has no role models consistent with prior experience and values, and may be unable to adjust to novel arrangements. Indeed, he commonly suffers loss of authority, for he is no longer the exemplar and instructor for his children or others who traditionally might have emulated him. He becomes a pathetic figure, treated with indifference or contempt by the young revolutionaries.

A fourth situation is that of contemporary modernized societies, including the United States. With extremely rapid change, the pace of collective experience becomes too rapid for the individual to keep current. He falls behind. Generational succession gives way to dependence on a steady supply of new entrants to the labor force, bringing fresh skills and capacities for creative adjustment, but the young innovators are quickly threatened in their turn. Again, if we take the example of the person technically trained, his rate of accumulated experience is far less rapid than the rate of innovation produced by the aggregate of experts. He may be able to protect himself by specialization—to know more and more about less and less. He may be able to restrict access to his specialty, enforce employment security through seniority or tenure provisions, or become an administrator because he is no longer technically competent. He may, however, become plainly obsolete, and require a period of retraining if he is going to continue a productive career.

In a society in which social change is organized and institutionalized, "stopping progress" for the sake of a privileged position is not highly regarded. The alternatives are poorly developed, because the problem is generally seen as special rather than endemic. One alternative, and probably a bad one in view of poorly developed use of leisure in constructive ways, is something like a creative but short-lived participation in the labor force—say, fifteen years. Another alternative is for adult retraining, on a cycle that is likely to become increasingly frequent during a normal career. But that will require genuine attention to needful skills, and intellectual habits, rather than (or in addition to) contract bridge, bookbinding, flower arrangement, Shakespeare, current events, and ballroom dancing. A third alternative, which does not exclude the others, is a radical revamping of the educational system as a preparation for adulthood. The capacity for continuous learning, continuous adjustment, and continuous creativity must supersede the capacity for repetition and recall.

Creative adjustment will not solve all problems of aging. The notion of an ideal solution is a mischievous myth. But the beginning of wisdom would be preparation for an uncertain future, and thus the abandonment of the notion that individuals simply flow through a stable order.

This is probably the best and worst time in the world history to be old. Or to be young.

References

1. See Theodosius Dobzhansky, *Mankind Evolving* (New Haven, Connecticut: Yale University Press, 1962).

2. Wilbert E. Moore, *Social Change* (Englewood Cliffs, New Jersey: Prentice-Hall, 1963), especially Chapter 1, "The Normality of Change."

3. Ansley J. Coale, "How the Age Distribution of a Human Population is Determined," *Cold Spring Harbor Symposia on Quantitative Biology*, 22: 83–89, 1957, quotation from p. 88.

4. *Ibid.*

5. Wilbert E. Moore, Reference 2, p. 14.

6. See Wilbert E. Moore, *Man, Time, and Society* (New York: John Wiley and Sons, 1963). See also R. M. MacIver, *The Challenge of the Passing Years: My Encounter with Time* (New York: Trident Press, Simon and Schuster, 1962).

7. For a perceptive, but essentially static, view of age grading in the contemporary United States, see Talcott Parsons, "Age and Sex in the Social Structure of the United States," in his *Essays in Sociological Theory: Pure and Applied* (Glencoe, Illinois: Free Press, 1949), Chapter X.

8. Wilbert E. Moore, *The Conduct of the Corporation* (New York: Random House, 1962), Chapteer XIII, "Climbers, Riders, Treaders."

9. R. M. MacIver, Reference 6, Chapter XII, "The Indifferent Interval and Other Protections."

10. I expressed this view, without qualification, some years ago. See Wilbert E. Moore, "The Aged in Industrial Societies," *in* J. Douglas Brown and others, eds., *The Aged and Society* (Champaign, Illinois: Industrial Relations Research Association, 1950), pp. 24–39. I now regard the view as partially mistaken, as the discussion in the text indicates. For a more extended discussion of an evoluationary view of

contemporary kinship, see Wilbert E. Moore, *The Impact of Industry* (Englewood Cliffs, New Jersey: Prentice-Hall, 1965).

11. On this point I *was* correct in the first part of Reference 10.

12. William H. Whyte, Jr., *The Organization Man* (New York: Simon and Schuster, 1956), Part VII, "The New Suburbia: Organization Man at Home," especially Chapter 21, "The Transients."

13. See, for example, Conrad M. Arensberg, *The Irish Countryman* (New York: The Macmillan Co., 1937), especially Chapter III, "The Family and the Land."

14. This discussion is based on Wilbert E. Moore, *Man, Time, and Society*, Reference 6, pp. 80–84.

15. See Moore, Reference 10.

PART IV

FORECASTING THE FUTURE

14

PREDICTING DISCONTINUITIES
IN SOCIAL CHANGE

It is commonly complained, and with some justice, that sociologists are better at reinterpreting events, in their own exotic tongue, than they are at predicting events in the first place. Actually, the scientific pretensions of the discipline are most readily justified by a substantial array of correlational propositions. For sequential relations, however, and thus for real prediction of the historic future, our aspirations are ahead of our achievements.

Yet it will be my claim that our present and prospective position is far from bleak. The rapid growth of the discipline's human and financial resources has produced a kind of two-way stretch of the empirical bases for generalization: a broadening of the comparative perspective on societies and their subsystems, and a lengthening of the time-period through longitudinal or retrospective observation. Though emphasis on methodological precision has often resulted in pettily localized studies, the purists have not deterred comparative sociologists and anthropologists from their fruitful pursuits. And, owing in large measure to prophets out of season, we have begun to make rather remarkable progress in the analysis of social sequences. With perhaps more daring than judgment, I shall even suggest that we have grounds for predicting change that is irregular in magnitude, rate, and direction, along with more orderly progressions.

The Bases of Prediction

I shall start by making two assumptions, neither of which has a perfect probability. The one is common to all predictions: that there will

SOURCE. Adapted from "Predicting Discontinuities in Social Change," *American Sociological Review*, 29: 331–338, June 1964; by permission of the American Sociological Association.
This MacIver Award Lecture was delivered at the meeting of the Southwest Sociological Association in Dallas, Texas, March 27, 1964.

be a measure of order in that portion of the universe under scrutiny. The interdependence of social actions and organizations validates the conceptual use of *systems,* a notion that informs the social sciences generally. If chaos rules, prophecy cannot, nor for that matter, can man survive. Social survival is my second assumption. It has a special uncertainty: the reliable techniques for total human destruction now at hand. The apostles of apocalypse and the armorers of Armageddon are somewhat persuasive, but I shall assume away oblivion along with chaos, for either would make our present pursuits unconscionably frivolous.

Correlations and Sequences

The principles of sociology, the propositions and theorems that formalize the relations among social variables, are mainly comprised of generalizations that are cross-sectional in character. At whatever level of generality—say, differential delinquency of contemporary American rural high-school dropouts or the universality of the nuclear family—these principles provide static predictability in the classic form: if (an independent variable), then (a dependent variable). Some available generalizations, however, involve sequential relations, with or without precise timing, and with or without the allegation that the later condition is caused by the earlier one. For example, in the course of modernization death rates fall before birth rates, as the two phenomena are unequally sensitive to the effects of modernization, taken as a global variable. Some unknown portion of the explanation of the eventual or prospective decline in fertility may be attributed to the influence of declining mortality in providing conspicuously higher survival rates of children, but other conditions and motivational elements are certainly involved. It must be noted, however, that much of the analysis of modernization is sequential in the gross, but not in the fine. Treatises on the social consequences of economic development rely in the main on before-and-after comparisons, with no information on the rates, routes, or timetables involved in getting from origins to destinations*

Components of Temporal Prediction

The art of prophecy, if it is to rest on scientific procedures rather than supernatural inspiration, requires some rather well-machined parts put together in a sensible order. To foretell the future, we should

---

* I do not exempt my own work from these strictures. See, for example, Wilbert E. Moore, "Industrialization and Social Change," in Bert F. Hoselitz and Wilbert E. Moore (eds.), *Industrialization and Society* (Paris and The Hague: UNESCO and Mouton, 1963), Chapter 15.

want first to identify probably *persistent* components of the present. Neither the impression of total flux, which may arise from rapid and extensive change, nor the allegation that there are universal "lags" or continuities, has much validity. It may be true that affective commitments are less likely to change than merely instrumental arrangements, that values are less volatile than the means for their attainment, that supernatural beliefs hold constant while worldly perceptions change. Yet contrary cases are not difficult to find, and a probability matrix by cultural categories has yet to be constructed. Prophecy, in fact, is surest on the basis of extensive stipulation of the present and past, and on a less grand scale than man's total experience. This is not to deny the reality or utility of conceptions of social evolution; it is only a question of the desired detail, and the detail I am looking for cannot, I believe, be derived deductively from so general a formula.

For smaller-scale but empirically richer forecasting, three other components may be mentioned rather briefly, as they all figure in "safe" prophecy, which we here eschew. For particular societies, or groups of societies having critically relevant common features, one would take account of: *continuation of orderly trends*—for example, rising rates of school enrollment, or the shift of labor force out of agriculture in the course of economic modernization; *planning*—the extensive use of deliberate change in all industrial societies and those attempting to join the group; and *recapitulated experience*—the partial repetition of historic trends, a valuable aid to prognosis of the social change that can be expected in newly developing countries.

These aids to vision will dispel part of the inevitable haze through which the future is seen. Can we do better?

The Challenge

The predictive problem that is especially difficult is how to handle sharp changes in the magnitude of change, and sharp (or at least clear) changes in direction. Certain conceptual aids are available, but their use must be explicated.

The theory of biological evolution offers us, in addition to variability and selective adaptation, the concept of *mutation*. In the sociocultural sphere *innovation* has perhaps an analogous influence on the system, and its explanation is somewhat more adequate than is the geneticists' explanation of mutation. Mutation, for the geneticists, is a kind of *deus ex machina*, only partially and retrospectively accounted for by environmental changes in such conditions as radioactivity.* Innova-

* Blum, however, hypothesizes that mutation rates for any species may show a sharp upward trend at the "beginning," followed by a marked damping off owing to a

tion, in contrast, can be explained by the combination of several facts: social actors are purposive; they are comprised in social systems, characterized by values imperfectly realized. The quest for these values, as well as adjustment to the nonhuman environment, is by no means merely mindless on the part of the actors, but rather calls forth the normative acceptance of both accidental discovery and ingenious design.

In what follows, the innovative, problemsolving character of human action in organized systems will provide a recurrent theme. Yet the term innovation is too general and too lacking in precise content to be of unqualified use as an explanatory or predictive principle. The task is to specify types and circumstances, and we should be about it.

Changes in the Rate of Change

Innovation is most evidently effective in changing *rates* of change. This may arise from the multiplier effect of innovations, including unintended consequences, or from deliberately rapid transformations, or from the emergence of new levels of action or performance.

Although innovation is organized and institutionalized in the contemporary world, some change is "accidental," and some of the consequences are unintended. At the very least, even with highly planned change, timetables are likely to share the universal fate of being subject to change without notice. The predictive problem here is that of assigning probabilities to classes of consequences.

Innovation may also be an "exogenous variable." Witness the rapid, emulative spread of both ideas and instrumental techniques from one society or subsystem to another in the contemporary world. Innovation of course may be social as well as technical. Sharp changes in rates may thus be due to "heroic effort"—witness the rise of integrated national planning and various "bootstrap" operations in newly developing areas.

Some innovations may give rise to the phenomenon of *emergence*, the creation of new levels of integration and potentiality for change. In retrospect, the evolution of human culture has provided many such Pandora's boxes: writing, administrative organization, organized technology, and institutionalized rationality. An attempt, now, to "predict" these discontinuities from prior evidence is likely to be pointless, as inevitability is too easy to assume after the event, and too difficult to

---

finite number of genetic alternatives. See Harold F. Blum, "On the Origin and Evolution of Human Culture," *American Scientist*, 51: March 1963, 32–47, especially pp. 43–44.

prove. The more difficult, and interesting, task is to try to descry innovations of comparable importance in the future, where at least the test of history has yet to be met.

Lawful Acceleration

The closest approximation to the simple extrapolation of orderly trends is the use of a multiplier (or divisor) to take account of orderly changes in rate. Perhaps the simplest example is an exponential curve, which makes the rate of growth proportional to the extent of the relevant universe at any time. This was Ogburn's classic formulation of technological change, his "explanation" being the accretion of elements into an ever-richer pool available for new combinations.[1] Blum, though referring to "tools," generalizes the exponential curve to cultural evolution as a whole.[2]

The processes of accretion and combination may be compounded by formation of supersystems. For example, despite barriers to communication including secrecy, it is probably sensible to view the world's technology now as a single system: a pool of practical knowledge from which withdrawals are made without depleting the principal and in which new applications supply new deposits along with the results of more organized inventive activity. Science and humanistic scholarship share to a degree the characteristics of a single pool, and there is some basis for considering political ideologies and techniques in the same way.

Such an "expanding social universe" leads to the possibility of secular acceleration, with particular reference to the complex of changes summarized as "modernization." By this principle, the later a country's (or a region's?) start toward modernization, the more rapid will be the change in rates of development. Examples of prospectively accelerating rates include shifts of the labor force out of agriculture, changes in agricultural technology, rising labor productivity in manufacturing, reduction of illiteracy, and reduction of mortality.

Note that this prediction of progressive acceleration is contrary to some conventional views, which assert that millennia are required for "Stone Age cultures" to catch up, whatever that could mean, or that special impediments to change are to be found in certain complex but traditional cultures. The "Stone Age" designation, it must be said in fairness, is more often used by journalists than by scholars, but anthropologists and sociologists have tended to cultural conservatism based on the supposed integrity of time-honored values and customs. Without arguing the case in greater detail, I think the resistances are exaggerated and the implied slowness of change simply wrong.

Thresholds

Resistances to change are of course real. Some may be based on a simple preference for the known over the unknown, some on a failure to perceive prospective benefits, some on clearly perceived prospective loss. But especially resistant components may still be subject to accumulation processes, to "hidden undermining." Birth rates in countries just beginning rapid modernization *may* provide an example. The seemingly appropriate neoMalthusian concerns of the experts rest upon the assumption of a considerable delay between declining mortality and declining fertility, and a slow rate of fertility decline even after it starts. But the ambient social conditions in currently developing areas scarcely replicate those that previously prevailed in countries now industrialized. Certainly all evidence points to a nearly universal and very rapid rise in aspirations, boosted by knowledge that the goals are not totally beyond man's power. Unprecedented rates of mortality decline are likely to sharpen the sense of excessive numbers of children, family by family. And, not least in importance, the worries of the experts are now communicated to governments and private welfare organizations, and deliberate propaganda and information campaigns are expanding rapidly. This looks very much like a threshold situation, where the example of a very small number of leaders in birth limitation may be quickly emulated.

The notion of a threshold stresses the significance that a small change in one element may have in producing greater change in the interaction of various analytically distinguishable elements and processes. The refinements of our technical skills have been mainly directed at analysis in the strict sense—to determine, for example, what proportion of the variance in some aggregate measure can be accounted for by factor A, how much by factor B, and so on. But synthesis is as much a part of scientific methodology as analysis. The summation and interaction of components is likely to be critically important in the attempt to translate analytical relations into the real world of historic experience. The example of prospective fertility rates in developing areas will serve once more. To the combination of unprecedented conditions already noted, a cheap, reliable, and esthetically acceptable contraceptive pill may be added. This will increase the probability of a rather sharp reduction in birth rates. Inevitably, some simple souls will then attribute the result solely to the technical innovation and more sophisticated souls will engage in a secondary analysis to sort out the component factors. All this is standard in the scholarly scene, and scarcely merits scolding. I should like, however, to rephrase the methodological moral. For forecasting one must somehow move from discrete necessary conditions to cumulative and sufficient ones, and that is likely to require the use of "systems" with genuinely dynamic dimensions.

Changes in the Direction of Change

Since adages impound the folk wisdom on human affairs, it is not surprising that formal statement of sociological principles may occasionally have a proverbial counterpart. Yet we should scarcely contemplate a general textbook comprised only of proverbs, in part because their terse generality leads to contradiction by other adages of equal merit. And some aphoristic wisdom is simply wrong. I refer, for example, to those sayings that reflect a grand sense of boredom, the impression of *déjà vu* writ large: there is nothing new under the sun; *plus ça change, plus c'est la même chose*. Novelty does occur, and the orderly progression of events may be interrupted by reversals of trend.

Reversals: Cycles and Swings

The nearest confirmation for bored familiarity with apparent change is to be found in various cycles that are short enough in term and similar enough in successive appearances to occur several times in a normal life span. In capitalist economies economic fluctuations have some quasi-cyclical features, though both the temporal regularity and the uniformity of sequential patterns may be questioned.

In many features of normative systems—the rules of conduct and their ethical evaluations—a genuinely dialectical situation prevails. I have argued previously[3] that most of the dichotomous classifications of forms of organization, norms, and value-orientations, with which our literature is replete, are to be most meaningfully viewed as paired alternatives, ". . . both of which are persistent in groups and societies. Emphasis on one alternative in the values and norms of any society or group does not dispel or dismiss its counterpart."[4] Thus consanguine principles of kinship persist in institutionally conjugal systems, status ascription underlies status achievement, and informal relations find a hospitable environment in formal organizations. I am even inclined to think that the nominally suppressed alternative tends to become activated to recurrent strength as successive attempts are made to increase compliance with the official norms. Similarly, administrative policies of centralization and decentralization illustrate this alternating emphasis. Each policy has distinct advantages and penalties, and in the quest for a mythical, ideal combination, the executives of such organizations introduce changes that turn out to be essentially cyclical in character. Though no doubt particular cases may be affected by idiosyncratic events such as the time of executive succession, my impression is that five years is about the life-span of either official policy before cumulative strains prompt a reversal.

It is also worth noting that various incidence rates (for example, births, deaths, crimes) are variable over time, and if the variations have some regular temporal pattern, they are cyclical by definition. Crime rates may go down as well as up, death rates up as well as down. Though I should not go as far as Sorokin's "principle of limit,"[5] to the effect that no trend or correlation can be extrapolated to all degrees and infinite time, an overly short historic perspective may conceal the evidence for possible reversals. For example, as nearly as I can read the long-term historical trends, economic modernization tends at first to reduce the direct economic participation of women, particularly after the very earliest stages of reliance on relatively cheap labor, but that trend is subsequently reversed and women play an increasing part in the labor force. There is nothing mysterious about this change of direction. After an initial period of "sweated labor," women tend to be supported by male breadwinners as housewives and mothers. With subsequent increases in female education and reduction in childbearing, women can, once more, combine economic and familial functions.

Reversals: Completion of Processes

Some reversals of trend can be best interpreted as occasioned by the completion of a process of social transformation, after which other influences on the phenomenon in question come to the fore. I think the "baby boom" in Western countries following World War II and still persisting nearly 20 years later is a case in point. At the beginning of the War, or a little before, the diffusion of knowledge and practice of contraception was virtually complete. Thereafter, one could more or less safely assume that three or more children had been desired (even given the use of little or inefficient contraception owing to religious scruples). Children were no longer a visible symbol of ignorance and error. Thus new determinants of fertility could take over, including the view of children as analogous with other consumption goods and available for conspicuous display of affluence. That the sharpest increases took place among the urban, high-income and highly educated groups lends credence to this interpretation.

The illustration I used earlier of a long-term "cyclical" shift from diminution to increase in female economic participation might perhaps better have been attributed to a kind of process completion. Though I have elsewhere[6] argued rather vehemently that "modernization" is a continuing rather than terminal change in societies, the broad onset of modernization is likely to represent, for any single society, a unique and discontinuous change. The major disruptions of prior social structures associated with this transformation have been extensively documented,[7] but I think we can now see evidence for partial restoration of some earlier structural features after urbanization and industrialism are far along. The initial impact is clearly to nucleate family units, to introduce a radical disparity between the occupations of the old and those of the young, and to sterilize market and employment relations of sentiment and informality. As the new forms of production, exchange, and mobility become very general, some partial restoration of the prior, richer fabric of social relations becomes evident. Perhaps the analogous processes of partial restoration following major revolutions are responsible for the view that revolutions really change things very little.[8]

But the conclusion claims too much. The urban nuclear family that stays in regular communication with relatives and even participates in various forms of mutual aid among siblings and between generations is not the same as a preindustrial extended kinship unit. The informal organizations and "human relations" policies found in complex bureaucracies are not the same as the preindustrial work organization. And so on. The wheel turns but it also moves across a changing terrain. The systemic qualities of social practices, though too easily exaggerated into a kind of functional determinism, have enough validity to prevent utterly anachronistic combinations of the major features of the social order. All I am arguing is that "advanced" (though never "complete") modernization affords opportunity for partial restoration of patterns previously suppressed but not entirely eliminated.

Tangents

Not all discontinuities in social change reduce themselves neatly to alternation of direction or recurrent cycles. Such changes do occur, but the implicit geometric pattern is too restrictive to account for all changes. In addition, we must, first, follow for a considerable measure of simple "fluctuation,"[9] owing to some degree of structural autonomy and autonomous variability within any society. Other changes of direction appear more enduring and may be called *tangents*. Substantial alterations in the structural modes of handling standard functional necessities, such as political organization or religious beliefs and practices, provide examples. Despite the optimism of true believers in, say, Christianity and Democracy, there is no substantial evidence for a long-term secular trend toward their gradual, eventual victory. What does appear, however, is that complex religions, offering rationalized meaning to life, death, and the troubles besetting the human condition, are likely to win or survive in competition with less comprehensive alternatives. Note the success of Buddhism, Christianity, and Islam in securing converts among animists and other "primitive" believers but not from each other's adherents. Note also the hardy survival, albeit not prosperous expansion, of Christianity, Judaism, and Islam in communist states, which offer a theologically poor alternative metaphysics. It is also probable that some form of "participatory politics" will displace true monarchies, despotisms, or oligarchies, but the power structure may still be one-party and essentially dictatorial. These structural substitutions I should call tangential changes.

The instigating sources of tangential change may be external: missionary activities, economic modernization, "imported" political ideologies, the lasting effects of colonial rule. Some adaptation or naturalization is also likely to occur, however, giving lasting effect to prior social structure and thus preserving some portion of the variety that proves exasperating to students of comparative analysis.

Honesty compels the admission that analytical distinctions may not neatly match the concrete world. Do emergents like writing or monetary systems represent changes in rate, or direction, or both? Do science and industrialization represent mere additional steps in man's long and incomplete mastery of his environment for his own purposes, or sharp discontinuities with archaic practices? The answers are not of crucial importance. Any analytic taxonomy is a matter of convenience in ordering phenomena, and is always subservient to theory, the true aim of which is the predictive proposition. The discussion so far has been marked—I hesitate to say "graced"—by a fair number of propositions that make allegations about prospective, discontinuous social changes. If those have merit, the predictive end does justify the analytical means.

The Problem of Revolution*

I turn, finally, to problems of predicting large-scale discontinuous changes in the social fabric of society, that is, revolution. I shall limit

* Although I am not using Smelser's detailed analytic scheme, I have found his treatment of collective behavior extremely useful. In particular, I agree with his emphasis on the *combination* of determinants such as "structural conduciveness" and "struc-

the term here to fundamental change in the normative order, including notably the forms of legality and, crucially, the basis of legitimacy for the state itself.† Excluded for present purposes are other sweeping social changes that are not primarily political in character and various political alterations, such as sporadic rebellions or *coups d'état*, that do not critically affect the political forms of legitimacy.

No science can be expected to predict unique events, but only to assign probabilities to individual occurrences within a class of events. A principal value, therefore, of systematic comparative analysis is the establishment of common features despite detailed diversity, and thus the accumulation of an "experience rating" or actuarial basis for prediction. It cannot be fairly said that our knowledge of revolutions is adequate by these tests, though the kind of systematic checklist of interacting determinants suggested by Smelser[10] marks a distinct methodological advance.

Revolutionary Potential: The Problem of Order

Although revolutions represent discontinuous change *par excellence,* their exceptional character is easily exaggerated in the statistical sense,[11] as is their distinctive departure from "normal stability." There are excellent theoretical reasons for expecting tensions and conflicts in all societies. I have argued elsewhere[12] for the utility of the conception of society as a tension-management system rather than a self-equilibrating one. Such a conception makes order itself problematical rather than assumed, and invites attention to sources of dissidence and deviation, controversy and conflict.

Disorder, however, is not equivalent to potential or actual revolution. Societies without strongly centralized polities, a substantial degree of urban agglomeration, and fairly effective internal communications (which, however, need not reach all areas and social segments) may well be marked by frequent but localized violence, including occasional rebellions against constituted authorities. They are unlikely to have genuine revolutions in the restricted sense of the term used here.

Likewise, any system of social inequality will produce equity strains

---

tural strain." This "value-added process" is akin to my comments above with respect to "thresholds." See Neil J. Smelser, *Theory of Collective Behavior* (New York: The Free Press of Glencoe, 1963), especially pp. 12–21 and Chapter 11.

† The specification of *legitimacy,* I believe, places my use of the term "revolution" in Smelser's category of "value-oriented movement" (see *ibid.,* Chapter 11), and the emphasis on changes in legality approximates Edwards' use of the term "revolution." See L. P. Edwards, *The Natural History of Revolution* (Chicago: University of Chicago Press, 1927).

and manifestations of dissatisfaction with the existing order of rewards. (The same would be true of an equalitarian system[13].) The more complex and multidimensional the bases of social differentiation, the less likely is a clear-cut confrontation. To take a simple example, the early stages of industrialization are marked by a radical polarity between the managers and the managed in the modernized sector. Marx perceived this correctly, and made a totally false extrapolation of inclusive class conflict. Early polarization characterizes only a relatively small segment of the social structure, and the more traditional differentiation rests on other bases. This duality prevents any strict and comprehensive set of social divisions. By the time that modernization has affected most of the social order its typical status gradations have multiplied, and status itself has become multidimensional. Thus revolution is not the *normal* consequence of modernization, though under certain combinations of circumstances it is not unknown. The contemporary speed of sharp rises in aspirations, combined with relative slowness in economic improvements, greatly increases the probability of revolution in "new nations."

Predicting Revolution

Polarization, then, is the key indicator of incipient revolution. It is, however, only an indicator and no more causes revolution than the thermometer causes temperature. But what we are looking for, taking account of other and more fundamental harbingers that I shall note presently, is the transition from fractionation and shifting coalitions to broadly divisive and enduring coalitions.

What are the more fundamental determinants of revolution? Certainly one is an objective and apparent deterioration in economic well-being or political rights. The deterioration may be relative as well as absolute, as when the rich get richer and the poor, if anything, poorer.

In particular, revolutions are probable wherever structural changes in the legally sanctioned distribution of power and social rewards have been slight or retrogressive. Thus the Republic of South Africa and the Rhodesias are safe bets for revolution, and most Latin American countries are odds-on favorites. It is extremely difficult for an entrenched elite to perceive that its days are numbered unless it makes concessions. The plea is for time, yet poor use is made of the time at hand. Indeed, the early perception of threat most commonly leads to repressive rather than conciliatory measures, and thus an acceleration of the process of polarization. A somewhat "integrated" ideology is formed, but it still contains rather arbitrarily selected differentiators ("Oh, you like spinach? You must be one of those communists."). The world of everyday experience becomes simplified though rather restrictive, for a time, whether the revolutionary movement succeeds or fails. Partisan identification defines nearly all social action. A balanced, or criss-crossing, or indecisive view is regarded by both polar camps with simple hostility.

Concluding Comment

There are, of course, other sources and types of social discontinuity: disasters, natural and otherwise; wars; fads, fashions, panics; and indeed the battery of social manifestations that we characterize as "collective behavior." It would be silly to say that these are inconsequential, and I hope that my inattentiveness to them will not be so regarded. What I have attempted to illustrate is an approach to prediction, and I have, I think sensibly, selected from the universe of assorted and frequently unpleasant prospects an unrepresentative sample comprising those that could be cleaned up for a public showing. Ample disorder is left for those who want to live dangerously either as participants or as observers.

References

1. William F. Ogburn, *Social Change* (New York: Viking Press, 1928).

2. Harold F. Blum, "On the Origin and Evolution of Human Culture," *American Scientist*, 51: 41–43.

3. Most recently, *in* Wilbert E. Moore, *Social Change* (Englewood Cliffs, New Jersey: Prentice-Hall, 1963), pp. 66–68.

4. *Ibid.*, p. 66.

5. See Pitirim A. Sorokin, *Social and Cultural Dynamics* (one-volume edition) (Boston: Peter Sargent, 1957), Chapters 38 and 39.

6. See Reference 3, pp. 105–112.

7. See for example, Wilbert E. Moore, "Industrialization and Social Change," *in* Bert F. Hoselitz and Wilbert E. Moore (eds.), *Industrialization and Society* (Paris and The Hague: UNESCO and Mouton, 1963), Chapter 15.

8. See, for example, Crane Brinton, *The Anatomy of Revolution* (New York: Vintage Books, 1958).

9. See Pitirim A. Sorokin, *Society, Culture, and Personality* (New York: Harper, 1947), Parts 6 and 7.

10. Neil J. Smelser, *Theory of Collective Behavior* (New York: The Free Press of Glencoe, 1963).

11. See Pitirim Sorokin, Reference 5, Chapter 35.

12. See Wilbert E. Moore, Reference 3, Chapter 1.

13. See Wilbert E. Moore, "But Some are More Equal Than Others," *American Sociological Review*, 28: 13–18, February 1963.

15
GLOBAL SOCIOLOGY: THE WORLD
AS A SINGULAR SYSTEM

The primary question raised here is whether we may now speak of civilization and its changes in the singular, and if so, in what respects. In the course of these comments, little attention will be given to civilization, somewhat more to sociology as a discipline that now and then, here and there, has interested itself in civilization. I shall even, toward the end, discuss briefly some small intersection between the course of events in the contemporary world and their reflection or interpretation by some segments of the sociological fraternity. A full-fledged *wissensoziologische* interpretation will not be attempted, however, partly because of some diffidence about my competence, partly because I have yet to encounter a predictive proposition yielded by such scholarly exercises.

We shall traverse some familiar terrain, with a sort of tourist's guide-book to the living remnants and fossil remains of bits of the intellectual history of our discipline, noting the partly dialectical and partly alternating emphasis on the global and the particular, the broad-brushed portrayal of mankind and its evolution, on the one hand, or the precise miniature cautiously constructed with a camel's-hair brush, on the other.

The Global and the Particular

By global sociology I shall mean sociology of the globe, of mankind. But there is another sense of the term that is worth passing comment. The discipline of sociology, though not firmly established in a variety of exotic places visited chiefly, and temporarily, by anthropologists, has

---

SOURCE. Adapted from "Global Sociology: The World as a Singular System," *American Journal of Sociology*, 71: 475–482, March 1966; by permission of the University of Chicago Press. Copyright 1966 by the University of Chicago.

itself become remarkably international. Sociology reached America chiefly from the European continent, being of slight academic consequence in England until relatively recently. But now British universities and those of the older British commonwealths are rapidly expanding their academic positions. A few older Indian sociologists are now being joined by large numbers of younger ones. A few older Latin-American sociologists, largely in the cultivated traditions of the *pensadores*, the thinkers, are now being overwhelmed by large numbers of younger sociologists, oriented to the strongly empirical strains in contemporary North American and European sociology—these are, if you will, the *investigadores*. The Near East, postwar Japan, and postcolonial Africa support at least a few sociologists. The discipline has even penetrated the Iron Curtain, though mainly in those fields that seem most immediately practical, rather than in conceptions of grand theory that might too frontally clash with current Marxist orthodoxy.

We may properly ask of this rapidly spreading sociological enterprise, "Is it adding to the common knowledge or only enriching the store of specialized knowledge?" Does the discipline share only method plus a kind of framework for analysis, so that the questions are similar but the answers different? Or do the answers resemble one another enough so that we gain a kind of collateral replication of cause and effect, or at least a confirmation of functional correspondences? The answer is "both," but in the nature of the case the rather small, specialized study of unknown transferability and thus of unknown broader import is more frequent among the sociological novices where they are pioneers, as compared with the careful testing of allegedly established principles in somewhat novel settings.

There is, however, some basis for hope, not that sociologists will themselves help unify the world, for they can scarcely unify themselves, but rather that the common features of human existence will be increasingly documented and otherwise verified along with the undoubted variability that makes the human experience so challenging to those of us who seek to understand it, order it, and predict it. Part of the present thesis is that the quest for common features will be aided not alone by the growing ubiquity of sociology, but more importantly by the growing ubiquity of similar problems and similar solutions in the world of events.

The Grand Tradition

A brief and selective reading of our intellectual history is now in point. At least some of the precursors of our discipline, the philosophers and the philosophers of history who wrote about the nature of man and society, had a kind of grand view of the unity of mankind. It is true that the unity seen by Polybius or Ibn Khaldun was one of common historic experience, not a richly factual appraisal of mankind at the time. Indeed, well into the nineteenth century it was the Judeo-Christian, Greco-Roman world and its historic heirs that enlisted the attention of at least those grand-scale theorists with which we have some small familiarity. (Incidentally, that familiarity owes much to Sorokin's *Contemporary Sociological Theories*,[1] which provided American sociologists with a window on European historical and sociological traditions that they sadly lacked at the time. But that is getting ahead of the story.) Several of the leading founders of sociology shared this global view of mankind. This was notably true of Comte, with what we should now call a "stage theory" of social evolution. Later, Spencer and Durkheim were also generalists, though by that time the awareness of societies or cultures not a part of the classical historic sequence had grown apace, so that their view of mankind could reach to Oriental civilization and tribal societies. Sociology was indeed the "science of society," as it was called by Sumner and Keller,[2] and though diversity kept getting recorded, the singular society, the common features of the human condition, continued to be given central emphasis.

Parochialism Rampant on a Field of Data

This grand tradition fell upon evil days. Emphasis on precision of conceptualization and of observation began to grow, particularly after the turn of the century, and, here and there, use of quantitative data appeared—though of course one can find precedents for all of these. A most important circumstance, in my view, was the Americanization of sociology. The burgeoning, state-supported higher-educational system began to introduce instruction in sociology, mainly following the lead of a rather new private university, Chicago, rather than an old one, Yale, which gradually withdrew from contact with the rest of the discipline. And despite the original, strongly Germanic orientation of Chicago's sociology as prolifically portrayed by Albion Small* his immediate successors and various independent developments in the large state universities pointed in other directions. The motto became, "Get out there and observe, record, measure, verify." The introduction and rapid expansion of rural sociology gave added weight to local studies.

The Americanization of sociology, though never complete, was en-

---

* Small was a principal contributor to the early issues of the *American Journal of Sociology* during the 1890's and 1900's.

hanced by the virtual rejection of the subject by the British academy and by the extremely modest flexibility of Continental universities. An even more severe influence was World War I, which virtually ended the Durkheim school in France and radically reduced Weber's heritage in Germany, while the Bolshevik Revolution ended the small but active development of Russian sociology. To exaggerate only slightly, sociology between the wars became the all-American science, and its focus was increasingly empirical and often minutely local. For several decades in most of the general texts, society was American society, the family was the American family, and so on. Park and Burgess's large text of 1921[3] was widely imitated in organization, but the imitators saw fit to exclude the historical and contemporary European materials of the original, and include, instead, data on Chicago and tables from the *U.S. Statistical Abstract*. By the early 1930's Sorokin's *Social Mobility*[4] and *Contemporary Sociological Theories*[5] and the Sorokin-Zimmerman *Principles of Rural-Urban Sociology*[6] had been in circulation for several years, and these were far from parochial books. But they had little early impact on the most widely used texts.

The Open Mind: Relativism and All That

Among the popular texts, the break in parochialism came in a different form, with attention, not to contemporary Europe or to historic civilizations, but to the ethnographic monographs produced by anthropologists studying tribal societies. Ironically, this meant a rediscovery of anthropology by sociology, a tentative and partial reunion of subject matter that Spencer and Durkheim had considered to be inseparable. With Sutherland and Woodward's *Introductory Sociology*,[7] the beginning student was given a kind of shock treatment. In the great outside world, other people have other beliefs and customs. The emphasis was insistently comparative, but also insistently relativistic: We do it this way, they do it that way. "Ethnocentrism" was introduced from Sumner's vocabulary as the cardinal sin. The compensating moral virtue presumably was tolerance, but the bare sociological message was morally neutral—it was simple diversity in the human experience. Such general theory as sociology had to offer survived in the chapter headings: somehow some of this diversity could be grouped under the rubric of the family and kinship, some more could be inclosed in a chapter on political institutions (which mostly dealt with political structures), and an additional part in a chapter on religion. What justified this sorting of descriptive data into conventional categories was not an explicit intellectual issue until somewhat later, and often is not

yet among the writers of introductory texts. Ethnocentrism was perhaps
defeated as an intellectual stance, though almost certainly not as an
evaluative stance. But anthropocentrism in the special sense of a focus
on man somehow got defeated too, though that had not been explicitly
identified as an enemy.

Sovereign Systems

Now matters begin to get complicated, and an even more radical
ellipsis will be necessary in order to encompass developments in the last
three decades. My specific focus will be on the central issue of the
singularity of civilization and therefore neglectful of the vast bulk of
continuing sociological investigation which, perhaps wisely, remains
unconcerned with that problem.

Two *somewhat* independent developments engage our attention. The
one development was Sorokin's reintroduction into sociology of the
grand tradition of large-scale concern for human civilization, with a
considerable overlay of modern technical sophistication as compared
with earlier protagonists. It must be said, negatively with respect to our
concerns here, that *Social and Cultural Dynamics*[8] is almost entirely,
and explicitly, limited to a reading of the evidence from the Western
world, in the classic, historic sense. It must be added, positively, that in
that monumental work Sorokin dealt with social and cultural *systems*
and *supersystems,* the latter, especially, transcending the mere boundaries of national states or small periods of history.

The other development involved the rediscovery of anthropology,
though it may not have grown out of that influence in any precisely
determinate way. Certain theorists—Parsons[9] as a persistent leader,
Davis[10] and Levy[11] as mature coconspirators—labored assiduously to
make of sociology a generalizing science of man's social conduct. This
development, which is still going forward actively, had consequences
that were also mixed. One emphasis looked like relativism revisited.
Cultures, in the language of anthropologists, or societies, in the tongue
of their sociological counterparts, became self-subsistent entities. Autonomy reigned wherever somewhat separable ethnic groups, tribal
enclaves, or, implicitly, national states were to be found. Durkheim's
sociologism—the explanation of social phenomena in terms of other,
presumably simultaneous, social phenomena—became the watchword.
With Parsons, social action became the universal element for analysis,
but social action was caught up in systems.[12] The highest level of such
systems, as more or less indicated in Parsons' work and explicitly in
Levy's,[13] was a society: either encompassing all social action or being

the mediator of that action if it transcended systemic boundaries. The kind of eclectic, almost scandalmongering, picking-up of odd practices for contrast with our own at the hands of the earlier relativists came to be exaggerated into a kind of rampant functionalism: everything must be seen in its immediate context. The cautionary qualification, "It all depends," had been taken out of the southern tier of counties in Iowa or the patients in a private mental hospital and spread across Oceania and subSaharan Africa, and had lost none of its stultifying effect by overseas transportation. We were really back where we had come in, save for the cash price of a field trip and the personal price of roughing it without water closets and drug stores.

Several further consequences of this particular, rather recent, intellectual tradition, need to be noted, however. One was the restoration of theoretical stature to the chapter headings of texts, by making explicit the common, functional features requisite for any society. Even if it be argued that those common features of society were *ex definitione* by a kind of extended derivation of the defining characteristics, they were at worst useful tautologies, sharing that designation with all other scientific uniformities, once verified, but still subject in principle to being nullified by evidence, if in fact the uniformities are not mere translations or equations. Another consequence, intrinsically dependent on the first but not always explicitly so in the theoretical works, was the formulation of particular propositions of great generality: the circumstances under which magical practices can be expected (Malinowski[14]), the universality of social differentiation for specifiable reasons (Sorokin,[15] Parsons,[16] Levy,[17] Davis and Moore[18]), the congruence between power and responsibility (Levy[19]), and the discrepancy between ideal and practical norms (Levy[20] and Moore[21]). A third consequence is especially noteworthy at this point because it can be carried further: the emphasis on *systems* as the proper focus of sociological inquiry. For it is only in social systems that one makes explicit the emergent qualities that derive from the interaction of the human actors in any social context, and thus avoids the kind of classical exemplification of the reductionist fallacy embodied in George Homans' presidential address to the American Sociological Association in 1964.[22] Social systems are real, they are earnest, and they may be both smaller and larger than societies, however defined.

In practice, society has come to be defined "operationally" either as units identified by anthropologists as "cultures," not always with explicit criteria, but duly recorded as separate entities in the Human Relations Area Files, or as coterminous with national states, which, though they may not be truly self-subsistent, do mostly get represented in the United Nations, and do form the principal takers of national censuses and assemblers of other aggregative and distributive social quantities.

Let us pass over for the moment the rapidly disappearing authentic and relatively autonomous primitive or tribal societies, for they move to the center of the stage a little later. Let us examine, rather, the equivalence of the modern national state with the models of those encompassing social systems called "societies" in our theoretical systems. That the fit is not perfect is not in itself disturbing, for it is the nature of theoretical models to be abstract and the function of theory to detect such verifiable elements of order as can be extracted from otherwise chaotic phenomena. But the discrepancies *are* instructive and by no means adequately attended to in our current theoretical writings.

First, the multicommunal state is the statistical norm, not the exception, in the contemporary world. The encompassing of two or more distinct and somewhat noncommunicative and even hostile segments within a national polity is often forgotton by American true believers in the somewhat ineffective melting pot. The Levantine states of Lebanon and Syria somewhat precariously survive deep religious divisions, but so do Belgium and The Netherlands. The former African colonies face nationhood with political boundaries formed with no regard to rather vague ethnic frontiers, but such ethnic and linguistic diversity still survives in Switzerland and the United Kingdom. India has problems of language, religion, and caste, but so in some degree does the United States. The "common value system" of these states may be extremely thin and essentially negative, comprising antipathy to the former metropolitan power and, by extension, other "colonial" or "imperialist" powers. Such negative nationalism figures prominently in new nations. This appears to be no more durable as a basis for consensus than the reliance on personal loyalty to a charismatic leader, which also appears frequently in newly independent or postrevolutionary states. In many communist states the "common values" may be superficial and strongly mixed with overt political power. In some of the seemingly most stable democracies, such as Switzerland, Great Britain, and the United States, a major part of the underlying consensus may rest on procedures for compromising and containing differences, rather than on substantive agreement.

Second, some of the seemingly strongest national polities have made a positive virtue of pluralism in various forms and degrees. Despite insistence on the political ascendancy of the Communist Party apparatus in the Soviet Union, the "cultural" protection of ethnic minorities has been a somewhat ambiguous and intermittent policy. Tolerance for diversity has been a strong feature of Anglo-American traditions, though also sometimes set aside in periods of extreme and paranoid anxiety. In principle, we tolerate almost every preference except national identity itself.

Third, some of these intrasocietal identifications are transitional in scope. From the possibly inconsequential shaping of national foreign policy in order to placate domestic ethnic groups to rather more consequential concerns with one form or another of "international conspiracy," the ways in which segments of human populations identify and differentiate themselves tend, perhaps increasingly, to criss-cross national frontiers.

The initial, methodological moral to be drawn from these considerations is to emphasize the importance of applying the *system* concept wherever it has some degree of empirical warrant, without assuming that society is both man's highest achievement, tardily discovered by sociologists, and that nonsocietal systems must necessarily be subsystems of that great piece of social architecture. This kind of elementary caution is given added point by attention to such empirically real and possibly theoretically significant phenomena as international political and technical organizations; private, nongovernmental, international associations such as those found in the learned professions; organizations such as the English-Speaking Union, or ecumenical organizations that seek to make common cause across some part of the spectrum of religious affiliations and beliefs.

Grand Themes Revisited

But is this global sociology? No, it is only a step in that direction, the essential preliminary of freeing the concept of system from automatic limits at the "boundaries" of societies or cultures.

We may "take a giant step" toward global sociology by returning once more to the exotic places, dearly beloved of ethnographers. The main, overwhelming fact about them is that they are losing their pristine character at an extremely rapid rate. Viewed at any particular time, the results may still be odd as judged by our precedents, but let us not get entangled with that now. The main negative point about our procedure for dealing with the modernization of traditional societies is that such simple, two-party transactional models as contained in the older theory of "acculturation" simply will not fit most of the evidence. More positively, what is happening is a great series of nationally directed programs of *deliberate* change (with its vicissitudes and unintended consequences). These programs take some account of local traditions and structures, and political leaders often seek, for understandable reasons of maintaining a national allegiance that is precarious at best, a distinctive nationalistic authenticity. But most of the elements are not autochthonous; they are drawn eclectically from a genuinely global pool of alternatives. Those alternatives include those of political ideology—Chinese Communist; Russian Communist; socialist of allegedly distinctive variety as the most commonly announced program; and, occasionally, mixed economies; or even free enterprise. But the alternatives also include the possibilities of wide choices in technology, in the mix between capital expenditures and consumer goods, in allocations between such options as national defense and public education, and even in the order of introduction of consumer goods available in the world's marketplace.

Viewed in one way, the world's new nations and their resurgent counterparts in such areas as Latin America have substituted a distinctly contemporary diversity for a rather more charming diversity that the ethnographers recorded. Viewed in another way, and that is the present perspective. we witness several elements of commonality that go beyond our hardwon detection of uniform functional features of societies. There is, first, a rather remarkable concurrence in the ideology of economic development, despite differences in technique and, often, despite differences in the more ultimate goals to which this essentially instrument goal is to be directed. There is, second, the fact that this diversity is the product of accidental *and eclectic* combinations from pools of options that are essentially worldwide in scope.

The world, then, is a singular system in these minimal senses and in one other as well: to an increasing degree, the life of the individual anywhere is affected by events and processes everywhere. This is as true within the seemingly initiating great powers as it is within the seemingly dependent small powers and new nations. Of course this is partly owing to the circumstance that the great powers compete for influence over others, but that adds to the singularity of the system, if not to its simplicity.

I am not arguing for the view that we are in the midst of a uniform and rectilinear process leading to world homogeneity or a singular civilization of mankind in that sense. Several years ago, Dr. Feldman and I indicated the kinds of structural similarities that could be expected from the continuing changes of industrial societies and from the addition of newcomers to that circle of somewhat ambiguous charm, and also the reasons for predicting that diversity, including diversity along cultural, societal, or national lines, might be expected to persist.[23]

I am arguing for the view that we must rediscover supersystems, some of which are even more encompassing than those to which Sorokin has insistently drawn our attention. Mankind may not survive long enough for us to study it as a complex entity, but that is scarcely an excuse for abandoning one of the oldest themes of our calling.

References

1. Pitirim A. Sorokin, *Contemporary Sociological Theories* (New York: Harper, 1928).

2. William G. Sumner and Albert G. Keller, *The Science of Society* (New Haven, Connecticut: Yale University Press, 1929), 3 Volumes.

3. Robert E. Park and Ernest W. Burgess, *Introduction to the Science of Sociology* (Chicago: University of Chicago Press, 1921).

4. Pitirim A. Sorokin, *Social Mobility* (New York: Harper, 1927).

5. Pitirim A. Sorokin, Reference 1.

6. Pitirim A. Sorokin and Carle C. Zimmerman, *Principles of Rural-Urban Sociology* (New York: Holt, 1929).

7. Robert L. Sutherland and Julian L. Woodward, *Introductory Sociology* (Philadelphia: J. B. Lippincott Co., 1937).

8. Pitirim A. Sorokin, *Social and Cultural Dynamics* (New York: American Book Co., 1937–40), 4 Volumes.

9. See especially Talcott Parsons, *The Social System* (Glencoe, Illinois: Free Press, 1951).

10. Kingsley Davis, *Human Society* (New York: Macmillan Co., 1949).

11. Marion J. Levy, Jr., *The Structure of Society* (Princeton, New Jersey: Princeton University Press, 1952).

12. Talcott Parsons, Reference 10.

13. Marion J. Levy, Jr., Reference 12.

14. Bronislaw Malinowski, *Magic, Science and Religion* (Glencoe, Illinois: Free Press, 1948).

15. Pitirim A. Sorokin, *Social Mobility*, see Reference 5.

16. Talcott Parsons, "An Analytical Approach to the Theory of Social Stratification," in *Essays in Sociological Theory: Pure and Applied* (Glencoe, Illinois: Free Press, 1949), Chapter VII.

17. Marion J. Levy, Jr., *The Structure of Society*, cited in Reference 12, pp. 157–166, 275–278.

18. Kingsley Davis and Wilbert E. Moore, "Some Principles of Stratification," *American Sociological Review*, 10: 242–249, April 1945.

19. Marion J. Levy, Jr., *op.cit.*, pp. 384–386, 468–503.

20. *Ibid.*, pp. 123–125.

21. Wilbert E. Moore, *Social Change* (Englewood Cliffs, New Jersey: Prentice-Hall, 1963), pp. 18–21, 77–81.

22. George C. Homans, "Bringing Men Back In," *American Sociological Review*, 29: 809–818, December 1964.

23. Arnold S. Feldman and Wilbert E. Moore, "Are Industrial Societies Becoming Alike?" *in* Alvin W. Gouldner and S. M. Miller, eds., *Applied Sociology* (New York: Glencoe Free Press, 1965), pp. 260–265.

16

FORECASTING THE FUTURE: THE UNITED STATES IN 1980

The job of the prophet presents unusual occupational hazards, and were it a full-time position, it is probable that life-insurance premiums would be very high. Though forecasting is a reasonable and even necessary part of life's orientations in the modern world, there are substantial uncertainties and possibilities of error in predicting the future, and, as we are well aware, some errors could be fatal.

The Bases for Prediction

Though the precise shape of the future is hidden by haze, there are several bases for at least rough and partial prediction, particularly if we can somehow appraise their interrelated influences. The first of these is simply *persistence* of the present and immediate past. It is said that in meteorology (note: a physical science) the elaborate calculation of winds, temperatures, and barometric pressures still yields less reliable short-run forecasts than the simple assumption that tomorrow will be pretty much like today. For much of our social conduct we can and do make the same assumption; if we did not, we should not know how to act or what to expect from day to day. Even over considerable periods into the future, customs, organizations, and values may be expected to survive the pressures of other changes.

A second basis for prediction is to be found in the *continuation of orderly trends*. Here especially is where the numerical manipulators have their say, and quite appropriately. The rate of urbanization and suburbanization has been increasing, but changes in the rate have been fairly orderly over three decades. The average age of marriage has been

SOURCE. Adapted from "Forecasting the Future: The United States in 1980," *The Educational Record*, **45**: 341–354, Fall 1964; by permission of the American Council on Education.

decreasing, but at a slowing rate of decline. The proportions of secondary school graduates have been increasing, as have the proportions going on to college. Women are entering the labor force at a gradually rising rate, particularly at ages over forty-five and under sixty. The amount of private savings increases as the economy grows and income increases, but the proportion of money saved remains remarkably constant.

A third component of forecasting is of special significance in industrial countries and those attempting to become so. I refer to the great and growing importance of *planning*. A remarkable amount of our energy and other scarce resources is spent on deliberate change. Though accidental and mindless change still occurs, change is also organized and institutionalized. We know the future in part because it will be the way we, or other planners and implementers, intend it to be.

Were we spreading our vision of the future to the whole world, and especially to those underdeveloped areas that currently differ from us so markedly, we should also want to use a fourth basis for prediction, *recapitulated experience*. Precise replication of rates and sequences of change need not always occur, and often will not. Still, we can go rather far in reasoning from the Western experience to major parts of the social organization and personal standards of those now seeking to become part of the modern world. Not that industrial societies will stand still while others catch up, for if preindustrial societies are rather static—and that presumption is easily exaggerated—industrial societies seem to change at an ever-accelerating rate.

Population

The failure of the demographers to predict the postwar baby boom and their reluctance to admit that it was still happening a decade and more later, have combined to make population experts shy about predictions. In general, they prefer the narrower term "projections," meaning future estimates based upon explicit assumptions about births and deaths.

Part of our task in reaching out to 1980 is eased by the fact that the adult population, and indeed the college population, is already born. Additional reductions in mortality are likely to be very slight for all ages under fifty, and even the solution to both cardiac disorders and cancer would add no more than one-fifth to the projected population over sixty-five years of age.

The population of the United States in 1980 should be in the range of 260 to 273 million.[1] Even the low estimate would represent more than a 70% increase over the census population of 1950 and about a 44% increase over the recorded population in 1960. As recently as 1958, a "reasonable" estimate of the population in 1980 was 230 million, or 30 million below the lowest estimate in the early 1960's.

Why are population estimates too low? The tale is a long one, and I shall not try to trace out all of the theoretical preconceptions that have led demographers into persistent, conservative errors. But, in a few words, the fundamental difficulty is that the American population is one that mostly limits its reproductive behavior voluntarily, and still persists in a fairly high rate of reproduction—or rather, having gone through a stage of very low natural increase typical of all the Western world as birth control finally spread throughout most elements of the population, has returned to somewhat earlier fertility rates.

The age distribution of a population is one way of recording its history, and some of that history can be projected into the future.[2] Starting at the upper ages, the number of persons over sixty-five may be expected to increase from 1960's 16 million to 25 million in 1980, an increase of some 56%. The population of college age, eighteen to twenty-two, is predicted to increase from approximately 12 million in 1960 to around 21 million in 1980, an increase of 75%. College enrollments will almost certainly show an even greater rate of growth, as the proportions attending college go on increasing. Assuming that trends in school enrollments of the mid-1950's continue to 1980, the college and professional school enrollment would reach 11.5 million, or almost triple the current registration of 4 million.

By contrast, that portion of the population that represents the bulk of the homemakers and the labor force, namely those aged twenty-five to sixty-four, is projected as increasing by less than 30%. A major factor in the relatively small size of that population, which is entirely comprised of people born before 1955, is that it includes the survivors of the small birth crops in the 1930's.

With mortality trends predictably stable, short of widespread disaster, the main uncertainty in predicting the population size is, of course, the problem of guessing birth rates. And that problem is exacerbated because historic trends and differentials no longer operate and we must try to puzzle out the significance of more recent experience.

The Baby Boom

Though current American birth rates have leveled off from their high plateau in the years just following World War II, they are still substantially higher than their prewar levels. The Taeubers[3] have provided a rather thorough analysis of the proximate sources of the increase—not where babies come from, which is no mystery, but what would account for their greater number. Comparing the first postwar decade (1945–54) with the depression decade of the 1930's, the number of births increased by 58%, though the birth *rate* per thousand population rose only from 18.4 to 24.9, an increase of 35%. Here is how the increased number of births was accounted for, in percentage terms:

Factor	Percent
Earlier childbearing	34
Earlier marriage (additional)	30
More women of childbearing age	24
Bigger families	12
Total	100

Except for the additional numbers of potential mothers, about which little could be done, short of killing or sterilizing them, each of the other components of the increase in births must be judged as reflecting changes in motivated action.

Earlier childbearing within "normal" families and earlier marriage combine to speed the rate of population replacement by shortening the span of time between generations. Despite the wondrous number of babies born, very few are born to women over thirty. By marrying earlier and decreasing the intervals between births, young mothers concentrate their childbearing and then, if you will, turn to other proper female concerns, like child-rearing, housekeeping, and some social activity outside the home.

Note, however, that part of the baby boom has been genuine—that is, bigger families. Though accidents undoubtedly happen, this change must be assumed to have been mainly deliberate. This assumption is supported by some additional facts. While the birth rate has gone up, there has been no reversal of the long-term downward trend in really large families of five or more children. On the other hand, childless families are much rarer, and the main part of the increase in births has been a shift from two children to three, and occasionally to four. (Thus, except for the finer nuances of interpersonal relations of interest to students of personality and group dynamics, we are not dealing with a major structural change in the family system. In fact, the small-family pattern has been accentuated, not abandoned.) Of perhaps even more significance have been the social characteristics of those who have mainly contributed to increased birth rates—precisely, the urban, professional, and college-educated sectors of the population whose predecessors were in the vanguard of the practice of birth control. Between 1940 and 1950 the highest percentage increase in fertility of women by educational attainment was among college graduates.[4] To repeat, these people have not abandoned family limitation, but they do appear to want several children produced in the very earliest years of married life.

Since sexual behavior is motivated behavior and one form or another of birth control is available to most sectors of the population and certainly to the educated dweller in various suburban fertile valleys, we may reasonably ask, what has happened, and will it continue? Although a definitive answer to the first question is not possible,[5] it does appear that there has been a genuine recrudescence of "familism," an emphasis on the family as the one institutionalized system where individuals are treated as something approximating whole persons and about the only place where an adult may legitimately display some emotion. In a complex social system where well-rehearsed actors are mostly playing bit parts, the family provides a drama with all starring roles. Far from disappearing from loss of functions, the modern family is called upon to perform one of the most crucial functions for human personality formation and reinforcement, and some families collapse under the strain.

Though the continuing importance of the family in the future cannot be seriously doubted, that alone does not tell us much about prospective birth rates. For that, we need still further analysis of the nature and implications of recent trends.

Fertility Differentials

In the historic transition from high to fairly low fertility rates, the practice of family limitation spread slowly from upper-income and occupational groups to other parts of the population. Thus, until the very recent past there was a negative correlation between socioeconomic status and number of children. Those best able to afford children had the fewest. Very large families are still mainly produced by the poor and by Catholics strongly oriented to the church as evidenced by attendance at parochial schools.[6] But for the rest of the population the historic relationship has been reduced, and here and there reversed. For a growing number of families, children have become a major category of conspicuous consumption—"consumer durables" with high upkeep costs.[7]

What apparently has happened, and may be expected to continue, is about like this: once pregnancy, or especially a second or third pregnancy, was no longer taken as automatic evidence of ignorance and error, but might be assumed to have been intended, then childbearing and child-rearing expenses could be allowed to compete with other income uses in families with comfortable or affluent resources.

The earlier basis for fertility limitations among business and professional groups was commonly attributed to mobility aspirations, both between generations and within careers. But note that these same groups have a kind of assured mobility at least within careers; that is, they have what amounts to tenure and a graded career in some large administrative organization, public or private, or an assurance of a steady or expanding practice if they operate independently. Note also that most expect a *rising* level of real income through time, hopefully adequate to meet future expenses, including education for their children.

Two or three further implications of present and prospective fertility patterns warrant comment. If the association between fertility and ability to pay becomes even stronger, a growing population may be as favorable to the economy as all of the business press assumes. But it must be remembered that as manufacturers of building materials, consumer goods, and textbooks look with favor on increasing markets, they must also contemplate a rising level of property taxation to provide the schools, playgrounds, youth centers, and juvenile courts that are also needed at an accelerating rate.

Similarly, if the historic association between large families and poverty is broken, then a larger proportion of children is afforded the advantages of material comforts and, hopefully, cultural and intellectual benefits in forming character and aspirations. (I do not assume that the biological or genetic quality of the population is thereby improved, for there is very little evidence that the rich are brighter than the poor, and none at all that their children are.) Again, however, let us turn this coin over. One long-standing component of openness in our society, of the possibility of intergenerational mobility, was precisely demographic: the circumstance that various elites did not reproduce themselves, to say nothing of filling the growing proportions of managerial and professional positions in the labor force as a whole.[8] If the advantages that the well-to-do can provide for their now-larger families means a growing inheritance of social position, even stronger measures to equalize opportunity than those currently under way will be required to avoid a major waste of talents among those relatively disadvantaged.

Temporal Patterns

Since fertility throughout the American population is generally under some form and degree of voluntary control, it is not surprising that birth rates are rather sensitive to current economic conditions. In fact, one of the very first harbingers of the recession of 1958 was the marriage rate, though this was probably an artifact of speedier reporting than was true, say, of portland-cement production or freight-car loadings.

The implication of this linkage, however, is far-reaching, for the rate of population growth is as stable or unstable as the economy itself. Thus school and other planners may be faced with rather uneven annual flows of recruits, often exceeding the architectural or administrative flexibility of the agencies involved.

Some rather longer-term strains are also foreseeable. As I have described the problem in a recent book,

> Many new suburban communities consist almost exclusively of young adults and their immature children. These homeowners (with mortgages) are precisely representative of current trends involving somewhat larger families rapidly produced, so that school construction represents a major part of community needs and tax-supported budgets. Without substantial residential mobility in the future, these homeowners and their children will grow inexorably older, and after the foreseeable high schools, and, possibly, community colleges have been built and staffed, what then? It would require an extensive rate of out-migration by parents as their children leave each stage of the school system and of inmigration of parents with children ready for that stage, or a marked extension of the number of children and period of childbearing in most families, to avoid a rather substantial oversupply of school facilities only a decade or so from now.[9]

The young parents who have contributed to the continued high reproductive rate since 1950 were themselves the survivors of very small depression birth crops, and thus faced a rather favorable labor market situation. Grauman[10] has suggested that we may be in the midst of a succession of twenty-year off-phase cycles, whereby labor shortages yield high wages and high fertility and thus labor surpluses and depressed wages when the bumper crop of children reaches maturity. Certainly those finishing their education now, ahead of the big increase of eighteen-year-olds for college or employment beginning in 1965, will have a comparative advantage in getting jobs.

I cannot leave the subject of population trends without sounding a note of alarm. Even if the economy can afford larger populations and, here and there, profit by the expanded demand, and even if affluent families can afford many children, the implications of growth for sheer massiveness of organization, density of settlement, and congestion of movement strike me as very grave. Local and private actions and solutions to problems may become increasingly difficult as numbers increase. I am enough of an unreconstructed neoMalthusian, and enough of a believer in openness and choice in social organization, to regard the production of more than two or three children by any family as simply socially irresponsible. Population growth has to stop sometime, and in my opinion it should have been about a decade or so ago.

Levels of Living and Styles of Life

I suppose that, after sex, the second major American preoccupation is money. But I think we should clear up one common confusion. In an economic system such as ours it is a mistake to equate an interest in money with mere materialism. "Money is useful for whatever it will buy, which may be quite non-material and even philanthropic. The world's materialists are perforce the have-nots and not the haves."[11] I shall return to the significance of discretionary income, but we should first establish a numerical base for looking into future patterns of expenditure.

Economic Growth*

Though there are short-term fluctuations in growth rates in the American economy, the "stagnation" hypothesis popular in the 1930's has proved at least premature and possibly fundamentally wrong. In any event, a more optimistic view of the future appears warranted by the period since the end of World War II, but not of course without soft spots and serious problems.

The 1980 gross national product may reach $1 *trillion,* or about double that of 1960. Dividing that by the prospective family units of 1980 would yield an average family income of $9,500, some 70% higher than 1960. (The median, the income level that would divide the range of families into equal halves, would be somewhat lower, as the arithmetic mean is affected by the small number of very high incomes.)

For such growth to take place, productivity gains will need to be made in various services as they have been made in manufacturing, and

* I owe my projections of economic magnitudes to Arnold W. Sametz, *The Economy in 1980,* one of a series of studies distributed in October 1958 by the General Electric Company under the general title "1980: The Basic Planning Horizon."

the rate of unemployment controlled by rapid transfers to expanding sectors of the economy. Sametz[12] assumes a leveling-off of defense expenditures in the "public sector," but an increase in other public construction and services—especially in schools, scientific research, health, and so on. He also assumes that residential construction will represent an even larger share of the family's budget, that other consumer goods (including automobiles) will decline somewhat in relative importance, and that services (including health, education, and travel) will increase.

The *spread* of income may not narrow much, particularly by reduction of upper incomes, but social policy is likely to continue to add social benefits for the very poor: wage and rent controls, medical care, retraining and relocation assistance for the unemployed breadwinner, possibly higher pension benefits for those beyond retirement age.

Making a Living

The reduction of the farming population has been one of the longest and strongest trends in the structural change of the American economy. From a figure of 72% of the economically active population engaged in agriculture in 1820, the proportion had declined to 38% by the turn of the century, to 12% in 1950, and under 8% in 1961.[13] Meanwhile, the volume of agricultural production has increased tremendously. Yet there are still a good many "marginal" producers among farm families, and even the bipartisan Federal farm policies that subsidize farmers at the expense of the rest of the taxpayers cannot prevent further reductions in the farm population. The South is a major target area for improved agricultural efficiency and decreased agricultural employment.

Another pattern is also beginning to emerge: the shift of farmers to towns and cities as residences, the farmstead house providing temporary shelter during brief periods of sowing and harvesting. Thus, some parts of the American countryside are beginning to resemble the classic European pattern of the agricultural village and town surrounded by uninhabited fields. The difference is that the American drives to his farm in a late-model car, and because of technological advances in mechanization, may not have to make the trip very often. He may even contract for plowing, sowing, and harvesting by mobile crews with expensive equipment, and arrange by telephone for another commercial service, that of spreading insecticide dusts by airplane.

The hardy, independent, small producer in the isolated rural region, exemplifying virtues not visible in the city, thus represents another bit of increasingly fictional nostalgia. Rural isolation was never as common or as highly valued as our folklore had it, and the second or third

agricultural revolution—along with roads and the mass media—
have radically reduced its statistical frequency.

Whether for farming or for other types of economic activity, another
trend will surely carry forward into the future. That is an increase in
minimum skills levels for labor-force participation. Though much of
the polemical literature on the effects of machines has emphasized the
splitting up of skills and degradation of the worker serving the
machine, the jobs most readily mechanized or "automated" are in fact
those that have been already routinized and stripped of all but the most
elementary decisions. With the advances in electronic observation and
information storage and computerized information retrieval and problem solving, occupations as diverse as supermarket checkers, junior
administrators, law clerks, medical diagnosticians, and teachers may
be under the threat of machine displacement.

The new machines need masters, not slaves: inventors, programmers,
responsible monitors, and diagnosticians of electronic troubles. The
machine has not made man obsolete. It has made automatons obsolete,
and requires of us that we behave within something like the distinctly
human qualities of intelligence, creativity, and constant adjustment to
novelty.

This way of stating the situation highlights the ever-increasing importance of education as a qualification for employment. But it also
subtly distinguishes between types as well as levels of education. The
simple storage of information—and that is what a barbarous proportion of our examinations seeks to test—is not using the human potential very efficiently. Information deteriorates very rapidly, even when
it is accurate in the first place. The skills of thinking, of knowing how
to find out, and of creating new knowledge are going to be at a
premium, and the skills of repetitive dexterity and simple recall are
sure to be increasingly unmarketable.

Let me give a concrete illustration that shows how various trends
intersect. We have noted the trends toward earlier marriage and
toward early childbearing and its termination by the age of thirty.
Thus there has been a recent marked increase in female labor-force
participation rates over the age of forty-five, when the youngest child
is safely in secondary school and one or more older children may be
already married. The Department of Labor forecasters, this time working with a 1975 deadline rather than 1980, predict an increase from
43.5% labor-force participation of women aged forty-five to fifty-four
in 1955 to a 56.0% rate in 1975—an increase of about 19%—and an
even sharper increase in the labor force participation of females fifty-
five to sixty-four, from 32.2 to 44.4—a 38% increase.[14]

Now it is difficult to provide a suitable secondary or even college education for males who start their careers immediately and may be able to adjust to changes by small stages. Consider the problem of the female college graduate who marries immediately after (if not before) graduation, perhaps uses some part of her education for a year or two before she starts bearing children, and then drops out of the labor market for twenty years. If her college years were not totally misspent— and that is a real possibility—they should equip her to stay intellectually alive while she is out of direct economic circulation, and able to refresh herself quickly for personally satisfying and economically rewarding employment when she seeks to refurbish her adult participation in the economic life of the community. For if there is anything predictable at all about future employment, it is that particular highly-trained skills will become obsolete at a very quick pace, while the demand for new skills will increase at least as fast.

Styles of Life

As we look at the emergent patterns in the ways people organize their lives—or live them out with varying degrees of disorganization—we are faced with an immediate paradox. One can make out arguments of almost equal persuasiveness for increasing homogeneity and for persistent diversity in life styles.

On the side of homogeneity, we can safely predict a growing similarity in standards of living and even in some actual levels of consumption, particularly for life's necessities and some of its comforts. Thus differences deriving from geographic regions, race, ethnic origins, and rural or urban residence may be expected to become narrower. And, in fact, the significance of income differences is likely to diminish over considerable areas of consumption: food and clothing, medical and educational facilities. Even in the area of adult toys, there is less qualitative difference between a jalopy and a Jaguar than between a jalopy and no car at all.

Yet the standardization that comes about in a relatively affluent economy has limits. Though luxuries have a way of becoming necessities through time, and the status symbols of the rich have an extremely short duration before they are widely copied, it remains true that moderate to high incomes produce the interesting phenomenon of *discretionary income*. Goods compete with services for the household's expenditures, and some of the services may take the form of experiences (art, entertainment, travel) rather than simply catering to creature comforts and lazy indolence. Money becomes useful for an ever-wider array of choices, and it follows then that the choices cannot be predicted from income alone.

The paradox is thus a true one, for both contradictory propositions are true. They are true for different segments of consumer behavior. And I should add that it is the worst form of snobbery, unfortunately widely indulged by a band of self-styled intellectuals, to maintain that culture widely shared is somehow debased, that the possessors of "true" culture must become more and more *outré* in their tastes in order to establish their distinction from the common run of mankind. Does Tchaikovsky become less tuneful because heard by a car salesman, Bach less contrapuntally mathematical when heard by an overhead crane operator, or Picasso less imaginative because a good print hangs in the primary school teacher's living room? The access to cultural wealth is one of the side benefits of an open society, and one wonders why it makes some people feel so insecure.

Residential patterns, too, exhibit clear trends that can be projected into the future. The American population was 46% urban in 1910,* 51% in 1920, and 70% in 1960—by a somewhat different criterion of urban areas.[15] But central cities have grown less rapidly than the rings —the suburbs. Between 1900 and 1950 suburbs grew one and one-third times faster than central cities, and in the decade of the 1950's suburbs grew at an astounding rate of five times the rate of increase of central cities. By 1960 suburbs accounted for nearly half (49%) of the total population in metropolitan areas.

Despite valiant attempts, here and there, at urban renewal, there is little reason to expect an end to urban decentralization over the next two decades. What the train did for urban centralization, the automobile has done for suburbanization, and some cities, such as Los Angeles, never had a substantial center.

When the spreading city reaches and overtakes an established community, the result is simply a more complex urban structure. But the freshly-created suburbs are something else again. Because they tend to be the creations of one real estate developer or at most a very few, they tend to provide a rather narrow economic range for residents as determined by housing prices. We are thus witnessing the phenomenon of the "one-class" suburb, with obviously negative implications for the range of social experience of children through schools and play groups.

The age-specialization of suburbs, which I commented on earlier, has another facet of present relevance. It is especially the suburban environment for child rearing that appeals to many, perhaps most, suburbanites. We may thus expect a growth of a trend already visible, namely reurbanization of couples whose youngest child has left the home, and

---

* The earlier definition of "urban" was a municipality of at least 2,500 inhabitants. The new definition is based on density, and includes areas contiguous to cities even though the actual locality is under 2,500 or has no organized local government.

whose enthusiasm for gardening, shoveling driveways after snowstorms, and several hours of daily commuting by the breadwinner has diminished radically meanwhile.

The reurbanization of older couples in middle-income groups is, in fact, about the only chance that central cities have to avoid the completion of a current process of radical polarization: the city as the dwelling place of the very poor, and, for part of the year, the very rich.

Still another important aspect of style of life is the use of time. Despite the suburban commuter's long day, the two-day weekend is nearly universal and the three-day weekend not unknown. Business managers, some of whom actually do carry home extra work in their slim attaché cases and actually do it, have benefited less from restrictions on the length of the workweek than have organized manual workers. For the salaried manager, pressures for shorter work hours and longer vacations may be expected, and some pressures will certainly succeed. The professional, on the other hand, tends to work even longer hours, but to draw less precise distinctions between enjoyable work and creative leisure. It does not appear that we are creating any great number of equivalents to the "new Soviet man," whose wide cultural participation and minimum occupational specialization is a kind of Marxian myth; but life styles that emphasize breadth and creativity at the work place and also in the home are certain to be increasingly articulated as goals of the affluent "middle mass" of the population.

Administrative Problems of Size

The steady bureaucratization of the labor force—some 85% of the economically active are now wage and salary earners—has its counterpart in virtually every aspect of life: government, education, entertainment, and even religion. Continuous population growth combined with the obvious advantages of coordinated specialization that organization affords, will certainly assure continuation of the trend toward an "organizational society."

I should not want to stop with only the negative implications of massive organization, however. Local, occupational, and other interests may actually be protected by size, since the administrative costs of centralization may be too great, and decentralized autonomy and areas of choice may be accorded by default if not by design. There is nothing so repressive to diversity as the tight little organization. Despite a libraryful of tendentious treatises by industrial sociologists, informal organization is likely to be far more restrictive of individuality than formal organization. "Bureaucracy" gets its evil reputation in large measure from mindless adherence to rules, but in a sufficiently large and complex organization the adept individualist can usually find a way of subverting the organization for its own good as well as his own. This may be one of the most highly prized social skills as organizations grow in size and individuals, hopefully, grow in ingenuity.

Some Educational Problems

Since the setting of this venture into prognosis is the academic community, I should like to make a few concluding comments about the higher educational enterprise over the next few decades. The three social functions of the college or university are preservation of knowledge, passing it on, and adding to it. But each of these functions is going to be steadily more difficult in view of an explosion in information that makes the population explosion seem like a very small noise.

First, with respect to preservation, college libraries are faced with book acquisitions that will shortly use up available space, even if a new building has just been dedicated. For any college library with anything like an adequate rate of current acquisitions, the median age of all its books—the age that divides the total population of books into older and younger halves—is almost certainly under five years, and will certainly go down: for a high literary fertility rate reduces the age of the book population as inexorably as prolific human populations grow younger. This presents storage problems for librarians and college fund-raisers, but it presents increasing *retrieval* problems for library users. We must almost certainly have to shift to an increased use of microphotography and computerized magnetic tape as an adjunct to scholarship.

But as I was not the first to remark—the comment has been attributed to Justice Oliver Wendell Holmes—information does not keep well. We may yet have to use something like Orwell's "memory hole"[16] in order to get rid of outworn "knowledge."

And that brings me to the question of teaching. Surely too much of the formal educational enterprise seems designed to treat students as information storage and retrieval units, of remarkable inefficiency. Should not the center and substance of a higher education be training for a world that, despite our best efforts, remains somewhat uncertain and for positions that are bound to change at a rapid rate? The capacity for continuous learning, perhaps now and then formalized by advanced courses for persons on leave from their normal duties, would seem to have highest priority. And I should also emphasize training for *creativity*. I am not suggesting great books or the *Synopticon*. This sort of approach strikes me as increasingly reactionary. What is needed is a habit of mind rather than a store of information. "Lightly" supervised independent work might well be made a universal requirement in college curricula, even at the expense of dropping as many as one-fourth of the ordinary number of formal courses.

Plans for dealing with the problem of teacher shortages are not entirely encouraging. Making lectures bigger and bigger is concentrating attention on the most questionable mode of communication. Despite the extremely favorable present and prospective market position of college teachers—they've never had it so good—the professors are made distinctly nervous by talk of the closed-circuit television, recorded lectures by outstanding authorities, and teaching machines. Why not use them all, if the professors are thereby freed for more creative scholarship and more creative supervision of the students' largely independent study and investigation? Professors might even be willing to spend more hours in the classroom—if they were given the kind of secretarial and clerical assistance that is accorded the most junior business administrators. But classroom hours, I am suggesting, may be a nearly outmoded aspect of higher education.

It was, I suppose, nearly inevitable that I should start making predictions and end up constructing a utopia. But that, too, is part of the business of prophecy, for some segments of the future will be what we intend them to be, given a little devotion of energy and resources to making dreams come true.

References

1. U. S. Census estimates, summarized and discussed by Philip M. Hauser, *Population Perspectives* (New Brunswick, New Jersey: Rutgers University Press, 1960), Chapter 2.

2. I have derived all of the future estimates of American population from Hauser, Reference 1.

3. Conrad Taeuber and Irene B. Taeuber, *The Changing Population of the United States* (New York: John Wiley and Sons, 1958), pp. 267–68.

4. See Clyde V. Kiser, "Differential Fertility in the United States," *in* National Bureau of Economic Research, *Demographic and Economic Change in Developed Countries* (Princeton, New Jersey: Princeton University Press, 1960), pp. 77–113; comparison from Table 6, p. 103.

5. See Charles F. Westoff *et al.*, *The Third Child* (Princeton, New Jersey: Princeton University Press, 1963).

6. *Ibid.*, Chapter VIII, "Religion and Religiousness."

7. See Gary S. Becker, "An Economic Analysis of Fertility," *in* National Bureau of Economic Research, *Demographic and Economic Change in Developed Countries*, pp. 209–231.

8. See Elbridge Sibley, "Some Demographic Clues to Stratification," *American Sociological Review*, June 1942, pp. 322–330.

9. Wilbert E. Moore, *Man, Time, and Society* (New York: John Wiley and Sons, 1963), p. 125.

10. John V. Grauman, "Comment" on paper by Frank W. Notestein, in National Bureau of Economic Research, *Demographic and Economic Change in Developed Countries*, pp. 275–282.

11. Wilbert E. Moore, *The Conduct of the Corporation* (New York: Random House, 1962), p. 274.

12. Arnold W. Sametz, *The Economy in 1980* (Schenectady, New York: General Electric Co., 1958).

13. For the trend from 1820 to 1950 see Simon Kuznets, "Quantitative Aspects of the Economic Growth of Nations, II: Industrial Distribution of National Product and Labor Force," Supplement to *Economic Development and Cultural Change*, Vol. V, No. 4, July 1957. For 1961, see U. S. Bureau of the Census, *Statistical Abstract of the United States, 1961* (Washington: Government Printing Office, 1961), p. 107.

14. See *Statistical Abstract . . . , 1961*, p. 204.

15. *Ibid.*, p. 23.

16. See George Orwell, *Nineteen Eighty-four* (New York: Harcourt, Brace, 1949).

17

THE UTILITY OF UTOPIAS

Never in human history have so many people, or has such a large proportion of mankind, been engaged in attempting to remake the environment, to increase our capacity to use the environment for human purposes, and to remodel the rules and social arrangements that govern man's interaction with his fellows. Some of these reshapers of man's destiny are honorable troublemakers in the context in which they find themselves—scientists and engineers, teachers and legislators, social planners and community developers. Others are faced with opposition from constituted authorities, and from the network of traditional restraints that discourage innovation. The first target of the malcontents in those situations is precisely the established social order, which is regarded as inhibiting if not iniquitous.

Man has always been a problem-solving animal, but in the course of his social evolution he has increasingly invented the problems to be solved, the novel goals to be achieved, rather than merely coping with ambiguity and adversity. It is this addiction to discontent and to the search for a better future that I want to explore here, particularly as this activity of the laity relates to the enterprise of sociology as the generalizing science of man's social behavior. Have we, in short, any obligation as social scientists to start taking account not only of the changeful quality of social life but also of the fact that some portion of that change is deliberate? And do we, still as social scientists, have anything positive to add to the fulfillment of human hopes for the future, or are we always fated to counsel the eager traveler that "you can't get there from here"?

SOURCE. Reprinted from "The Utility of Utopias," *American Sociological Review*, 31: 765–772, December 1966; by permission of the American Sociological Association.

This chapter was originally prepared as the presidential address delivered at the annual meeting of the American Sociological Association in Miami Beach, August 31, 1966.

All Is Vanity

Utopias have fallen on evil days. The derogatory designation "utopian" signifies unrealistic assumptions and unrealizable aspirations.

Some of this ill repute is justified. Utopian constructs often violate fundamental principles of social discourse and human survival.

Item: Utopias are sexless or provide for unlimited sexuality. The former alternative clearly bodes ill for continuity beyond the lifetime of the founders. The latter alternative might possibly work, but it has a considerable weight of contrary human experience as at least cautionary evidence that would counsel examination of the importance of enduring emotion in the relations of males and females.

Item: Utopias are unconscionably peaceable, and thus miss the utility of difference and conflict, as well as its realistic probability in any human aggregate.

Item: Mostly their inhabitants appear to be rational adults of somewhat depressing uniformity. Thus differences in abilities and motivations are given little play, and the uncertainties of childhood socialization are evaded.

Item: Utopias are almost invariably millenialist and consequently static, since where would one go from perfection?

Despite these and other damaging defects, I shall argue that a vision of the future is not vain, or vanity in the Biblical sense. And I shall further argue that, despite serious intellectual inhibitions, sociologists have some scientific stake in forecasting and even in implementing the future that is hopefully better than the present.

It is in this sense that I use the term utopia, that is, a future state of human affairs that more nearly realizes individual and collective goals. Thus no real distinction is drawn between utopia and ideology[1] as long as ideology is future-oriented and not a mere rationalization of the current state of social arrangements.

Because many ideal goals may be approximated but not fully attained, and because goals actually attained do not preclude the creation of new ones, there is no necessary presumption of static perfection. Once the practice of planning the future is firmly established it is likely to persist, if for no other reason than to introduce variety in human experience.

The older intellectual traditions of sociology favored the use of current knowledge for remodeling as well as merely describing the social order. Whether one dates sociology from Plato or from Comte,

the *Republic* or the *Parliament of Man* represented attempts to en-
vision a future form of social organization that would draw on the
best knowledge and wisdom concerning human affairs. What happened
to that tradition deserves some brief comment, for the inhibitions I
referred to earlier are still very much with us.

There Is Nothing New

One of the restraints on sociological utopias has been the type of
analytic machinery that many sociologists have used. Analysis of the
relations among social phenomena by treating them as parts of a
system does not intrinsically require that the system remain in a steady
state. The analysis is usually easier, however, if that assumption is
made. Almost all of our analytic methods, which are being developed
far beyond the capacity of some of us to keep technically competent,
are designed to extract more and more information about covariance.
Very little inventive skill is devoted to probability chains in sequences
of social actions. Theorists and methodologists, despite their manifest
differences in other respects, have been remarkably atemporal, and thus
seem to deserve each other.

There is surely no need at this point in our intellectual history to
beat functionalism over the head once more. No analytic science could
dispense with models that are in some way or some degree unrealistic
representations of the phenomena that they are designed to put in
order. The danger lies not in abstraction but in the use of one model
of reality to the exclusion of others. There *are* notable elements of
persistence in the way social behavior is ordered. There are likewise
notable elements of what may be called self-regulation in social systems
once established. And there are even notable elements of assuring
persistence through socialization of the young into predetermined adult
roles. A model of social systems containing only these elements distorts
reality in various ways and degrees. And the seriousness of the distortion will differ in time and place. It is probably true that the fit
between this analytic model and social reality has been closest in small
and relatively isolated tribal societies prior to their being swept into
the contemporary world social system. In newly modernizing societies
and in postindustrial societies the distortion is rather severe. Not only
is large-scale structural change left out of account, but also there is no
room for a type of order that rests upon the balancing of discordant
interests rather than upon complementarity and mutuality.[2] It must
be noted, however, that attention to conflict is properly viewed as a
corrective to social-system models and not as a substitute.

It may be well to remind ourselves, in passing, that Durkheim, the reputed father of functionalism, did not hold a purely static view of the universe. It is true that he identified correlation as the prime sociological method,[3] which he exemplified brilliantly in his analysis of suicide.[4] But it is also true that in *Division of Labor*[5] and in *The Elementary Forms of the Religious Life*[6] his approach was evolutionary. And Durkheim even permitted himself to look into the future and indeed to express some preferences as to its course.[7]

The mindlessly mechanical versions of functionalism have little affinity with Durkheim. In other versions, individuals are endowed with drives, interests, and ends, but collectivities are not. The fear of fallacy (the group mind) has led to the neglect of such realities as national purpose, including individual sacrifices for its realization.

I am suggesting that there is always something new under the sun, some of which was intended. There is nothing unseemly about systematizing our knowledge of coexistence in social phenomena as long as we are not precluded from an analysis of sequences and behavior oriented to the future.

Let Them Have Dominion

Another intellectual model, and one explicitly dynamic in orientation, has had the paradoxical effect of inhibiting attention to the future and particularly of constructing more desirable future states. That model is social evolution, which has recently had renewed attention after some decades in disrepute.[8]

The theoretical scheme of evolution—resting upon variability, differentiation, and selective adaptation—has been linked here and there with notions of progress: The fittest survive; more highly organized forms have competitive advantages over simple organisms. Intelligence and culture can be viewed as evolutionary emergents, lending reality over the long term to the Biblical promise to men: "Let them have dominion . . . ."

Although innovation may be viewed as the social equivalent of biological mutation in accounting for variability, the evolutionary model is poorly designed to include purpose. Chance rather than design is the principal feature of evolutionary change. Que será, será. Were some utopian social order to emerge from the processes of evolution, it would be a long time coming, and essentially accidental. Human impatience is manifestly increasing, and though the creation of the future will surely be marked by trial and error, the trials will be mainly deliberate and any success can scarcely be credited to chance.

Press Toward the Mark

The purposive, goal-oriented, future-oriented character of social life has been a bit embarrassing to social analysts. This embarrassment, we have seen, derives from the use of mechanical and ecological models of social processes, not to mention instinct theories long abandoned. Yet there has been another source of unease also, and that is the worry over "subjectivism." By a classic semantic confusion, it was supposed by some that if one took account of subjective states of actors under observation, the objectivity of observation itself would be destroyed. To the behaviorist, or positivist in that sense, human behavior is determined, but not self-determined.

What remains true is that, almost uniquely, human action is purposive and oriented to the future. (I know about ants relative to grasshoppers, and the alleged forehandedness of squirrels, who often cannot find their caches carefully put by for a less opulent time. Lacking innovative qualities, these behaviors appear more instinctual than purposive.) At the possible risk of reductionism, I suggest that this propensity of human beings to be goal-oriented, and future goal-oriented at that, probably has something to do with genetic intelligence. However that may be, the propensity is pretty common to mankind, even if the future goals are otherworldly—worldly goals having failed for the common run of mankind. The anesthetic qualities of conventional theology exasperated Marx—properly—because a supernatural set of aspirations was likely to quieten discontent over current injustice.

The intellectual and ideological revolution of our time is that fate has lost standing as an explanatory principle in accounting for poverty and suffering, and the (often whimsical) will of God has fared little better. Mundane explanations are increasingly demanded and mundane solutions earnestly sought. Chance still plays a part in explanations, but chance is essentially an expression of ignorance and is therefore subject to curtailment as knowledge increases.

Even some of our cherished determinism is subject to suspicion. This has been eloquently expressed by Manning Nash in the final passage of his book on the industrialization of a Guatemalan village:

... the human tolls of industrialization are not built into the process itself. They are the result of an image of man in social change which delineates him as the passive agent mechanically responding to immutable forces, or as the pawn in a political chess game, or as the expendable material in an economic vision. The questions we must ask of the process of industrialization cannot be phrased apart from the ineluctable fact that man makes himself, or he is not made at all.[9]

The options of course are not completely open, but they allow for considerable variability and thus for discretion in both structural terms —the exact mode of social arrangements—and in sequential terms— the order in which our more stately mansions are built.

Men act *in* and often *for* social collectivities. Nothing else makes sense of the human condition, and no attempt to reduce this nearly invariant fact of man's behavior to individual actions can do anything else but denigrate and deny the whole meaning of man's life as a social, and occasionally even as a cultured, animal. The exceptions are clearly on the tails of the distribution in a statistical sense, and clearly patho- logical in terms of man's survival as a species, and certainly as the most successful evolutionary form in the competition among species.

As sociologists, all of us are relativists but also determinists. "It all depends," or "Under what conditions?" are phrases that properly abound in our literature. But we are also generalists: "In every con- tinuing society roles must be so allocated that essential functions are performed by qualified persons." Or, if that is regarded as tautological, as many useful generalizations may be, we may affirm: "An industrial system is dependent on a monetary system of exchange." And we also, more or less secretly, harbor the thought that we may be of practical relevance: "If the goal is to secure rapid but balanced economic growth in Xanadu, under conditions 1 through n, then major investments should be made in the training of primary school teachers, at the possible expense of a new cement plant." Note that here we assert some deterministic views, some sense of priorities in social causation, for which we have a rather too meager basis in well-established se- quences. In this role we either accept the goal, or evade the issue under the guise that we are technicians. As a practical matter of motivation, however, technicians are likely to feel uncomfortable, and may do poorly, in the service of ends that they do not share. All of us have been rehearsed to repeat that the motives for undertaking an inquiry have no bearing on the validity of results, and there is no reason to alter the aphorism. Yet it is surely proper to note the probability that some of the fascination in studying the aspirations and tribulations of new nations and other developing areas is that thereby some of us can indulge suppressed missionary impulses, as we share at least vicariously in a worldly quest for human salvation.

One concrete manifestation that the sociologists' blindness to change and extreme reluctance to admit the phenomena of deliberate change are not shared by men of public affairs is the abundance of 5-year,

10-year, and even longer integrated national plans. These plans may not be the construction of utopias, properly speaking, but they are viewed as steps toward a future seen perhaps dimly. Their first consequence is a deliberate allocation of resources in order to implement the goals.

Though centralized planning does not easily fit the institutional structure of a pluralist society, this does not mean that there are no shared visions and no men and organizations dedicated to their realization. And, to a growing extent, there will be a demand for *monitoring* social change in the dual sense of close observation of trends and of initiating corrective action when trends are going the wrong way or at the wrong pace.[10]

Sociologists are in danger of being priced right out of the market. Political leaders, their active opponents, and other organized collectivities across the social landscape are trying to remodel political and economic arrangements, and social arrangements not elsewhere classified. On occasion, representatives of organized interests seek the counsel of social scientists on organizational matters, on questions of priorities, on troublesome uncertainties about maintaining a modicum of order while rapid change is set on its way. But what about helping to shape the grand design from the beginning?

Dennis Gabor asserts that we cannot predict the future, but that we can invent it.[11] The specific concerns of this thoughtful physical scientist are all-out war, overpopulation, and the challenge of technology. He makes a strong case for optimism. The distinction between predicting and inventing is spurious, however. If we invent the future, we thereby predict it, for deliberate acts will be taken to implement the invention, and we shall be able—no doubt with some slippage—to do what we set out to do.

The Trumpet Shall Sound

There is another tradition in our intellectual heritage, which at first glance was not religious in its orientation to the future, and which at second glance was also not scientific, contrary to the founders' claims. This is the Marxist version of man and his future, which has suffered many amendments and reinterpretations. The details of the crosscurrents in this particular theology can interest only the faithful, and, since they are split into sects, only some of them. Yet certain points in the Marxian tradition have had a kind of continuing viability, despite the best efforts of orthodoxy to make them meaningless.

The principal enduring features of Marxist theory are the emphasis on conflict and particularly the role of conflict in producing structural change. To these features one may properly add an emphasis on utopian idealism, for the Marxian tradition has been as utopian as those socialists that Marx criticized. Neither the future foreseen by Marx nor the process of getting there occurred in the places where the prediction was applied. It is as ideology and not as deterministic theory that Marxism has relevance for the future, where the ideology is accepted. The irony of this reversal of Marxist doctrine will not detain us.

Revolutions thrive on utopian images, and without such images they will fail. Nihilist rebellions may be provoked for the single purpose of deposing existing rulers, but unless there is a kind of ulterior purpose, a positive rather than a purely negative goal, institutions will not be changed and a revolution will not have occurred. Indeed, a new set of rascals will have succeeded their predecessors.

Marxist theology has a hardy survival power, not because of its scientific accuracy, but because it is a worldly eschatology. It promises mundane solutions and mundane rewards. It has probably produced more bad sociology than even the mindless functionalists, for the latter had a kind of honor about verifiable relationships and a sense for what constitutes a predictable concatenation of events. The Marxists generally have been deluded into thinking of a social system as held together by a conspiratorial group wielding overt and subtle power, and barely containing the deep-seated conflicts of unwilling or unwitting participants. Yet in utopia, after the revolution, good social arrangements will replace evil ones, and man will no longer set his hand against the commissars, who are his friends, as he formerly did against the bosses, who were his enemies. When the state withers away, he will be truly master of his destiny. The derogatory use of the term utopian seems especially apt for this particular and powerful ideology.

The fascinating feature of contemporary revolutions and the ideology of new nations is their eclectic quality, as men go about constructing images of the future. The predominant role of the state in economic and social planning is justified under the rubric of socialism, though often political participation by the ordinary citizen is radically limited or manipulated. And continuity with a precolonial past is sought, or continuity with a time prior to a deposed regime. National identity is cultivated, especially where it scarcely exists in multitribal and multicommunal states. And it is precisely the future orientation of the ideology that glosses over current conflicts and complaints. The vision of the future counsels patience with the present. One of the utilities of utopias is that they work, from a pragmatic political view.

And a New Earth

I pose now a fundamental question. Can we help mankind survive for the next twenty years, or, to be safe, until the end of this century? If we can, and it does, the implication seems clear: that we shall have got over the hump of solving international disputes without resort to ultimate weapons, that the burden of population growth will have been alleviated in rich lands as in poor ones, and that technological change, which is never an autonomous variable, will stop threatening its creator.

As I put it in a recent publication, can an evolved, intelligent species survive the reliable means for its own destruction?[12] Comparative interstellar sociology offers no evidence on this. The history of man is ambiguous to the point of absolute uncertainty. But all this presupposes a kind of mechanical fatalism, to which we have been too long addicted, out of fear of our humanity. Of course we can make the future, for no one else is in charge here.

The utility of utopias is simple. In the degree that utopias are taken seriously, they determine the course of present action and become, in a restricted sense, self-fulfilling. This is the point that Wendell Bell has underscored with respect to "images of the future."[13] The future *is* the cause of the present in substantial degree, and it is only the failure of sociologists to come to terms with human purpose that has hidden this verity from their view. When sociologists have dealt at all with sequences, their view has tended to be that of the pool table, with the cue ball set in motion by accidental acts. Surely we know better.

What if we were to construct a new earth? Could we pretend to any technical competence, and could we, even more pretentiously, lay claim to setting human values?

In advance of evidence, I should not suppose that sociologists were exceptionally qualified or exceptionally disqualified for giving advice on the scenario for utopia. Let me comment first on disqualifications, just to get done with it. To the extent that we are embarrassed by human purpose, read it out of our conceptual schemes, and permit no change because that would disturb self-equilibrating systems, we are simply out of the business of constructing utopias or implementing them. Even so, our incompetence is not total and universal. To the extent that we do take account of social values, goal orientations, and purposive action we can at least examine individual and collective aspirations for the future. Our strong point has been an emphasis on connections, and interrelations. And, it must be noted, this has often prompted a cautionary attitude on visionary schemes. But once our attention turns to sequences rather than static connections, our stance may be cautious but it does not need to be negative.

At the very least the sociologist can properly play the role of observer, including the observation of trends that permit him to be a prognosticator. And because he, the sociologist, is strong on relationships, he may claim some expert capacity to identify secondary and tertiary consequences of action programs initiated by others. Incidentally, there is no reason to suppose that all of the side-effects carry negative signs, though the conservatism implicit in equilibrium models has led to exaggerated caution.

The real crux of the issue, however, is the value question. What model of utopia are we talking about, and who determines the choice? Can a value-free social science say anything about goals, or is it confined to mere instrumentation? The questions are valid enough, in principle, but I suggest that their practical significance has been exaggerated.

The only effective enemy of man is man himself. Now that must give us pause. Is it then the law of the jungle, or social Darwinism that still explains our state? No, I suggest that mankind has common goals. Given scarce resources at any given time, there is likely to be a bit of a dispute—perhaps with bloodshed—over their allocation, and indeed over priorities in goals.

Despite cultural differences—and some of these are rapidly disappearing in the contemporary world—men everywhere prefer health to sickness and longevity to early death. Men everywhere also prefer material well-being to poverty. I am aware of contrary doctrines, and it is always possible that voluntary poverty for the sake of spirituality may command the allegiance of a minority. But the spiritual values of poverty have been vastly exaggerated. Viewed empirically, values extolling poverty and fixity of social position—values often deeply embedded in religious doctrine—have been readily abandoned when alternatives have been presented, or indeed when the mere existence of alternatives elsewhere has become known. We have, in effect, exaggerated the significance of cultural differences in human values, for many of these differences simply do not survive the extension of communication that makes the world a single system in important respects.*

If the common values alleged so far smack of crude materialism, two comments are in order: First, health and material well-being are not only valued as such, but also are likely to be essential conditions for more intellectual and esthetic concerns. Second, there is some basis for suggesting the existence (or perhaps emergence) of less materialistic

* See Chapter 15.

values that unite mankind. One of these might be expressed as the rule of law, that is, the quest for orderly ways of resolving conflicts without bloodshed. The universality of this value may be disputed, but it is certainly one mark of a civilized polity in the maintenance of internal order, and it now appears as a kind of necessary value in international relations. Konrad Lorenz has noted that man, almost uniquely among animal species, has ritualized destruction within the species rather than ritualizing its prevention.[14] What remains to be seen is whether man's superior reason is an adequate substitute for the instinctual rituals that inhibit lethal conflicts within other species.

Another value that is even less certainly universal but seems to have spread rapidly in this century is the extension of the common rights of citizens as contrasted to the differential privileges deriving from wealth, power, or mere lineage.[15] Some of those common rights are, once more, access to health services, income maintenance and economic opportunity; others relate to political participation and encounters with the law. And is it not fair to view the end of colonialism as an extension of the concept of citizenship in the world community?

What I am suggesting is that these more or less common goals provide a sufficient basis for building preferable futures and alleviating anxieties about the "value problem." Value problems will still abound, including the sticky questions of who pays the costs and who gets the benefits. Yet these questions will not deter political leaders from planning the future—note, often a future that these leaders will not live to see. And it is not clear that social scientists should shrink from complexity. Were that the proper course, we should abandon our calling forthwith and try to find the simple life doing something else.

It is true of course that any future we now seek to construct must take account of present conditions and also of trends that would be extremely difficult to alter. For example, short of a morally untenable destruction of people, many demographic dimensions are already fixed for the rest of this century and beyond. And though technology is never an autonomous variable, it would be difficult now to prevent continuing development of computerized data storage and retrieval, with the technical potentiality of developing complete dossiers on every inhabitant within a country so equipped. Yet dangers foreseen are possibly dangers that can be alleviated or prevented.

The utility of counterutopias, such as Orwell's *Nineteen Eighty-Four*,[16] is precisely admonitory, encouraging prior preventive action to dampen and redirect trends of change. The future will not be exactly as we intended it to be, even if we now had consensus and concerted conduct in the attempt to bring it about. It will be closer to the future that engaged individuals and spokesmen for collectivities hoped it would be if we make those hopes explicit than if we take refuge in silly notions of the inevitability of autonomous forces or of "natural evolution." Although we have been schooled not to exaggerate human rationality, we have perhaps failed to emphasize, and assist, the human potential for sensible action. The picture of man driven is no more intrinsically valid than the picture of man driving on a course at least partly chosen by himself.

It would be improper as well as useless to suggest that every sociologist drop his current intellectual concerns to devote his talents exclusively to building a better world. Even if that were the sole acknowledged rationale for our existence as a discipline, which is pretty dubious, we are not well equipped with knowledge as to just how a better world would look, or how it might be brought about. Some of our current careful work is bound to be useful in constructing, and reconstructing, utopias, even if we have no such lofty ambitions or reject them as professionally improper. My only plea is for indulgence toward our brethren who think that man is worth saving and his lot in life worth improving. A little activism of this ambitious kind will do us no harm at all.

References

1. See Karl Mannheim, *Ideology and Utopia* (New York: Harcourt, Brace, and World, 1949).

2. See Ralf Dahrendorf, *Class and Class Conflict in Industrial Society* (Stanford, California: Stanford University Press, 1959).

3. Emile Durkheim, *The Rules of the Sociological Method*, translated by Sarah A. Solovay and John H. Mueller (Glencoe, Illinois: Free Press, 1950).

4. Emile Durkheim, *Suicide*, translated by John A. Spaulding and George Simpson (Glencoe, Illinois: Free Press, 1951).

5. Emile Durkheim, *The Division of Labor in Society*, translated by George Simpson (New York: Macmillan, 1933).

6. Emile Durkheim, *The Elementary Forms of the Religious Life*, translated by Joseph Ward Swain (Glencoe, Illinois: Free Press, 1954).

7. Especially in the Preface to the Second Edition of the *Division of Labor* Reference 5.

8. See, for example, Marshall D. Sahlins and E. R. Service, *Evolution and Culture* (Ann Arbor, Michigan: University of Michigan Press, 1960); Talcott Parsons, "Evolutionary Universals in Society," *American Sociological Review*, 29: 13–18, June 1964.

9. Manning Nash, *Machine-Age Maya: The Industrialization of a Guatemalan Community* (Glencoe, Illinois and Chicago: Free Press and University of Chicago Research Center in Economic Development and Cultural Change, 1958), p. 116.

10. See Wilbert E. Moore and Eleanor Bernert Sheldon, "Monitoring Social Change: A Conceptual and Programmatic Statement," American Statistical Association, *Proceedings of the Social Statistics Section*, 1965, pp. 144–149.

11. Dennis Gabor, *Inventing the Future* (New York: Alfred A. Knopf, 1964).

12. Wilbert E. Moore, *Social Change* (Englewood Cliffs, New Jersey: Prentice-Hall, 1963), p. 117.

13. Wendell Bell, "The Future as the Cause of the Present," Plenary Session Address to the American Sociological Association, Miami Beach, August 30, 1966.

14. Konrad Z. Lorenz, *On Aggression*, translated from the German by Marjorie Kerr Wilson (New York: Harcourt, Brace and World, 1966).

15. See T. H. Marshall, *Class, Citizenship, and Social Development* (Garden City, New York: Doubleday and Co., 1964), especially Chapter IV, "Citizenship and Social Class."

16. George Orwell, *Nineteen-Eighty-Four* (New York: Harcourt, Brace, 1949).

INDEX